BHAJANAMRITAM

Devotional Songs of
Mata Amritanandamayi

VOLUME I

MATA AMRITANANDAMAYI CENTER
San Ramon, California

BHAJANAMRITAM
Volume I

PUBLISHED BY:
Mata Amritanandamayi Center
P.O. Box 613
San Ramon, CA 94583-0612
Tel: (510) 537-9417

Printed in the United States of America

FIRST PRINTING November 1992
SECOND PRINTING November 1994

ALSO AVAILABLE FROM:
Mata Amritanandamayi Mission Trust
Amritapuri P.O., Kollam Dt., Keralam
INDIA 690525

ISBN 1-879410-57-5

The Significance of Devotional Singing

"Darling children, to gain concentration in this spiritually dark age (Kali Yuga), bhajan is better than meditation. By loud singing, other distracting sounds will be overcome and concentration will be achieved. Bhajan, concentration, meditation . . . this is the progression. Children, constant remembrance of God is meditatation.

If bhajan is sung without concentration, it is a waste of energy. If sung with one-pointedness, such songs will benefit the singer, the listener and also Mother Nature. Such songs will awaken the listeners' minds in due course.

Bhajan is a spiritual discipline aimed at concentrating the mind on one's Beloved Deity. Through that one-pointedness, one can merge in the Divine Being and experience the Bliss of one's True Self.

It matters not whether one believes in Krishna or Christ, Mother Kali or Mother Mary; a formless God or even a flame, a mountain or an ideal such as world peace can be meditated upon while singing. By letting the mind expand in the sound of the divine chanting, each one can enjoy the peace born of one's inherent divinity."

-MATA AMRITANANDAMAYI-

A Word About Pronunciation...

The following key is for the guidance of those who are unfamiliar with Oriental transliteration codes. Although the only accented letters that appear in the *bhajans* are Ā, Ī, Ū, Ñ and Ś, all the accented letters appear in the *Thousand Names of the Divine Mother* at the end of this book.

<u>*Vowels*</u>

A	-as	*u*	in b*u*t
Ā	-as	*a*	in f*a*r but held twice as long as a
AI	-as	*ai*	in *ai*sle
AU	-as	*ow*	in h*ow*
I	-as	*i*	in p*i*n
Ī	-as	ee	in meet but held twice as long as i
O	-as	*o*	in g*o*
Ṛ	-as	*ri*	in *ri*m
U	-as	*u*	in p*u*sh
Ū	-as	*u*	in r*u*le but held twice as long as u

<u>*Consonants:*</u>

K	-as	*k*	in kite
KH	-as	*kh*	in Ec*kh*art
G	-as	*g*	in *g*ive
GH	-as	*gh*	in di*g-h*ard
Ṅ	-as	*n*	in si*n*g
P	-as	*p*	in *p*ine
PH	-as	*ph*	in u*p-h*ill

B	-as	*b*	in *b*ird
BH	-as	*bh*	in ru*b-h*ard
M	-as	*m*	in *m*other
Ṁ	-a resonant nasal sound like the *n* in the French word bo*n*		
Ḥ	-coupled with a vowel, *aḥ* is pronounced like *aha*,		
iḥ	-is like *ihi*		

T & Ṭ	-as	*t*	in *t*ub
TH & ṬH	-as	*th*	in ligh*th*ouse
D & Ḍ	as-	*d*	in *d*ove
DH & ḌH	-as	*dh*	in re*d-h*ot
Ṇ	-as	*n*	in *n*aught

These letters with dots under them are pronounced with the tip of the tongue against the roof of the mouth, others with the tongue against the teeth

C	-as	*ch*	in *ch*air
CH	-as	*ch*	in staun*ch-h*eart
J	-as	*j*	in *j*oy
JH	-as	*dge*	in he*dge*hog
Ñ	-as	*ny*	in ca*ny*on
Ṣ	-as	*sh*	in *sh*ine
Ś	-as in the German *s*prechen		
S	-as	*s*	in *s*un

TABLE OF CONTENTS

Songs *1*
Slokas & Mantras *271*
Sri Lalita Sahasranama Stotra *273*
(The Thousand Names of the Divine Mother)
Index of Songs *309*

SNEHA SUDHĀMAYI

Vol. 1, A-1

sneha sudhā mayī amrita mayī
prema sudhā varshinī devī
sneha sudhā mayī amrita mayī

O Goddess of Love and Immortal Bliss, Thou art Divine Love Personified, O Goddess of Love and Immortal Bliss.

mohana sangīta sammodinī
hridaya sadā nandinī devī
hridaya sadā nandinī

Thou art the Power behind enchanting music ever giving bliss to the heart, ever giving bliss to the heart.

sauhridam tulum bunna sauparnnika yile
saubhaga sangīta saundaryame
nin manda hāsa prabha pushpa śobhayil
en ātma dīpam kolu tidatte

In the river of Love Thou raisest the waves of divine music and beauty. Thy smile radiates cooling light in which my inner self gets immersed.

ul kamalarchite chit prabha sāgare
ul palatā pushpa lochanī
madhura sudhā rasa hridaya vilāsinī
mridula sudhā varshinī devī

Thou art worshipped within the lotus flower of the Heart, O Thou with eyes like the petals of the blue lotus. Thou sportest in the Heart filled with Immortal Bliss, Personification of softness and immortality.

ĀNANDA MAYI

Vol.1, A-2

ānanda mayī brahma mayī
ānanda mayī brahma mayī
atulita saundarya rūpinī
ānanda mayī brahma mayī

O Blissful One, O Absolute One,
O Blissful One, O Absolute One,
Whose form is of unsurpassed beauty.
O Blissful One, O Absolute One.

ā rā dhārangal kadannu yogikal
amūlya nidhi ninne ariyunnu
analpa śakti ninnude prābhavam
avarum alpam ariyunnu

Crossing the six mystic centers, the yogis come to know Thee, the invaluable Treasure. Thy Glory, O Infinite Power, is however, only slightly known to them.

matavum jātiyum ivideyī marttyende
madamūyarttān mātram upakaricchū
manuja mrigādiyil okkeyum jīvanāyi
manassinde yadi tattil nī śayippū

Religions and castes have only helped to increase the arrogance of man. As the Life of all humans and animals Thou rest at the bottom of the mind.

VANDIKYUNNEN

Vol. 1, A-3

vandikyunnen amme ennil nritta māduvān
vanda nīya prade vannadi panīyunnen

In order that Thou should dance within me, O Mother, O Adorable One, I bow and surrender to Thee.

jīvātmi kayāyi ninnu jīvi pikkyum śaktiye
nī vedinnyu poyāl nischala makhilavum

Existing as the Power of Life within the individual soul, if Thou should leave, all would become still.

parayām śakti vā vā pari pūrnānand ātmike
parama jyoti sevā piriyā tennil ninnum

O Universal energy, the Self of Perfect Bliss, come, come. O Supreme Light, remain never abandoning me.

jñāna kadale vā vā nānā srishti kārane
akhilā dhāra murte alavillātta satte

Come, come, O Ocean of Knowledge, the Cause of the Diverse Creation, Embodiment of the Substratum of the Universe, Measureless Essence.

anuvilu manuve vā vā akhila vyāpta vastu ve
āyira dala padmattil āvāse nī vā vā

O Thou Atom of atoms, Who pervades the Universe, Dweller in the Thousand-petalled Lotus, come, come.

kodi divākara śobhe en tadiyil vārum ambike
adiya navide layīkkyuvān amma tanne yāśrayam

Whose brilliance equals millions of suns, Dweller within myself, that Mother alone is the only hope for getting merged in Her.

amrita jyotir mayame ānandābdhe ninnil
mānasa manīśam līna mākān tunayikkanam

O Ambrosial Light, Ocean of Bliss, may my mind merge in Thee forever.

nirmmala me nirguna me anudinam namikkyunnu
dīna dayālo ende dīna taya kattuka

O pure and qualityless Being, I bow to Thee again and again. Compassionate to the afflicted, rid me of my distress.

arivin arive satte abhaya pradame śive
ariyā nari villamme kundalinī śakti

O Knowledge of knowledge, Essence, Shive (Consort of Shiva), giver of shelter, O Mother, Kundalini Śakti, I have not even the knowledge to know.

śanka kala kattān śankarī nī yettanam
peyā kolla enne māyike nīye gati

O Śankari, Thou must come to remove my doubts. May I not have the fate of a madman, O Maya.

KĀRUNYA VĀRIDHE

Vol. 1, A-4

kārunyavāridhe krishnā
nitya merunnu jīvita trishna
illā manasinnu śānti ayyo
vallā teyāyi vibhrānti

O Krishna, Ocean of Compassion,the thirst for life is ever increasing. There is no peace for the mind and alas, confusion is so much.

tettukal ellām poruttu - vannen
netti viyarppu tudaykkyū
kanna mattilli nīya valambam - ninde
patamalar chevatiyennum

Forgiving all wrongs, wipe off the sweat from my brow. O Kanna, now I have no support other than Thy worshipful Lotus Feet.

tonda varalunnu krishnā
kannu randum patarunnu krishnā
pādangal randum talarnnu - mannil
vīnu pokunnu śri krishnā

O Krishna, the throat is drying up, the eyes are failing, the feet are tired, and I am falling to the ground, O Krishna.

MANASE NIN SVANTAMĀYI

Vol. 1, B-1

manasse nin svantamāyi ttoru ttarumillenullā
paramārtha mellāyiporum smarikkyuka nī

Remember, O mind, this supreme truth: nobody is your own!

artha śūnya māku moro karmangale chetu kondu
vyarthamāyi samsārattil alayunnu nī

Because of doing meaningless actions, you are wandering in the ocean of this world.

ārādhi chekyām janangal prabho prabho yennu vili
chāya talpa kālam mātram nila nil patām

Even though people honour you crying, 'lord, lord', it will be for a short time only.

**itra nāl mattulla janam ārādhicha ninde deham
prānan pombol upekshipān idayāyidum**

Your body, which has been honoured for so many days, must be cast off when life departs.

**etuprāna preyasīkyu vendiyitra yellām ningal
pādu pedunnundo jīvan vedinyu polum**

For which sweetheart have you been struggling all this time, not even caring for your life?

**ā pen mani polum tava mrita deham kānun neram
pedicchu pin mārum kūde varikayilla**

Even she will be frightened by your dead body and will not accompany you.

**māyatande valakyāka ttaka pettu kondu jagan -
mātā vinde nāmatte nī marannī tolle**

Trapped in the subtle snare of Maya as you are, do not forget the sacred Name of the Divine Mother.

**neti neti vādam kondo veda tantrātikal kondo
darśanangal ārukondo sādhya māyitā**

The Vision of God cannot be attained by the Veda, Tantra, Vedanta or other philosophies.

**nityānanda nimagnanāyi jīva jālangalilennum
satyasvarūpa nāmīśan kūdikollunnu**

Immersed in Eternal Bliss, God, Whose nature is Truth, resides in all beings.

sthāna māna dhana mellām sthira mānennorti tolle
satya vastu onne ullu jagadambika

Position, prestige and wealth are all impermanent; the only Reality is the Universal Mother.

bhakti lābham kotichallo māmunimār ekkālattum
śuddha mānasanmārāyi tapam cheyunnu

In order to gain devotion, even the ancient sages did penance with a pure heart.

kānta mirum pineppole ākārshīkyu mallo jagan -
nāthan bhaktiyuktanākum jīvātmāvine

The Lord will attract devotion-soaked souls like a magnet attracts iron.

kālimātā vinde nāmam kāmanakal vittu konde
āmodattāl pādipādi nritta mātitām

Renouncing all desires, let us dance in that bliss singing the Name of Mother Kali!

GOPĀLA KRISHNA

Vol. 1, B-2

gopāla krishna rādhā krishna
krishnā gopāla krishna
kannayā gopāla krishna
śrī krishna śrī krishna śrī krishna śrī krishna
krishnā gopāla krishna
kannayā gopāla krishna
satro kuru nām sakha pāndavā nām
krishnā vāsudeva

śrī krishna śrī krishna śrī krishna śrī krishna
he nāta nārāyana vāsudeva

gopāla=The Protector of the cows or Lord of the senses
krishna=The Lord who attracts irresistibly
rādhā=Krishna's consort, the Divine Energy or Power
kannaya=Darling child
satro kuru nām=The enemy of the Kurus
sakha pāndavā nām=The friend of the Pandavas
vāsudeva=Son of Vasudeva, Krishna's father. Also the One who dwells in all
he nāta=O Lord
nārāyana=The form of Lord Vishnu which reclines on the serpent Ananta
govinda=Lord of the cows.
hare=The Stealer of our hearts.
murāre=Slayer of the demon Mura.

KANNENDE KĀLOCHA

Vol. 1, B-3

kannende kāloccha kettūannoru
velli nilāvulla rāvil

Kannan's (Krishna's) footsteps were heard on a silvery moonlit night.

pullānkural vilikettūenmanam
tankaki nāvil layicchū...

Hearing the notes of the flute, my mind merged in a golden dream.

ī vennilāvinde tuvenmayilpūtta
hemanta saugandha me... kannā
tentukumā mandahāsatilen manam
sānandamāyi lasippūkannā...(kannende)

Manifesting this pure, bright moonlight, O fragrance of the winter season, seeing that honey-laden smile, my mind is shining blissfully, O Kanna.

undanekam katha chollāneni kende -
kannā nī pokarute...kannā
en matiyil ullorunmāda poykayil
vannu nīrāti nilkkū- kannā...(kannende)

I have innumerable stories to tell. Kanna, please don't go!
In the blissful lake of my mind, please stay for a bath.

AMRITĀNANDAMAYI

Vol. 2, A-1

amritānanda mayī mātā
amarā dhīśe namo namā
akatāril vannudayam cheyuka
amritānandamayī mātā amritānandamayī

To Mother Amritanandamayi, the Goddess of the Immortals, salutations again and again. May Thou dawn in my inner mind, O Mother Amritanandamayi!

ariyillamme vārttān ninnude
apadānangala moghangal
amale tava tiru vachanam tanayar -
kkamritam jīvanu kulir megham

O Mother, I don't know how to sing Thy sinless praises. O Pure One, Thy holy words are nectar to Thy children and are to life as cool clouds.

virāgini vidhi dayini
viśva vimohini nadanam tudaru

sudhā mayi mridu smitā bhayāle
sudhā rasam tulumbunnullam

O Detached One, Bestower of destiny, Universal Enchantress, continue Thy dance. O Ambrosial One, by the radiance of Thy gentle smile my heart is overflowing with sweet nectar.

sneha manantamām śaktiyen ennamma
otunnu pratyaksha mākitunnu
ammatan vātsalya dugdham nukaruna
dhanyarkku mattendu bandhanangal

"Love is eternal power", thus saith my Mother and She shows it to be so. For the blessed ones who have drunk the milk of Mother's divine Love, what other bonds are left?

ātura nālamba hīna navaśanum
āśrayam ammatan sneha mantram
ajñāna sindhuvil vīnuralunnavarkkā
lambam avidutte jñāna mantram

For the afflicted, Mother's words of love, the prop of the weak, are their only support. For those who are fallen and struggling in the Ocean of Ignorance, Thy words of wisdom are the only support.

ŚAKTI RŪPE

Vol. 2, A-2

śaktī rūpe ninde nāmam śravikyumbol
chitta morunmatta bhāvamentum
hrittil pulakangal taliritunnū
etrayo ramyam hā ninde rūpam
etrayo ramyam hā ninde rūpam

O Thou whose form is Power, while listening to Thy Name, the mind becomes divinely intoxicated, the heart trembles; O how very beautiful is Thy form!

nāmangal otunna nāvuvantyam dhyāna
pūjakalum varenyam
ninnil layikyunna buddhiya ganyamā
nalengil janmam vyartham bāhya
karmangalum vrithāvil

Holy is the tongue that utters Thy Name and worthy of attainment are meditation and worship. Invaluable is the intellect that merges in Thee. Without these, this birth and all external actions are but in vain.

ambike yennu vilikyunna nāvā
lasatyangal otu mengil
ambe paraninda yānanda mekukil
nāmattāl entu phalam... bhakti -
bhāvam kapatamalle

O Mother! What is the use of prayers if, with the same tongue that calls upon You, one tells lies and delights in reviling others? Is not this kind of devotion hypocritical?

ninne ninacchu kondanyare drohicchāl
nin chintayentinānu
nin chinta yālanya seva chetītukil
nin seva yentinammā... karma -
yoga matāvukille

What is the use of thinking of You if, while doing so, one hurts others? O Mother, what is the need of serving You if one serves others while thinking of You? Is this not equal to Karma Yoga?

pūjakal arppikyum kaikala śuddha mām
nīcha karmmangal chetāl
pūjāri yentinu vyājamāyi mārunna
pūjayi tentinānu kalla
kānika yāvukille

If one does impure, mean actions with the same hands that offer worship, what is the use of such deceitful worship and the one who does it? Is that not a false offering?

kovililere pradakshinam chetittā
vātilil ninnukondu
mārennoti picchakāreccha vittunna
bhāvam vichitramalle jñāna
yogam dushikyukille

Is it not strange if, after reverentially walking around the temple, one stands at the doorstep and kicks the beggars away? Is this not an abuse of the Path of Knowledge?

bimbam namikyum śirass ahambhāvatā
lengum vinaya mattāl
ambike sarvatra vyāpta chaitanyame
dambham nin munnil alle mada
matsaram ninnodalle

O Mother, all-pervading Awareness, is it not deceitful to humbly bow one's head to Thee though full of pride? Through self-importance, is not this one actually competing with You?

vyāmoha pātayil mātramalayunna
mānasa mottu neram
mātā vine smari chīdāykil hā kashtam
mohattāl śokam phalam antya
māśayil tanne nūnam

O, what a pity that one wanders only in the path of vain desires without remembering Mother even for a moment. The fruit of desire is misery. Surely this one will die in desire.

lokatti nādhāra māyullo rammayil
ekāgramāya chittam
vegam vishayatil odi rasichālum
ākeya śuddha mākum
rāja yogam nishidha mākum

The mind which concentrates on Mother the Substratum of the World, becomes completely impure if it rushes to delight in sense objects. Then Raja Yoga will be forbidden.

artha manārtha mundākkunna tinentum
marttyan bali yarppikkyum
kartavya pāśattilāyi bhrāntan pole
krityam marannidunnu mrityu
potti chiri chidunnu

Man will sacrifice anything for profitable and unprofitable things, binding himself with the noose of obligation. He forgets his duty like a madman and Death bursts out laughing!

chāla teruvil śūnikal kanakke
yalayunnu māyayāle
tāye nin makkal ānennu rachāl
loka vairuddhyam sneha mākum
dharma mengum ānanda mekum

Like the dogs in the slum streets, man wanders in Maya. O Mother, if one looks upon all as being Your children, the contradictions of the world will be transformed into love and Dharma will bring happiness everywhere.

PIRAYENTU CHETU

Vol. 2, A-3

pira yentu chetu nyān amme
erayām nin makan pira yentu chetu

O Mother, what error have I committed?
What error has Thy poor child committed?

alavattu mohikkyu nillā nin
darśana bhāgyam koticchu nyān
atinum tadassangal nī devi
entinu srishticchu loka māte

I am not longing for many things but only for the good fortune of Your Vision. Why did You, O Goddess and Mother of the World, create

abhayam tedi vannadiyan amme
aśarana nāmī nindya putran
anpulla ambike tāye nī
kanivotu śaranam tāye

O Mother, this unfortunate one has come seeking refuge, this helpless, mean son. O Mother, loving Mother, show compassion and save me.

śaranam śaranam nin charanam śive
nī yallā tilla vere śaranam
nin pāda padmam namikyān adiyanu
anugraha mekane karunā maye

My refuge, my refuge is Thy Feet. Other than You, refuge there is none. To enable me to bow at Thy Lotus Feet, bless this suppliant, O Compassionate One.

KANNĀ NĪ YENNE

Vol. 2, A-4

kannā nī yenne marannu vo mukil
varnna nī yenne marannu vo
dannam perukunnu kannane kānān
nonnum tiri yāttoren hridi

O Krishna, have You forgotten me? O Thou with the color of a stormy cloud, have You forgotten me? Not seeing You, my suffering increases and my heart is unable to understand anything.

engo maranyu kalanya to kanna
nenne vetinyu natannato
kannīr kata lile kenne nī kannā
mungā nayachu maranya to

Where have You disappeared to? O Krishna, have You walked away leaving me behind? O Krishna, have You sent me to drown in the ocean of tears?

nin pāda dāsanāyi ninnu nyān dina
menni karinnyu dayā nidhe
kannā nīyen mana mandire vara
nenteya māntam kripā nidhe

O Merciful One, counting the days, I have stood at Your Feet as Your servant. O Krishna, Treasure of Compassion, why are You delaying to enter the temple of my mind?

NIN PREMAM

Vol. 2, B-1

nin premam kond enneyun matta nākku
kendamme avīdunnu sneha purvam

O Mother, make me mad with Thy Love!

jñānavum yukti vichāravum koneni
kedum prayojanam mundo tāye

What need have I of knowledge or reason?

tāvaka prema śudhā bhuji pichenne
unmatta yākki kondālum amme

Make me drunk with Thy Love's Wine!

bhakta jana manohārinī nī yenne
mukkuka nin prema vāridhiyil

O Thou who stealest Thy devotees' hearts, drown me deep in the Sea of Thy Love!

samsāra mākum nin bhrāntālayam tannil
ānanda nrittam ādunnu chilar
etra murakke chirikyunnu kechana
dukhichu kerunnu mattu chilar

Here in this world, this madhouse of Thine, some laugh, some weep, some dance for joy.

gaurāngan śrī buddhan yesu moses ivar
nin premon matta ram punyātmakal

Gauranga, Buddha, Jesus and Moses, all are drunk with the wine of Thy Love.

dhanya mayīdum tadīyasam gālivan
dhanya nā kunna nā lennu tāye

O Mother, when shall I be blessed by joining their blissful company?

ENTE KANNUNĪR

Vol. 2, B-2

ente kannu nīr etra kandālum
manassaliyuka ille amme nin
manassaliyuka ille

Though seeing my tears, O Mother, how is it that Thou feelest no compassion, Thou feelest no compassion?

etrayo nālu kalāyi nin pāda manayunnū
yennittum angulil prasādam ille amme
angullil prasādam ille

Though it is many days since I came to Thy Feet to seek refuge in Thee, why aren't Thou pleased, O why aren't Thou pleased?

nin bhakta dāsarkku mana śānti engilum
nalkuvān entinamme madi kāttunnu amme
entinu madi kāttunnu

O Mother, why art Thou remiss in granting at least peace of mind to Thy devoted servants, why art Thou remiss?

nin pāda śaranārtham anayūmī yadiyanu
śaranam nalki ānugrahikyu amme
śaranam nalki ānugrahikyu

Thy Feet are the sole Refuge of this poor soul. Therefore, granting me refuge, bless me, O Mother, granting me refuge, bless me.

GOPĀLA GOVINDA

Vol. 2, B-3

gopāla govinda krishna vāsudeva
rādhikā chandra chakora krishna vāsudeva
dāmodara achyuta murali manohara
vāsudeva hari vāsudeva hari vāsudeva

devakī nandana srīnivāsa vāsudeva
jishnu hrishikeśa śauri vāsudeva
narada munīndra nud ānanda yashod ānanda
vāsudeva hari vāsudeva hari vāsudeva

śyāma sundara manohara vāsudeva
padmanābha kama lekshana vāsudeva
śyāmala komala anga seśa śayana keśava
vāsudeva hari vāsudeva hari vāsudeva

nanda nandana janārdhana vāsudeva
dīnanātha dukha bhanjana vāsudeva
jayasindhu dhara nīdhara sundara mukhāravinda
vāsudeva hari vāsudeva hari vāsudeva

gopinātha madana mohana vāsudeva
navanīta priya dadhi chora vāsudeva
krishna kamala lochana gopī lolla vanamāli jaya
vāsudeva hari vāsudeva hari vāsudeva

nitya nirguna niranjana vāsudeva
ati madhura sundara rūpa vāsudeva
chāru chandrāvatamsa chanda nālepa nānga
vāsudeva hari vāsudeva hari vāsudeva

mukti dāyaka mukunda hari vāsudeva
yādavendra yadu bhūshana vāsudeva

kevala gopāla ghana śyāma ramā vallabhā
vāsudeva hari vāsudeva hari vāsudeva

bhakta mandāra vara tīra vāsudeva
paramānanda divya sundara vāsudeva
bhava bandhana vimochaka dvāraka nāyaka
vāsudeva hari vāsudeva hari vāsudeva

nava navanīta rasikā vāsudeva
aganīta loka nāyaka vāsudeva
bhavya yogi paripālaka bhakto dhārana
vāsudeva hari vāsudeva hari vāsudeva

gopāla=Protector of the cows
govinda=Lord of the cows
vāsudeva=Son of Vasudeva
hari=Destroyer of samsara
rādhikā chandra chakora=The chakora bird that drinks in the moonbeams of Radha's face
dāmodara=Who was bound to a mortar
achyuta=Unshakeable
murali=Flute player
manohara=Enchanter of the mind
devakī nandana=Son of Devaki
Srīnivāsa=Abode of Sri (Lakshmi)
jishnu=Arjuna
hrishikeśa=Lord of the senses
śauri=Born in the clan of Sura
narada munīndra nud ānanda=The bliss of great sages like Narada
yashodānanda=The bliss of Yashoda
padmanābha=Lotus-navelled
kama lekshana=Lotus-eyed
shyāmala komala anga=Limbs of the hue of a blue lotus
sesha sayana=Reclining on the serpent of Time
keshava=Slayer of the demon Kesi
nanda nandana=Son of Nanda

dīna nādha dukha bhanjana=Destroyer of the misery of the afflicted
jaya sindhu dhara nīdhara=Who victoriously raised the earth from the bottom of the ocean
sundara mukhāravinda=Beautiful lotus-faced One
gopinātha=Lord of the Gopis
madana mohana=Enchanter of even Cupid
navanīta priya=Fond of butter
dadhi chora=Stealer of curds (yogurt)
kamala lochana=Lotus-eyed
gopi lola=Soft hearted towards the Gopis
nitya nirguna niranjana=Eternal, without qualities blemishless
atimadhura sundara rūpa=Exquisitely sweet,beautiful form
chāru chandrāvatamsa=Moon-like face
chanda nālepa nanga=With limbs smeared with sandalwood paste
mukti dayaka=Giver of Liberation
mukunda=Bestower of Salvation
yādavendra=Lord of the Yadus
yadu bhūshana=Ornament to the race of Yadu
kevala=Sole Reality
ghana śyāma=Of deep blue hue
ramā vallabha=Lord of Goddess Lakshmi
bhakta mandāra vara tīra=Boon-giving tree to the devotees
paramānanda=Supreme Bliss
divya sundara=Divine Beauty
bhava bandhana vimochana=Destroyer of the bonds of becoming
dvāraka nāyaka=Lord of Dvaraka city
nava nava nīta rasika=Enjoyer of butter
loka nayaka=Lord of the world
aganīta=Innumerable
bhavya yogi paripālaka=Sustainer of humble yogis
bhakto dhārana=Who uplifts the devotees

AMRITĀNANDA SVARŪPA

Vol. 3, A-1

amritānanda svarūpa manohari
mātā amrita mayī

hridaya saroruha dala madi lennum
amritam tūkiyor amritamayī

Enchanter of the mind, whose nature is Immortal Bliss, O Ambrosial Mother, the petals of the heart lotus are ever sprinkled with nectar by You, ambrosial One.

pranava porulayi vilasum tava mridu
charana sarojam mama śaranam
talarum jīvanu tanal arulītum
sura taru vallo mama jananī

Let Thy delicate Lotus Feet, which shine as the Essence of OM, be my refuge. To the weary soul Thou art the shade- giving Celestial Tree, aren't Thou, O my Mother?

janmāntarangalil mungum manujarkku
unnati yennum nīye
en mānasamadi lennum ninnude
chinmaya bhāva munarttu devī

For the man drowning in the repeated cycle of birth and death Thou art the refuge forever. May Thou always awaken in my mind Thy Divine Consciousness, O Devi.

MANASĀ VĀCHĀ

Vol. 3, A-2

manasā vāchā karmmanā
nirantaram ninne smarikyunnu
ennittu menotu kanivukāttān
amānta mente ponnamme
amānta mente ponnamme

Through my mind, speech and actions I am remembering Thee incessantly. Why then are Thou delaying to show Thy mercy to me, beloved Mother?

āndukal palatu karin yittum
svastata yillen manassinu
ittiri āśvāsa mekuvān
amānta mente ponnamme
amānta mente ponnamme

Years have passed but still my mind has no peace. O darling Mother, please grant me a little relief.

kāttila kappetta toni pole
alayunamme yen mānasam
chitta rogiyāyi mārā tirikyān
ittiri manaśānti nalku amme
ittiri manaśānti nalku amme

My mind sways like a boat caught in a storm. O Mother, give me a little peace of mind lest I become a lunatic.

vayya yendamme sahiyātā
venda īvidha jīvitam
nin parīkshanam tāngān atiyanu
āvatilamme āvatilla
āvatilamme āvatilla

I am tired Mother; it is unbearable. I don't want such a life.
I can't stand Your tests. O Mother, I can't endure it!

pāvam nyān oru tunayatton
amma yallāteni kyārumilla
parīkshanam nirtti yennamme nī

karam nītti yenne kara kayattū
karam nītti yenne kara kayattū

I am a miserable destitute. I have none but You, Mother. Please stop Your tests, extend Your hand and pull me up.

KANNANE KĀNĀN

Vol. 3, A-3

kannane kānān ulkannegu nī kannā
mannilum vinnilum kannāya nī
vennil āvellunna puñjiri pūnda nin
ponmukham kānuvān kanneku nī

O Kanna, give the inner eye to see Thee. O Kanna who art the eye (soul) of earth and heaven, give the eye to see Thy bright face which bears a smile that surpasses the moonlight.

kandillayo ende sankata minnu nī
mindillayo kannā ennotonnum
kandituvān karal nonditunnen kannā
kandillayo iniyum

Didn't You see my sorrow today? O Kanna, won't You say anything to me? O Kanna, my heart is aching to see Thee. Haven't You noticed me yet?

engum niranya nī ingillayo nyān
onnum tiriyātta kunyallayo
ingu nī porumo mangumen mānase
tingunna śokam ketān

O Omnipresent One, are You not here? Am I not a child who knows nothing? Will You come here to rid me of the sorrow that fills my mind?

SRISHTIYUM NĪYE

Vol. 3, A-4

srishtiyum nīye srishtāvum nīye
śaktiyum nīye satyavum nīye
devī...devī...devī

Creation and Creator art Thou, Thou art Energy and Truth...
O Goddess, O Goddess, O Goddess!

anda katāha vidhātāvum nīye
ādiyūmantavum nīye

Creatress of the Cosmos art Thou, and Thou art the beginning and end.

paramānu chaitanya porūlūm nīye
pañcha bhūtangalum nīye

The Essence of the individual soul art Thou, and Thou art the five elements as well.

BHAKTAVALSALE DEVI

Vol. 3, A-5

bhaktavatsale devī ambike manoharī
bhakta janārtti tīrppān śaktayāyi mevūm devī

O Devi, O Ambika, Beauty Personified, O Thou Who art affectionate towards devotees, may Thou dwell here in order to end the sufferings of the devotees!

mātāvāyedum nīye tātanāyedum nīye
mātulla brātākalum gurunātheyum nīye

Thou alone hast become the Mother, Father, Uncle, Elders and Guru.

enalla īkkānunna sarvvavum nīyānenne
ennute guru arul chetator tirunnu nyān

Not only that...I have sat listening to my Guru who says that Thou art, in fact, everything that is seen.

nītanne sarvvasvamen dīnata tīrppān śakta
nītanne ellāttinum nārāya verāyatum

Thou art everything, powerful enough to end my misery,
the Tap Root of all.

nītanne sarvva bhūtanātayāyi nilkunnaval
nītanne sarvvasvavum kāttu rakshīku nolum

Thou standest as the Ruler of all beings.
Thou art everything and its Protector as well.

viśvasi chevam bhaktyā stutichu bhajikyunnen
viśvaika nāte ninne kānuvān āśikkyunnen

Believing this, I am praising Thee with devotion.
O Goddess of the Universe, I desire to see Thee.

etra nālāyi ninne kānuvān āśichu nyān
ittiri neram polum tettāte bhajikyunnen

Since how many days have I been desiring to see Thee?
I am praising Thee without losing even a moment.

ennil nin endengilum tettukal sambhavicho
ennute dukham tīrkkān ishtam illāyi kayāllo

Did some mistake happen on my part or is it that Thou hast no mind to end my sorrow?

ennaka kāmbu vendu vennī rākatte yenno
onnume yariyāte sambrānta yākunnu nyān

Or perhaps Thou wishest that my inner self get burnt to ash.
I am getting confused...I know nothing.

dīnarāyi mevunnore svāntana pettuttīdum
dīnavatsale yallo nīyamma mahāmāye

O Mother, the Great Illusion, art Thou compassionate to the afflicted, consoling those who dwell in misery?

ammakyu makkal ellām tūlya mennulla satyam
ulppūvil daricchatu mityayāyi bhavikyumo

Will the truth which I keep in my heart, that all the children are equal to the Mother, become false?

nyān onnapekshichīdum enne nī trikanparttu
dīnata tīrppān alpam kārunyāmritattināyi

In order to end my misery, I will request a little of the nectar of Thy Grace pouring from the glance of Thy holy eyes.

nin mukham kani kānān ninnati kalil vīnu
janma sāphalyattināyi varatte yāchicchitum

I will fall at Thy Feet in order to see Thy gracious face and beg for the boon of the fulfillment of life.

nin arikattu vannu vīnuke napekshikyum
enne nī upekshicchāl ennute gati yendu

Coming near, I will beg of Thee.
What will be my fate if I am forsaken?

dīnere kāttitunna nin tirumirikale
kānumārā kename mānasa kannil sadā

O Protectress of the afflicted, I must see Thee in the eye of my mind always.

ajñāna kūrirulil petturalunno renne
vigñāna dīpam kātti kāttu rakshikkename

Showing the Lamp of Knowledge, save me who is groping in the darkness of ignorance.

sarvasvarūpe devī sarva mangale devī
sarvadā kanikānān kāttu rakshikkename

O Devi Who art everything, the All-Enchantress, save me so that I can see Thee always.

en manakkannil ninne kanikandānandippān
nirmmala bhaktyā nityam ninnute nāmam oti

I worshipped Thee with pure devotion by singing Thy Name always in order to gain Thy blissful sight in my mind's eye.

kalmasha nāśiniyām ninneyum bhajicchu nyān
nin mahītalam tannil nāl enni kariyunnu

Worshipping with pure devotion Thee who art the Destroyer of sin, I am counting my days on the surface of this earth.

torāte nitya moti arādhana cheyuvān
kārunya mundākane ambike bhagavatī

O Ambika, Bhagavati, be compassionate so that, always worshipping Thee, I may enjoy the sight of Thee in my mind's eye.

**kānunnatellām ninte komala rūpamāyi
kānuvānulla bhāgyam tarane nārāyanī**

O Narayani, bless me with the good luck
to see everything as Thy own form.

**cheyunna karmma mellām satkarmmamayi tīrān
ī eraykekītane kārunya pīyūshame**

Deign to give the nectar of Thy Grace
that all of my actions may become virtuous.

**ennute karnnangalil kelpattu sarvam ninde
danya nāmangalāyi tīrkkane kārtyāyanī**

O Katyayani, let whatever I hear with my ears become Thy blessed Names.

**ennute bandhukalāyi ninnute bhaktanmāre
enaru kattu nityam kānu mārākītane**

May I see near me always as my own relatives, Thy devotees.

**en duritangal ellām enne vitta kaluvān
nin tirunāmāmritam oushadhamāyidane**

May the nectar of Thy holy Name be as medicine
to cure me of all my miseries.

**tripāda seva cheyān enikku varameki
ammayām ninnarukil enneyum cherttītane**

Granting me the boon of serving Thy holy Feet
O Mother, keep me near Thee.

tripāda patmangale sevicchu vānitunna
tvalbhakta sāmūhattil cherkkane kārunyābdhe

O Ocean of Mercy, let me join the group of Thy devotees who live serving Thy holy Lotus Feet.

ādināthayām devī trailokyanāthe ende
ātanga śāntikyāyi nyān engu poyitendū

O Primal Being, O Devi, Goddess of the three worlds, where must I go to get relief from my misery?

AMBIKE DEVI

Vol. 3, B-2

ambike devī jagannāyike namaskāram
śarmadāyike śive santatam namaskāram
ambike devī jagannāyike namaskāram

O Mother, Goddess of the Universe, I ow before Thee.
O Giver of happiness, I bow before Thee.

śānti rūpinī sarva vyāpinī mahāmāye
andhā dihīne ātmā rūpinī namaskāram

O Thou whose form is Peace, Who is omnipresent, Thou art the Great Deluder, without beginning and end. O Thou whose form is of the Self, I bow before Thee.

buddhiyu marivum nī vākku mambika tanne
chittatte nāyippatum avidunnallo devī

Intelligence, knowledge, and speech, all are Thee only.
O Devi, it is Thou who leadest the mind.

sevano chīdam bīja mantra nyā narivilā
bhāvane kyanye puram prābhavam bhavadīyam

I do not know the appropriate bija mantras for serving Thee. Thy glory is beyond imagination.

evar kum gati amba etinu mavalambam
pāvanī durge bhaktavatsale namaskāram

O Mother, Thou art the sole Refuge and Support for everyone. O Durga, O Pure One who art most affectionate to Thy devotees, I bow before Thee.

engu nyān aho mantan ānanda svarūpinī
enguvān bhavaroga beshajam bhavadrūpam

O Blissful One, I am a dullard standing at a low level. Everywhere I am seeing the disease of repeated births and deaths. Thy Divine Form is the only remedy.

ningal en naham chittam niruttum bhaktanmāril
vankanī adivegam ambanī choriyunnu

Shower Thy mercy without delay on those devotees who incessantly fix their minds on Thee.

mangal ātmike satyam īvidha mirikkyumbol
engane vārttum ninne chinmayī namaskāram

O Goddess, Thy very nature is Auspiciousness. Being the Truth, how can I adore Thee? My salutations to Thee.

KANIVIN PORULE

Vol. 3, B-3

kanivin porule karunā māyane
krishnā abhayam ekūkrishnā abhayam ekū

O Essence of Mercy, Compassionate One,
O Krishna, grant me refuge.

urukī yorūkumī kannīr kanangal tan
katha yariyunille krishnā katha yariyunille
kāliya sarpatte medicha nin pādattil
pūvitām pūjikyām śrī krishnā

O Krishna, is the story of these burning tears that flow out, unknown to Thee? Offering flowers at Thy Feet that have crushed the serpent Kaliya, I will worship Thee, O Krishna.

dushta samhāra murtte kumārā
śishta rotalpavum karuna yille
pāl katal varna nin pādāravindattil
pūvidām pūjikyām śrī krishnā

O Embodiment of the Destroyer of the wicked, have Thee no mercy towards Thy devotees? O Thou Who art the color of the Ocean of Milk, O Krishna, I will worship Thy Lotus Feet with flowers.

matsya kūrma varāhavum nītanne
narasimha vāmana bhārgavanum
śrī rāma kalki janārdhananum nīye
lokaikanāthā śrī krishnā

Matsya, Kurma, and Varaha are Thee only as are Narasimha, Vamana, and Bhargava. Thou art Sri Rama, Kalki and Janardhana, O Sri Krishna, Lord of the whole world!

kurukshetrattil pārthasāratiyāyi vannu
satyavum dharmmavum kāttavane
satyavum dharmmavum pālikkyu mīsvarā
nyangal odittiri karuna kāttū

Thou came as the charioteer of Arjuna at Kurukshetra and protected trth and righteousness. O Lord who preserves truth and righteousness, show a bit of compassion to us.

gītā nāyakā sangīta priyane
nin gītam chollān karuttu nalkū
ullinde yullil ninuruvitum nin nāmam
kelkunille nī bhajana priyā

O Lord of the Gita, Lover of music, give the capacity to sing Thy song. O Lover of devotional singing, hearest not Thy sacred Names uttered from the innermost heart?

ULAKATTI NĀDHĀRA

Vol. 4, A-1

ulakatti nādhāra porul nīyamma
guna miyalunna nayanattinoli nīyamma

O Mother, Thou art the Essence of the Substratum of the world. O Mother, Thou art the Light of virtuous eyes.

takarunna hridayattin abhayam amma
ari vinnum uravāyo rarivum amma

For breaking hearts Thou art the Refuge, O Mother. The Wisdom that is the Source of all knowledge art Thou, O Mother.

arulīdu vadinulla takhilum nīye
akhilarkum abhayam nin padatār amma

Give me all that is needed for that (Wisdom).
Thy Feet are the Refuge for all.

kanivinnu kanivāya karunānidhe
tellu kripayenni larulīdu kripāmbudhe

O Source of all mercy and Treasure of compassion, grant a bit of Thy compassion to me.

KĀRUNYA MURTE

Vol. 4, A-2

kārunyamurtte kāyāmbūvarnnā
kannu turannitane
dukha nivāraka nallo nīyen
tāpama kattītane...tāpama kattītane

O Embodiment of compassion Who art of black color, deign to open Thy eyes. Art Thou not the Destroyer of sorrow? This being so, do remove my sufferings.

ulakil āśrayam nīye
chen tāmara kannā mani varnnā
pūja kyanu dinam pushpangal ende
kannunīr ānu krishnā kannunīr ānu krishnā

In this world Thou art the shelter, O bright-colored One with eyes like the petals of a red lotus. I worship Thee forever with the flowers of my tears, O Krishna.

irulil uralukayāyi nyān
mānasa mohana gopālā
īreru lakilum niranya śrīdhara
kannu tura nīdhane tāpama kattitane

O Gopala, enchanter of the mind, I am groping in the darkness. O Thou Who fillest the fourteen worlds, O Sridhara, open Thy eyes and rid me of sorrow.

VIŚVA VIMOHINĪ

Vol. 4, A-3

viśva vimohinī anaśvara rūpinī
śāśvatānandam nalku śakti rūpinī

O Enchantress of the Universe, Indestructible One, grant us the Eternal Bliss, O Thou Whose Form is Energy.

kali yuga kalmasha makal ānāyi
kārana vastu vila nāyanāyi
kāmini kāñchana bhogā śakti
kala kale kaleyūmarttyā

O mankind! Throwing away lust, greed and the desire for enjoyment, be rid of the sins of the Kali Yuga and unite with the Supreme Cause.

mahatva merum mānava janmam
itetutta tentinu nammal
atutta janmam ati lātāyi viśuddha vastu vilettān
tatuttitūnī mānasa bhikshuve
pañcha grahangalil ninnu

For what have we taken this noble human birth? In order to reach the Pure Being and avoid another birth, prevent the wandering mendicant of the mind from entering the house of five elements.

rāvum pakalum itorupol layiccha rāmakrishna deva
vedānta sāgara tirakalu yarttiya viśva kesariye
pavitra pāvana māmā pātayi livare nayikyaname

O Lord Ramakrishna who is immersed in That day and night, O Light of the Universe who raised the waves of the Ocean of Vedanta, deign to lead these people along the holy and purifying path.

pala mata sāravu monne notiya parama sadguruve
paramārthangale yariyā turalunni varkku trāni tarū
pavitra pāvana māmāppātayi livare nayikkyaname

O Supreme Sadguru who told that the Essence of all religions is the same, strengthen those who wander, not knowing the Truth. Deign to lead them along the holy and purifying path.

VEDĀNTA VENAL

Vol. 4, A-4

vedānta venalilūde
oru nādānta pānthana lannyāl
nītān tunakyu mavane enna
gītārtha mippol evite

Now where is the truth of the Gita that proclaims that Thou wilt help a traveller to Brahman through the summer of Vedanta?

śāntātmanā padaprāptikayi
kāntāra sāmya padhattil kūti
nīndān tutangi ennālum
chintunnu chittam vyathayāl

Even though I am swimming through the forest-like way with a peaceful soul, for the attainment of Thy Feet, my mind is filled with sorrow.

entino vendi hridantam sadā
venturu kunnārtta bandho

chinta ninakki tilille ende
santāpa mokkeyum māttān

O Friend of the miserable, my heart is always burning for something, I know not what. Haven't Thou the mind to remove all of my sorrows?

amme bhagavatī devī ninde
chinmoha nasvarūpatil
vannulayikāte śāntiyi
lenamme yariyunnatille

O Mother, O Bhagavati Devi, aren't Thou knowing that without merging in Thy mind-enchanting Being, there is no peace?

PARASAHASRA

Vol. 4, A-5

parasahasra hridayangalil dhyānikyunnū
paramahamsa chittil sadā jvalichuyarnū

O Thou Who art meditated upon in thousands of hearts, Thou blaze forth forever in the minds of those who have realised God.

mana marinyu madama katti malar choriyūamme
makane ninde rūpam kātti māla kattuka

Knowing as Thou do my mind, rid me of the ego by showering flowers. O Mother, showing Thy form to this child, rescue me from all sorrow.

jani maranam rogam dukham patana
maihikam mātti charana talam cherā
nāyi kanivu nalkanam

Ridding me of this world which consists of birth, death, disease, sorrow and humiliation, show Thy mercy that I may merge in Thy Feet.

akhilaśakti nalku devī ninne vārttān
bhajanam ende nariyātta vanil olivitarenam

O Devi, shedding thy Light on me who knows not how to pray, give me the power to praise thee.

vijanamāya deśam pūki tiriyu mennālum amme
mohanamī driśyamupekshi chengane vārum

How could I live leaving this enchanting sight of Thee here and go to a lonely place to seek Thee within?

varika hrittil nrittam mātittarika darśanam
lahariyilāratte kālidāsane pole

O Thou Who dances in my heart, letting me get divinely intoxicated like Kalidasa, grant me Thy Vision.

OMKĀRA DIVYAPORULE–I

Vol. 4, B

omkāra divya porūe varū
omana makkale vegam
omanayāyi valarnā mayangal nīkki
omkāra vastu āyitīru

Come quickly darling children, you who are the Essence of OM. Removing all sorrow, grow as endearing ones and become one with the sacred syllable OM.

enile nyān ānu nīyum pinne
ninnile nī ānu nyānum
kannu kānāyi keyāl bhinnamāyi tonnunnu
bhinnam alennāl ītonnum

You are the 'I' which is in me and I am the 'you' which is in you. The feeling of difference is due to the blindness of ignorance. In truth, nothing is separate.

bheda vichāram valarnāl manam
māyāntakāratil ārum
mārgum manavum namukāgayāl nammal
āren nada ārān yarīyu

If the attitude of duality increases the mind will fall deep into the darkness of illusion. Therefore, let us seek the Self and know who we are before the mind loses its lustre.

ulla tekātma svarūpam pakal
allennu milloru bhedam
tellumagaleya lullil nirantaram
minni telinyulla sippū

The non-dual Self alone exists which knows not the difference between day and night. It is not far away but abides within us constantly shining forth with brillance.

ātma sarovara nītil
kūlichātma samtripti varuttū
śāśvatānanda tinādyam manasine
svāyatem ākkān sramikyū

Find satisfaction by bathing in the Lake of the Self. In order to enjoy Immortal Bliss, first try to attain the Self.

ninnil alinyenni lākūsadā
ninnil ānandam tireyū
kanmasham poyi janma sāphalya meluvān
nirmal ātmāvil layikyū

Merge in your Self to become one with Me and always seek happiness there. In order to remove all sorrows and to fulfill this birth, get absorbed in the Pure Self.

dāsarku dāsiyā namma
namukillore damsvontamāyi
ningal tan antarātmā vingal ānende
svonta sthalam santatavum

Mother is the servant of servants and has no abode of Her own. Her real dwelling place is in your innermost Self.

picha nadakunnu ningal amma
otu nadakunnu kūde
uttamarāyulla makkale ningalku
nityadā bodham valartān

Stumbling as you are, my children, Mother walks beside you in order to develop the consciousness of Eternity in you.

vyomatin nīlima pole dūre
nīrala pole maruvil
kānum prapañcham verum tonal ānitu
māya tan jālam ennorkū

Like the blue of the sky and the water of the distant mirage in the desert, remember that this world is unreal brought forth by the magic of Illusion.

**tūlya bhāvamkayi varānyāl
namukilla sukam tellu polum
amma chollu natal kollān kariyukil
ullatullatil teliyum**

Without gaining equanimity of vision, even a bit of real happiness cannot be enjoyed. That which IS will dawn within you if you are able to imbibe the utterances of Mother.

**kālam vridāvil ākkolle vanna
kāryam ārum mara kolle
oro nimeshavum kevalātmāvine
bodhi padinnāyi sramikyū**

Don't spend your time uselessly forgetting the purpose for which you have come to this world. Try to be aware of that Absolute Self each and every moment.

**nāma mantrangal japiche chitta
rāgādi rogam kedutī
dhyāna yogam tanvasam varuttīdukil
jīvitam dhanyamāyi tīrum**

Blessed will be this human birth if the technique of meditation through chanting the Divine Name and mantras of the Lord is learned, thereby extinguishing the disease of attraction and repulsion.

**tyāgam manasil varānyāl kodum
tāpam varum māya mūlam
āsa tīrāy kilo klesam erum sarva
nāsam varum bhūvil ārkum**

If the mind is devoid of renunciation, great suffering will befall one through illusion. If desire is not uprooted, affliction follows which will culminate in the utter ruin of anyone in this world.

sneham ānīśvara nennu makkal
orkanam ullatil ennum
sneha svarūpate dhyānichu ningalum
sneha svarūpamāyi tīrū

Dear children, always remember in your heart that God is Love. By meditating upon that Embodiment of Love you also will become Love personified.

pāricha chintakal poki makkal
prāpikanam svātmabodham
sthānamānangalku sthānamillātmāvil
ātmānubhūti varānyāl

Casting off the burden of thoughts, attain the awareness of your own True Self. If the intuitive experience of the Real Self is achieved, there will be no place for self-importance and self-conceit.

loka śāntikyu takāte makkal
jīvitam pārākidolle
gñāna sukha pūvil cherniru nittiri
ten mantra rāgam porikyū

Children, lead not a fruitless life by not giving peace to the world. Abiding in the blissful Flower of Knowledge, lightly sprinkle the honey of the melodious mantra.

nityam etennu darippān
makkal epporum mettam sramikyū
chitta pūvingal patar nirikyum
moha nidraye nīkki teliyū

Children, always strive to know That which is eternal. Become illumined by removing the pervading darkness of delusion from the mind.

pakshi mrigādikal pole prapañchatil
pirannu chākāte
lakshyam nirūpichu rachu sammodamo
dulpūvidarttān sramikyū

Don't get trapped in this cycle of birth and death like birds and animals. Be firm in your goal and joyfully try to open the Heart Lotus.

sattine nannāyi grahichāl ellām
svattāyi mārum namukku
nishtayil ninnalpam tetti tā teporum
satchidānandam smarikyū

If the Essence is known well, everything will become valuable to us. Without making even a slight error in the observance of your spiritual disciplines, remember Being-Awareness-Bliss Absolute.

veshattil alla mahatvam dhana
lābhattil alla prabhutvam
ekantamāyi manam ekātma vastuvil
ekāgramākān padikyū

Greatness is not in the dress nor is lordship in the acquisition of wealth. Be in solitude and learn to concentrate the mind on the One Self.

śuddha hridayarāyi kelkekkal
śraddhayodī tattva sāram
śuddha bhakti pravāha tingal ārukil
apore janma sāphalyam

Dear children, attentively listen to this essential truth with a pure heart. The fruit of life is immediately gained if one gets immersed in the continuous flow of pure devotion.

poruka makkale ningal vegam
bheda mattā harichīdān
inamma nalkunna tāharichīdukil
tīra vyatakalum tīrum

Come quickly dear children and eat everything without distinction. All the never-ending afflictions will cease if you eat what Mother provides today.

sāhodaryatinde tenum pinne
dīnānu kambatan nīrum
āvola mundi vidātmā vilekulla
pāteyum śobhichu kānām

Here you can find the sweet honey of brotherhood and the stream of mercy to the afflicted. One can also see here the shining path unto the Self.

āśrama jīvitum dhanyam ennāl
āśramatil kariyenam
ātmāvil āśrayam nedān mika vārnor
āśramattil murukenam

Blessed is life in an ashram, yet one should always be making 'that effort' (ā śramam). Absorb yourself in that excellent effort which will gain for you the Supreme Self as your sole refuge.

nārī janatinde munnil ninnu
nānam kunungolla makkal
vedānta vedyan padābjatil etuvān
kāminī kāñchanam pokkū

Children, don't flirt before women. Abandon women and gold (lust and greed) in order to reach the Lotus Feet of the Bestower of Vedantic Knowledge.

nāri mār ningalum nere venda
tetennu chinti churachu
pāril anarthada jīvita til ninnu
pāramārthyate grahikyū

Oh women, you also should think over and decide what is really wanted in this life. Free yourself from the clutches of the meaningless world of diversity and apprehend the Supreme Reality.

allenkil ellām orīśan tante
sallīla yānennu rakyū
sarvārpanattāl manas ātmavastuvil
sarvadā viśramikyate

Otherwise be firm in the conviction that everything is the sport of the One God. Let the mind always rest in the Self with complete surrender to Him.

makkale ningalku vendi amma
etra janmateyum pūgām
chitta rāgangal koratta millāyikayāl
śraddhichu jīvikya makkal

Darling children, Mother is ready to take any number of births for you.
Endless are the mental fluctuations, my children, so always live with utmost alertness.

śāśvatānandamte vegam
makkal sākshātkarikyān padikyū
dhyānichu sākshāt karikyāte yanyarkka
tekuvān ārkenge nokkum

Children, quickly learn the way to realise Eternal Bliss. How to transmit it to others without realising It through meditation?

ishta daivatte bhajikyān ārkkum
nishta venum yatākālam
ātma svarūpa mānennu rachāl tattva
bhaktikyu vignamilletum

One can worship one's Chosen Deity but in doing so regularity is necessary. If one has the strong conviction that devotion is identical with one's own True Nature, then there is no harm in practising devotion while established in Knowledge.

tattva mūlatte grahichu bhakti
tattvatil ettunna neram
muktikyu vere bhajikyāte bhaktiye
bhaktyā bhajikyunnu bhaktar

When the state of real devotion is attained apprehending its basic principles, the devotee, without worshipping anythig else, devotedly worships Devotion for the attainment of Liberation.

SADGURO PĀHIMĀM

Vol. 6, A-1

sad guro pāhimām jagad guro pāhimām
śrī rāmakrishna deva pāhimām pāhimām

O Perfect Guru, bless me, O Guru of the World.
Bless me, O Lord Ramakrishna, bless me, bless me.

jīva rahasyamām śānti dharmam
śānti svarūpa niyoti tenam

Tell me the Dharma of Peace which is the secret of Life,
O Thou whose very nature is Peace.

dharma rahasya mām karma margam
satya svarūpa niyoti tenam

Tell me the Path of Action which is the secret of all dharmas, O Thou whose nature is Truth.

satyam dharmatte nayichitenam
premattin śānti labhicchitenam

Let Dharma be led by Truth,
Let the peace of Love be achieved.

rūpamārūpamāyi tīrnitenam
tinmaye nanmayāyi māttitenam

Let form become formless,
Let vice be changed to virtue.

ETRAYO NĀLĀYI

Vol. 6, A-2

etrayo nālāyi kātirikyunnu nyān
vyarthamā yīdumo jīvitam īśvara

I am waiting for so many days, my Lord.
Will my life pass in vain?

lokangal kellām adīśan ānangunnu
kevalam nyān oru nissāra jīviyum

Thou art the Lord of all the worlds and I am only an insignificant creature.

sādhu vāmenude chittatil angaye
vārikyuvānulla moham vritāvillo

How can I ask Thee to come and dwell within my poor heart?

kollaru tāttoru par kudilengilum
āśayoden chittam nokku nitangaye

My heart's humble cottage door stands open wide and down the path of hope I gaze with longing day and night.

audatya mennatu tonnaru tīśvara
tellida nīyitil viśramam kollumo

Will Thou feel it presumptuous, O Lord, on my part to desire Thee to rest in my humble heart?

alpa mennākilum viśramam kollukil
dhanyamā mennude jīvitam īśvara

Lord, even if Thou come for a moment my life will become blessed.

RĀDHĀ RAMANA

Vol. 6, A-3

rādhā ramana mām hridayeśā
ādi vināśana nikhileśā
en mānasa madil maru vīdu natu
chinmāya nākiya nī yalle

O Beloved of Radha, Lord of my heart, Destroyer of misery and Support of all, is it not Thee only, the Embodiment of Consciousness, who has occupied my mind?

sukhavum śāntiyum ārivum ninavum
tikavum bhāvana vibhūtikalum
inni vanī vaka mikavu samastham
tannu tunachatu nī yalle

Pleasure and peace, the intellect and mind, all household goods and a means of livelihood, is it not Thee who has kindly blessed me with all these?

bhūvanum mūnnilum īvaniloru varum
āvanam chaivadil nīyenye
īha paramāyatum guruvara nāyatum
jananiyu māyatu nī yalle

In the three worlds, there is no one to save me except Thee. To me, Thou art this world and the world beyond. Thou art my Guru and Mother.

nityānanda vidāyaka nāyum
nityopāsita devatayāyum
hridyopāya mupeya vumāyum
vidyo dīpadu nī yalle

Thou art the Giver of Eternal Bliss. Thou art That which is worshipped eternally, and Thou art the Goal of Life and the means to reach it, and Thou art the Light of Knowledge as well.

ARIKIL UNDENKILUM

Vol. 6, A-4

arikil undenkilum ariyān kariyāte
alayunnu nyān amme
kannun dennālum kānān kariyāte
tirayunnu nyān ninne amme tirayunnu nyān amme

O Mother, even though Thou art near, I am wandering unable to know Thee. Even though I have eyes, I am searching unable to see Thee.

hemanta nīlani śīdhiniyil pūtta
vārtingal nīyāno
vānile tīduvān kariyāte tīrattil
tala tallum tira māla nyān amme
tala tallum tira māla nyān

Art Thou the beautiful moon that blooms forth in the blue winter night? I am a wave that, unable to reach the sky, beats its head against the shore.

iha loka śudha mellām vyārtha mānenulla
paramārtham nyān arinyapol
iravum pakalum kannīr orukki
ninne yariyān kotichūamme
ninne yariyān kotichū

When I came to understand the truth that all worldly comforts are worthless, I longed to know Thee shedding tears day and night.

dukha bhārattāl talaru norenne nī
āsvasippikyān varille
ettīdu mennulla āśayode nyān
nityavum kātirikyunnu amme
nityavum kātirikyunnu

Won't Thou come to comfort me who am weary of the burden of sorrow? With the desire that Thou wilt come, I am waiting always.

ŚYĀMA SUNDARA

Vol. 6, B-1

śyāma sundara madana mohana rādhe gopāl
brindāvana chandra krishna rādhe gopāl

he giridhāri he avatāri rādhe gopāl
brindāvana chandra krishna rādhe gopāl
krishnā...rādhe gopāl
kanayā...rādhe gopāl

he mana varī kunja vihāri rādhe gopāl
navanīta chora nanda kumāra rādhe gopāl
krishnā...rādhe gopāl
govindā...rādhe gopāl

rādhika lola venu gopāla rādhe gopāl
karunāla vāla chitta chandana rādhe gopāl
krishnā...rādhe gopāl
kanayā...rādhe gopāl

bhakta vatsala madana gopāla rādhe gopāl
murali vāla dīna dayāla rādhe gopāl
krishnā...rādhe gopāl
govindā...rādhe gopāl

janārdhana madana mohana rādhe gopāl
dayā sāgara ati sukūmāra rādhe gopāl
krishnā.....rādhe gopāl
kanayā.....rādhe gopāl

sanātana dīna janā vana rādhe gopāl
pāvana bhakta urachandana rādhe gopāl
krishnā.....rādhe gopāl
govindā.....rādhe gopāl

kambukandādhara govārdhanadhara rādhe gopāl
dayā sāgara ati sukūmāra rādhe gopāl

krishnā.....rādhe gopāl
kanayā.....rādhe gopāl

gopa kumāra gopi jana priya rādhe gopāl
govardhanadhara gokula nandana rādhe gopāl
krishnā.....rādhe gopāl
govindā.....rādhe gopāl

avatāri=Divine Incarnation
atisukūmara=The most beautiful
bhakta urachandana=Cooling like sandalpaste to the devotees
bhaktavatsala=Who is fond of the devotees
brindāvana chandra=The moon of Brindavan, the sporting ground of Krishna
chitta chandana=Who is as cooling as sandalpaste to the mind
dayā sāgara=Ocean of kindness
dīnadayāla=The Compassionate One
dīnajanāvana=Protector of the grief- stricken
gokulanandana=Son of Nanda of the village of Gokula
gopakumāra=Son of a cowherd
gopijana priya=Beloved of the Gopis or cowherdesses
gopāl=Protector of the cows
govardhanadhara=Holder of the Govardhana Hill
govinda=Lord of the cows
he giridhari=O the One who held the mountain on His hand
janārdhana=Oppressor of the wicked
kambukandādhāra=Who holds a lotus in His hand
kannaya=Darling
karunālavāla=The kind one
kunjavihāri=Who plays in the grove of trees
madana mohana=Enchanter of even Cupid
madana=Like Cupid in His beauty
manavari=One who releases one from the bondage of mind
muralivāla=Who plays the flute
nandakumāra=Son of the cowherd Nanda
navanītachorā=Stealer of butter
pāvana=The Holy One

rādhe=Beloved of Krishna
rādhikalola=Who has a soft heart towards Radha
sanātana=Eternal
śyāma=Blue-black color
sundara=Beauty
venugopāla=Who plays the flute

UYIRĀYI OLIYĀYI

Vol. 6, B-2

uyirāyi oliyāyi ulakattin muratāyi
urapongum umaye nī yevide
kāttāyi katalāyi kanalāyi nilkum en
kalaye nin kanive nilille

O Goddess Uma, where art Thou Who art said to be the life, light and firmness of the earth? O artful One Who exists as wind, sea and fire, have Thou no mercy on me?

ari vellām akalunnu piravippol tudarunnu
ari vellām ura vākunnū
kura vellām tikayunnu tikavutta nī yenye
mara yellām maravākunnū

All wisdom has fled to a distance and repeated births continue. Unreality has become reality and all defects are increasing in the absence of Thee who art the Real Knowledge concealed.

rudhi rāsti māmsatāl paritāpa durgandha
puriye samrakshikyunnū
puri vātil pura mellām pari pāvana mākunnū
puri nāthane ariyunilla

Thou art protecting this pitiful city (the body) stinking with blood, bone and flesh. We clean the surface of the body alone knowing not its Lord.

mana mākum vānaran mada menna kaniyumāyi
nina villā turarīdunnū
tan rūpam ninayāte kālattin kanivil nām
kālannūnāyi mārunnū

The monkey of the mind wanders ceaselessly holding in its hand the fruit of conceit. Reflecting not on its Real Nature it becomes food for the God of Death.

BANDHAM ILLA

Vol. 6, B-3

bandha milla bandhu villa svonta mallonnum nammal
kantya kālam bandhu vennatu svonta mātmāvu

No one is ours and there is nothing to call as our own. In our last days only the True Self will remain as ours.

kanda tonnum kondu poyi kanda tillārum pinne
entininnī kandatellām svonta mākkunnū

We can take nothing with us during the last journey.
Why then this madness for earthly possessions?

ulla tonnundulli lallā talla mattengum atu
kandi tānāyi ulli nullil chellanam nammal

That which truly exists is within us.
To see That, we must go within.

alla lin kallola monnum tellu millangu ellām
ullapol ullinde yullil ulla sichīdum

There is not even a trace of sorrow there.
There the True Self shines in Its own glory.

ullunar nullālariyān ullamārgate nerāyi
chollitām nyān enna bhāvam nalla pol ponam

The awakening of the Inner Self and True Knowledge comes only when egoism is completely gone.

ullatallā tullatil nin nullatil chellān nammal
kullinakkam nalla polellārilum venam

We go from untruth to Truth when we love and serve all living beings.

JAYA JAYA DEVI

Vol. 6, B-4

jaya jaya devī dayāmayiyambe
karunārnnava sudha yarulukayambe
arumara yotuka yadi yangalkāyi
amritānandamayī mama devī

Victory! Victory to Mother who is full of kindness. O Mother, kindly give the bliss of Thy ocean-like Compassion. Utter the Vedas for Thy servants, O my Goddess Amritanandamayi.

ana varatam tava charana smaranam
bhava bhaya haranam pāpa vināśam
avi kala dharmma parāyani śubhade
amritānandamayī mama devī

The remembrance of Thy lotus face destroys sin and the fear of becoming, O Thou Who art attached to the Pure Dharma, Giver of auspiciousness, O my Goddess Amritanandamayi.

naśvara loka sukhangal tyajikyān
niśchaya dārdhya modarulun ambe
viśva vidhāyaki vimala svarūpe
amritānandamayī mama devī

O Mother Who emphatically says to give up the comforts of the mortal world, Creatress of the Universe, whose Nature is Purity Itself, O my Goddess Amritanandamayi.

bhaktajanār chitta pāvani mahite
śudha manohara susmita vadane
śaktiyerātta mahatva padattil
varttikyum amritānandamayī

O great Holy One worshipped by devotees, with a pure enchanting smile on Thy face, in the Supreme State, untouched by desire dwellest Thou, O Amritanandamayi.

śokāmaya miha dūreya kattān
śāradayāyi jani yārnnavalo nī
śobhikyum hridayangalil nityam
amritānandamayī tava charanam

To rid us of this sorrowful world Thou has taken birth as the Goddess of Wisdom O Amritanandamayi, Thy Feet will shed brilliance in the heart forever.

patitarkāyi nī janma meduttu
parahitame nin pāvana lakshyam
nara rūpam sachinmaya rūpam
amritānandamayī mama devī

Thou has taken birth for the sake of the miserable. Thy holy aim being the well-being of others, Thou with a human form, Whose real Form is Being-Awareness, O my Goddess Amritanandamayi.

ātma viśuddhikyāyi tava makkal
kātmānātma vivechana marulum
svātma nimungi yorukum tava mridu
vākyam tān amritānandam

For gaining a pure mind Thou bestowest the discrimination between Self and non-Self. Immersed in the Atman as Thou art, Thy soft words flow out in an ambrosial stream.

ĀNANDĀMRITA RŪPINI

Vol. 8, A-1

ānand āmritā rūpini yamme
akhilāndeśvariye
ānanda tira mālayil nin nadha
yenneya kat alle

O Immortal, Blissful Mother, Goddess of the Universe, deprive not Thy worthless child of bliss.

andaga nadiga sīmani yetti
dandhu chura tumbol
nin tiru vadi mala rallā tilloru
chinta yeni kappol

My mind knows naught but Thy Lotus Feet. The King of Death scowls at me terribly. Tell me Mother, what shall I say to Him?

enno den doru tittinu bhīshani
hanta kadichu kritāntan
chonnī duga nī yivan odu sadayam
bhairavi devi bhavāni

It was my hearts desire to sail my boat across the ocean of this mortal life, O Durga, with Thy Name upon my lips.

āram kānnātta lagada lāmi
samsār ormmi yilenne
tārā nida nīyā kidu mennoru
nila nyān orttadu mille

I never dreamt that Thou wouldst drown me here in the dark waters of this shoreless sea.

nin tiru nāma smarana manārata
mendu vadundo hridantam
ennittum punar enden svāntam
tāndama tāvu nidāntam

Both day and night I swim amongst its waves, chanting Thy saving Name, yet even so O Mother, there is no end to my grief.

durgati yidu vidha mānī bhaktanu
tan arulīdu vadengil
durgā nāma mura padi narum
mutiru kayil ini meli

If I am drowned this time in such a plight, no one will ever chant Thy Name again.

KĀLINA KĀNĀN

Vol. 8, A-2

kālina kānānde kannu kalā hanta
kālunnu kāyāmbūvarnnā
kālika lotum kural vili yotum nī
otivā tāmara kannā

O dark-colored One, my eyes are pitifully burning for the sight of Thy Feet. O lotus-eyed One, come running with the cows and the music of the flute.

vennayum pālum tarānilla nyān kure
vedanakal kārcha vekkyām
kannīr kanangalām muttukal nyān ende
kannā nin kālkalarpikkyām

Having no butter and milk to offer Thee, I will offer Thee a little of my pain. O Kanna, at Thy Feet I will offer the pearl drops of my tears.

etra nālāyi vilikyunnu nyān nina
kittiriyum kaniville
itra melendu pirachūnyānayo nī
bhaktajana prīya nalle

For how many days have I been calling Thee? Hast Thou not even a bit of compassion? What great error have I committed? Art Thou not the Lover of the devotees?

kenu kenayo nyān vīnitum mumbe nī
venu vumāyingu vā vā
kevala nām ninne kānāte vāruvān
āvadi layyo nī vā vā

Before I fall down crying deign to come with Thy flute unable to live as I am without seeing Thee who are the sole Reality, come, come.

pīlikal chūtiya kārkūndal kettu mā
komala pon chāndu pottum
chelerum tūmanya pattu meni konnu
kānnuvā nen nini kittum

When will I be able to see Thy hair with a peacock feather stuck therein, the lovely bright mark on Thy forehead and Thy lovely pure silk cloth?

kārana pūrusha kāmida dāyaka
kāyambūvarnā nī vā vā
kālam kalayāte khedam valarttāte
kārunyamūrte nī vā vā

Fulfiller of desires, Cause of all, O dark-colored One, come,come. Without wasting time and increasing my sorrow, O Embodiment of Compassion, come, come.

ĀGATANĀYI

Vol. 8, A-3

āgatanāyi āgatanāyi vishnu devan
āśamsakal nalkuka nām devanu nityam
lokādhi nāyakan vannallo
lokati nāśvāsa meku vānāyi

Lord Vishnu has come! Lord Vishnu has come! Let us offer worship to the Lord always. The Supreme Lord of the world has come for giving comfort to the world.

mannil vārum martyarute kleśa makattān
mannilekitā devan vannu nilkunnu
śānti nāyakan devan kārunya pūrnan
moksha mārga meku vānāyi vanni rangi yo

The Lord has come to the earth to rid the men of earth of sorrow. Has the Lord of Peace, full of compassion, descended to show the way to

Ā JĪVANĀNTAM

Vol. 8, A-4

ā jīvanāntam bhajikyām nyān
ā tanga minnu nī tīrttu taru

ādi parāśakti yā devī
ā mayam nīkki anugrahikyu

I will worship till the end of my life but rid me of my sorrow today. O Goddess, Primal Supreme Power, bless me, remove my grief.

sarvā bhīshtavum nalku mamme
sarvārtha sādhike loka māte
sarvāvalam bayām śakti rūpe
śarvarī śāśvate satyamūrtte

O Mother Who grants all desires, O Universal Maya Who fulfills all desires, Thy Form is Energy, the Support of all, Parvathi, the eternal Embodiment of Truth.

tyāgangal etra sahikyunnu nyān
tāmasam ende katākshikyuvān
tāye nin māyayil ārti tolle
tāvaka pādam namāmi nityam

How many sufferings I am bearing Why art Thou delaying to cast Thy gracious glance? O Mother, drown me not in Thy Maya. I bow to Thy Feet always.

NIRAMILLA

Vol. 8, B-1

niramillā maraville manamatta malare
kanivinā yennum nī karayunno karale
karayunno karale

A rainbow without colors, a flower without fragrance, when such is my heart, why cry for compassion?

venalillā manyukālam mātramo ī jīvitam
vedanayāl nādamatta vīnakal pole

Life has become full of coldness without even a trace of warm feeling like a veena which has no sweet melodies but sorrowful silence alone.

katiravende karam ettā vāna madhyatil
cheriyo raruvi yullatil nali nangal
vitarārundo vitarārundo

Can the lotus flowers in a small rivulet deep within the forest blossom where the rays of the Sun cannot reach?

vānil megham kandu kekikal
pīli nivartti verute
jala kanattinu verāmbal tapas irunnu tapas irunnu

Seeing the clouds in the sky, the peacock spread its wings to dance, but in vain, and a chataka bird waited for drops of water.

NB: It is told that the chataka bird will drink only raindrops as they fall during the rains. It does not relish any other water. The idea is that both the peacock and the chataka feel happy at the sight of clouds but become miserable in the absence of the rain. Likewise, waiting for God alone to make us happy seems to be in vain after prolonged search and spiritual practice not yielding its fruit.

VEDĀMBIKE

Vol. 8, B-2

vedāmbike namo nādāmbike
vande surasangha sevya pādam

O Mother of the Vedas, O Mother of Sounds, I bow to Thee. I bow to Thy Feet which are adored by the Gods.

kāma pradam kama lābha pradam
kada nāri katattuken rāga priye

Bestowing love, bestowing the radiance of the lotus,
O Lover of music, take me across this ocean of misery

vidye śive sarva loka hite
madahatye jaya bhavanāśa kartre

O Goddess of Wisdom, O Parvati Who does good to all the world,
Destroyer of pride and rebirth, be victorious.

māyā mayam mana mārāl gatam mama
ālambanam tava pādāmbujam

Thou Who art full of Maya, by whom the mind exists,
Thy Lotus Feet are my support.

prānikal kokkeyum prāna namma
kārya tinokkeyum kārana mamma

Mother is the Life of all creatures. Mother is the Cause of all things.

gora samsāra makattitenam
dīna nāmenne nī kattitenam

Deign to rid me of this terrible cycle of birth and death. Protect this miserable one.

muktide muktide haste namo
śakte namaste mahā prabhāve

Bowing to Thee with joined palms, I pray, give me Liberation.
O Powerful One, Great Radiance, I bow to Thee.

KANNUNĪR KONDU

Vol. 8, B-3

kannunīr kondu nin pādam karūkām
kātyāyanī nī kāyivitalle

I shall wash Thy Feet with my tears. O Katyayani, forsake me not.

etranāl venamen ambike
tvadrūpa darśanam ekuvān

How many days are wanted, my Mother,to grant me the Vision of Thy Form?

avadhikal kettende ātmāvu
āśvasikyunnu nin māyayāl

Though Thou delayest in giving what I want,
my mind sits satisfied because of Thy Maya.

oru chenniramalar appada taliril
arppikyuvān nī anuvadikkyū

Will Thou allow me to offer a red flower at Thy Feet?

vijana māmī vīdiyilūten
varade teti alayunnu nyān

Through this forlorn path I wander in the hope of finding Thee.

kāmarāja priye nin mana sailattil
kārunya mundo cholla chollu

Is there any kindness in Thy hard heart, tell me, O Beloved of Śiva?

VANNĀLUM AMBIKE

Vol. 8, B-4

vannālum ambike tāye manoharī
tannālum tāvaka darśanatte
sañchita saubhagamen chitta patmattil
nin chāru rūpam vilangi tatte

Come, O Mother, Who art the Enchantress of the mind. give me, O Ambika, Thy Vision. Let Thy Form shine in the lotus of my heart.

ennullil bhaktiye chemme yunartunna
dhanya mām ponnusha senudikkum
nāmam japichu samtruptayāyi ennu nyān
ānanda bāshpabi vilolayākum

When will dawn that blessed day when my heart will become full of devotion to Thee? Satiated with the repetition of Thy Name, when will blissful tears flow from my eyes?

māmaka chitta mātmāvum viśuddhamāyi
mevunna nālennu vannu cherum
mānavum māmūlum lajayum kleśavum
nyān upekshikyunna nāl varumo

When will that day dawn when my mind and soul will become pure?
Then vain pride, possessiveness, bashfulness and affliction will be relinquished.

bhakti yākum madhu motti kutichu nyān
chikennu premattāl matta yākum
potti chirichu nyān ānanda magnayāyi
pettennu kannīruvannu kerum

When will I drink the nectar of devotion and becoming intoxicated, laugh and cry immersed in bliss lost in Thee?

MANAME NARA JĪVITAM

Vol. 8, B-5

maname nara jīvita mākum
vāyal elakal varalukayāne
oru parudum krishi yillāde
tari sāyadu mauvukayāne

O mind, the human birth is like a field... if not cultivated properly, it becomes dry and barren.

vidhi polatil vittukal pāki
krishi cheyuva tavida mennāyi
arivilla ninakoru lesam
ariyān otti labhilāsham

You know neither how to sow the seeds in the proper way nor how to grow them well. Not only that...you don't even have the wish to know also.

vala mit oda nūradu marichum
nala modadha kalakal parichum
pari chodadha pāli polum
vila koyyām madi yāvolam

By removing the weeds, putting fertilizer and by taking care properly, you could have gotten a good harvest.

kadana meru nortu kāraya līnāl
vika līdamayi nin kaumāram
tarunī viharana radha nāyi
takaru kayāyi nava tārunyam

The early part of life is spent in helpless cries and youth is spent in lustful attachment.

kārivukal muruvan kiravākum
kiravan ni yoru puruvākum
torilil ninnute norivākum
kuriyum nokki yiripākum

Now old age is coming and all of your strength will be taken away. You are going to become like a helpless worm and without any work, will spend the time looking forward to the grave.

IDAMILLA

Vol. 9, A-1

ida millā talayunna vari pokkanāyi amme
śaranārttha mannayunna vari kāttitū
nila yillā torukunna nadi tanni lalayāte
karayettā nutakunna gati yekitū

A wanderer am I here, who has no hearth or home. O Mother, give me refuge and lead me towards Thee. Let me not get tossed about in the deep waters, but extending Thy helping hand, take me to the shore.

chita tanni leriyunna hrita menna pol manam
eriyunnu pitayunnu bhuvi tannilāyi
chira katta para vayiku nila mundukel ī
manuja noravalambam minni yārammā

Like butter poured in fire, my mind is being burnt in this world. A bird can at least fall to the earth, but for a human being, who but Thee art the Support?

tirupāda malar tannil amarnītuvān amme
koti vanna taha mennu karu tāvato

mama mātā tiru nāmam oru neramen
akame nin nutirnnāl nī vetiyāvato

Wishing to come to Thy Lotus feet, O Mother, calling Thy Name but once, I thought this simple child would not be forsaken by Thee. Was that wrong? I know not, O Mother.

ini yennu tarum ninde pada darśanam amme
atināyi natiyende mana mekuven
avakāśa matinille bhuvaneśvarī
en akatāril ini yennu prabha tūkitum

When will I be blessed with the Vision of Thy Feet which my mind ever craves to reach? O Mother of the Universe, do I not deserve that much at least? When, O when will Thy Presence illumine the mind?

AMME BHAGAVATI

Vol. 9, A-2

amme bhagavatī nitya kanye devī
enne katākshi pān kumbitunnen

O Mother Divine, the Eternal Virgin,
I bow to Thee for Thy gracious glance.

māye jagatinde tāye chidānanda
priye maheśvari kumbitunnen

O Maya, Mother of the Universe, O Pure Awareness-Bliss, O Beloved Great Goddess, I bow to Thee.

bāle chaturveda mūla mantrāksharī
mele mele ninne kumbitunnen

O Source of all the mantras in the Four Vedas,
I bow to Thee again and again.

omkara kūttile paingili paitale
nin kālinayitā kumbitunnen

O Thou, the parrot in the nest of Omkara, I bow to Thy Feet.

nān mukhan tan mukha pankaja vāsinī
nān mara kātale kumbitunnen

O Thou Who dwellest in the lotus face of Lord Brahma, O Essence of the Four Vedas, I bow to Thee.

nānā nigamo dyānatil madī chittu
gānam murakunna kokilamme

Thou art the cuckoo singing intoxicated and sporting in the garden of the various Scriptures. I bow to Thee.

bhārga viyāyatum pārvatī yāyatum
durgā bhagavatī nītānallo

O Goddess Durga, it is Thou Who became Bhargavi and Parvati.

mūrtikal mūvarum devatā sanghavum
kārttyāyanī śakti nītānallo

O Katyayani, O Sakti, Thou art the Three Murtis (Brahma, Vishnu and Śiva) and the host of other gods.

chāyā svarūpinī chaitanya kārinī
māyā maye devī kumbitunnen

O Thou whose nature is as the shadow of the Real, the Cause of Life, O Thou who art full of Maya, I bow to Thee.

lokam chamakyayum rakshicharikyayum
lokeśvarī ninde līlayallo

O Goddess of the world, it is just Thy play to create the world and save it by undoing it.

bāle manonmani ponamme ninnute
līlayil nyānu manuvutane

O Mind of the mind, O Dearest Mother, I am just a mere worm in Thy play.

tān onnum cheyāte sarvam chetītunna
dīna dayālo torunnen ninne

O Thou who art merciful to the afflicted, who doest everything without doing anything, I bow to Thee.

brahmānda kotikale sevicchīdunna
brahma svarūpini kumbitunnen

O Thou of the nature of Brahman, who serves tens of millions of universes, I bow to Thee.

lūtam kanakke bhuvanam chamakyunna
mātāve nin pādam kumbitunnen

O Mother who creates the world like a spider, I bow to Thy Feet.

kālī karālī mahishaghni śankarī
nālī kalochane kumbitunnen

O Kali of black hue, Destroyer of the demon Mahisha, Sankari, whose eyes are like the petals of a lotus, I bow to Thee.

kaumārī sankata nāśini bhāskarī
bhīmātmaje ninne kumbitunnen

O Thou who art ever young, Destroyer of sorrow, O Thou of Great Soul, Bhaskari, I bow to Thee.

āpattu nīkki tunachekyen ambike
nin pattu sampattu nalkitenam

O my Mother, save us by removing all dangers and give us the ten kinds of wealth.

ŚRI RĀMA NĀMAMU

Vol. 9, A-3

śrī rāma nāmamu
yento manchi madhuramu
madhurādi madhuramu
mana kande amritamu

tāta kama jim jim munula
kāpādina nāmamu
rāvanādi rākshasūlanu
gedi inchina nāmamu

ĀRUNDU CHOLLU VĀN

Vol. 9, A-4

ārundu cholluvān ninnatuttambike
kātara nākumen dīnā vilokanam
prema svarūpinī mānava nākumen
jīvita mīvidham tīrukayo vidhi

O Mother, other than Thee, to whom can I tell my distress? O Thou whose nature is Love, is my fate that my human birth should end like this?

sankalpa gopuram kallola jālattāl
tallitta karkkunna tente dayāmayī
sneham pakarumā ponnilam kaikonden
kannīr tutakyuvān bhāvamillāyikayo

O Compassionate One, why art thou shattering the imaginary tower that I have raised? Aren't Thou ready to wipe my tears with Thy gentle hand that pours out love?

jātanāyi vannanā linnolavum bahu
śokam bhujicchu nyān vannu nin nandike
nīrum manovyātha ārunna tinnamma
snehakktir vīśi cherkkumo nin pade

I have come near Thee after suffering great sorrows from the time of my birth until now. Sprinkling the Nectar of Love, won't Thou merge me in Thy Feet?

mohichu nin rūpam chārattu kanditān
māya kondene nī mohita nākkole
ātma sumangale amme hridi sthite
ātmānandam tarān tāmasam entini

For relief from mental distress, I have longed to see Thee near me. Enchant me not with Thy Maya, O Auspicious, Eternal One. O Mother, who dwells in the heart, why art Thou delaying to give the bliss of the Self?

ORU TULLI SNEHAM

Vol. 9, B-1

oru tulli sneham en jīva santushtikāyi
varalunnī hridayattin nekukamme
entinā nentinā neriyunna tīkori
kariyunnī vallikku valamitunnu

O Mother, for the satisfaction of my life give a drop of Thy love to my dry burning heart. Why, O why dost Thou put burning fire as fertilizer to this scorched creeper?

potupote potti karanyu nyān etrayo
chutu kannīr nin munnil arpicchu poyi
netu vīrpil mātramo tungi pitayu men
utal tingum karal vingal kelkunille

Bursting out crying, how many hot tears have I offered before Thee? Hear Thou not my heart throbbing and agony coming out as suppressed sighs?

pāte patar norā chandana kātati
lūde katanagni nrittamāti
ītum balavumī śokāgniyil
takarnnotāyi terikyān ninna chitolle

Let not the fire enter and dance through the forest of sandalwood trees. Let not this fire of sorrow show its strength and burst forth like shattering tiles.

durgga durggeti japichen mati mattu
mārgangal okke marannu devī
svarggavum vendāpavarggavum vendende
durgge nin nirmmala bhakti mātram

O Devi, chanting the Name 'Durga, Durga' my mind has forgotten all other paths. O my Durga, I want neither heaven nor liberation. I want only pure devotion to Thee.

MARTYARE SAMSĀRA

Vol. 9, B-2

martyare samsāra vāridhi kyakare
ettī chīdum bhava tārini ambike
ī prapañchattin muradāyi mevidum
aprameyo jvala śakti svarūpinī

O Mother, Thou art the Redeemer of mankind taking us across the ocean of the world. Thou art the Primal Cause of the world, the Power behind the Universe.

nī yallayo trigunādhārayāyi jīva
bhāvamāyi mevunna teja svarūpinī
nyān ariyunnu bhaval prīti yonnutān
mānava janmam kritārthama kīduvān

Thou manifest as the three gunas and the Supreme Life Force too. I know, O Mother, that Thy love for us makes the fulfillment of human life possible.

nyān arinjīdunnu nin kripālepanam
dīna samtrānanam chevaden ulladum
śānti jagatilunārti nin puñchiri
pūtingalāyi parīlasikunnadum

The moonlight of Thy smile gives light and peace to this world of misery and darkness.

pañcha bhūtangal prapañcha ghatanayil
panku vahīpatum nin kripa vaibhavam

pūrna kumbatilum arghya putatilum
bhūtangal anchilum ādi mūlatilum

Out of the five elements the Universe is made to manifest by Thy gracious Glory. Thou art the holy waters, the elements and the Root Cause.

sākārayāyum nirākārayāyum ī
loka tilengum vilangunna devi nī
enne tyajichāl ā rakshanam entinu
mannittil ī vāranam cholluken ambike

Thou fillest the whole Universe manifesting with and without form. If for even a moment Thou abandonest me, tell me then, O Mother, what is the use of this life on earth?

ĀDIYIL PARAMEŚVARIYE

Vol. 9, B-3

ādiyil parameśvariye
akhila loka jananiye
ārumilla gadi yenikku
amma yallā tīyu lakingal

O Primal Supreme Goddess, O Mother of all the worlds, I have no goal in this world other than Mother.

pālikyunnu mūnnu lokangal
nīlavāri jalocha nayamma
mālakattu kale kamalālaye
mūla kārinī māye manohare

Mother, of beautiful eyes like the petals of a blue lotus, preserves the three worlds. O Dweller in the lotus, Maya, O Beautiful One, the Source of everything, rid me of all sorrows.

kāttu kollana menne kripāmayī
ārtti nāśinī samsāra tārinī
bhakti mukti pradāyinī yambike
kīrtti rūpinī kārttyāyanī namo

Protect me, O Gracious One, O Destroyer of greed, who takes one across the tract of transmigration. O Mother, giver of devotion and liberation, O Far-famed One, Katyayani, I bow to Thee.

vishtape sarva buddhiyum vidyayum
tushti pushtiyum srishtiyum nī tanne
ishta sādhike dhārshtya makatti yen
klishtata povān chitte vasi kyanam

O Goddess of the earth who art Wisdom and Knowledge, delight, nourishment and creation are Thee only. O Fulfiller of desires, ridding me of pride, dwell in my mind in order to remove my distress.

ANANTAMĀM Ī LOKATIL

Vol. 9, B-4

anantamām ī lokatil oru
anuvāmī yenne nī
āśvasippikkān varūdaivame
āśvasippikkān varū

O Lord, come, come, to console me who am a mere atom in this infinite world.

innende munpil varename
innende dukham tīrttitename
īreru patinālu lokam bharikunna
īśvara jagadīśvara

O Lord, Lord of the Universe who reigns over the fourteen worlds, come before me today and end my sorrows.

uttamapāta nī kāttitarū
uttama chintakal mātram tarū
uttam tonni karuten manassil
urinyu tayavan tamburāne

Show me the sublime path. Give me only sublime thoughts. O Lord Who art the Creator of this world, may I never feel any pride in my mind.

ennennum nin gītam pātuvānum
ennennum en munnil kānuvānum
ekāntamāyi ninne dhyānippānum
erām svarggasthā nī kāttitane

O Thou who exists in the seventh heaven, show me the way to sing Thy praises forever, to see Thee before me always and to meditate upon Thee in solitude.

ŚRI KRISHNA ŚARANAM

Vol. 10, A-1

śrī krishna śaranam mamā
śrī krishna śaranam mamā
śrī hari śaranam mamā
śrī hari śaranam mamā

Sri Krishna is my Refuge.
Sri Hari is my Refuge.

satchidānanda rupāya viśvot patyādi hetave
tāpatraya vināśāya śrī krishnāya vayam namaha

Prostrations to Sri Krishna Whose nature is Existence-Awareness-Bliss, the Cause of the creation, preservation and dissolution of the Universe, the Destroyer of the three types of suffering.

vamsī vibhūshita karāt navanīra dābhāt
pitāmbarāt aruna bimba phalā taroshtāt
purnentu sundara mukhāt aravinda netrāt
krishnāt param kimapi tatva maham na jāne

I know no Reality other than Sri Krishna whose hand holds the flute, who is beautiful like a fresh raincloud, who wears yellow robes, whose lips are red like an aruna bimba fruit, whose face is charming like the full moon and whose eyes are elongated like lotus petals.

śrī krishna nī perento madhuramulā
nandalāla nī perento madhuramulā
brindāvana chandrā
śrī krishna tera pyāra nāma he
śrī krishna tera pyāra nāma he
tera pyāra nāma he

Sri Krishna, how sweet is Thy Name.
O Son of Nanda, how sweet is Thy Name.
O Moon of Brindavan, Sri Krishna is the Name dear to Thee.
Radha, Govinda, Sri Krishna are Names dear to Thee,
These Names are dear to Thee.

rādhe govinda jai rādhe gopāl
rādhe govinda jai rādhe gopāl
govinda govinda gopari pāl
govinda govinda gopari pāl

Victory to Radha Govinda
Victory to Radha Gopal

Govinda, Govinda, Goparipal (Protector of the cows).

koyi kahe vasudevaki nandana
koyi kahe nandalāla
koyi kahe nandalāla

Some say that Thou art the Son of Vasudeva,
Others call Thee the Son of Nanda.

yamunaki nāre krishna kannaya murali madhura bhajāre
śrī krishna tera pyāra nāma he
natavaralāla tera pyāra nāma he
munijanapāla tera pyāra nāma he
śrī krishna śaranam mamā
śrī hari śaranam mamā

On the banks of the Yamuna river the child Krishna plays the flute so sweetly. Sri Krishna is a Name dear to Thee. Nadavaralala (one who loves to dance) is a Name dear to Thee. Munijanapala (Protector of the sages) is a Name dear to Thee.

KARUNĀLAYE DEVI

Vol. 10, A-2

karunālaye devi kāmita dāyinī
kārttyāyanī gaurī śāmbhavi śankarī

O Goddess, Abode of Compassion, Giver of desired things, O Katyayani, Gauri, Sambhavi, Sankari...

omkāra porule
ammā...ammā...ammā
omkāra porule nī
omkāra nāda priye
om śakti mantram kettāl...ammā

om śakti mantram kettāl
oti yettum mahāmaye

O Essence of OM, O Mother...Mother...Mother,
Thou who art the Essence of OM, Lover of the sound of OM, when Thou hearest the mantra 'OM Śakti', O Mother, Thou wilt come running, O Great Maya (Power of Universal Illusion).

srishti sthiti laya mellām nin chetikal
ellām nī yammā nī tanṇe yellām ellām
nī yallā tilla vere...ammā...ammā...ammā
nī yallā tilla vere agatikyu gadi yammā
ānand ātmike...ammā
ānand ātmike aruluka nal varam

The creation, preservation and destruction of the Universe are all Thy doings. O Mother, all is Thyself, Thou Thyself art all. There is none other than Thee, O Mother. O Mother, this suppliant has no other support except Thee, the Self of Bliss. O Blissful Self, grant me a good boon.

NĪLĀMBŪJA

Vol. 10, A-3

nīlāmbūja nāyane amme nī arinyo
ī nīrunna chittattin tengalukal

O Mother with blue lotus eyes, will Thou not listen to the sobbings of this sorrowing heart?

eto janmattil chetoru karmmattāl
ekāntanāyi nyān alayunnu

Perhaps due to the deeds of some past birth I am wandering alone.

yugānta rangalilūde oruki nyān ī
yuga sandhyayil piranyu vīrān
punarnītumo vārī pulkītumo
nin mati tattil kitatītumo amme
nin mati tattil kitatītumo

I have passed through ages and ages before taking birth now. Will Thou not take me to Thee with a motherly hug and put me in Thy lap?

yogyan allennālum mātāvu putrane
samtyaji chītumo toga dātri
vannītumo arikil anachītumo
nin kripā leśam tannītumo amme
nin kripā leśam tannītumo

I may not be deserving but, O Mother, will Thou forsake this child for that reason? Won't Thou come and, taking me close, give me a merciful glance?

KANNILENKILUM

Vol. 10, A-4

kannilenkilum karalin kannināl
kannane nyān innu kandūende
rādhā ramanane kandūende
rādhā ramanane kandū

Though not with these eyes, today I have seen my darling Krishna, the Beloved of Radha, with the Inner Eye!

sankalpa chorane saundarya rūpane
sangīta kārane kandūende
sāyūjya nāthane kandūende
sāyūjya nāthane kandū

I have seen the Stealer of the mind, Beauty Personified, the Divine Musician. I have seen my Lord of Oneness.

nīla katal varnna mundo āvo
pīlichurul mutiyundo
otakkuralinde nādattilūte nyān
komala rūpane kandū

Was He the blue color of the ocean? Did He have a peacock feather adorning His curly locks? I can't say but, through the sound of the Flute, I have seen His gracious Form.

ĀGAMĀNTA PORULE

Vol. 10, B-1

āgamānta porule jaganmayī
ārariyunnu ninne vidyāmayī
ānandātmike nitye nirāmayī
ādiśakti parāśakti pāhimām

O Essence of the Agamas (revealed Scriptures), Thou who fillest the universe, who knows Thee who art full of Wisdom? O Self of Bliss, Eternal Being devoid of sorrow, O Primal Power, Supreme Power, protect me.

sarvvāntaranga nivāsini sarvagnya
nirvvāna saukhya pradāna parāyani
dushtar korikkalum kandu kittāttaval
śishtartan dhyānatil ennum vilanguvol

Thou art the Dweller in all hearts knowing all, eager to offer the bliss of Liberation, who cannot be seen by the wicked but who always shines in the meditation of the virtuous.

satvādi śaktiyāl lokangal okkeyum
kāttukalpānta mellāmorikku vol

apparā śakti devī bhagavatī
kelppu nalkuken buddhikanāratam

Protecting all the worlds with potencies like sattva, Deliverer from the Universal Deluge, O Powerful Goddess, strengthen my intellect always.

nityayāyi niranyu vilangunna
satyarūpini devī sanātanī
martyaril mandanennil telinyu nī
mukti mārggam paranyu tannītanam

O Thou who shinest forth in full in the form of Eternal Truth, O Devi, Eternal One, showing the Path of Salvation, shine in me who am a dullard among mankind.

ipparā śaktiyā nidrādi devakal
kepporum māśraya bhūtayāyullaval
pāri loru vanāru bhavadīya
pārāvāra samānta ralīlakal

This Supreme Power is the Support of all the gods like Indra who perform Thy actions which are comparable to the ocean.

vyaktamāyi parayunnu nityavum
chittil vannu teliyu kayambike
tval charitrangal varttānetukuka
muktayākukī māyayil ninnu nī

Clearly I tell Thee, Mother... deign to enter and shine in my heart. Choose me to praise Thy story and liberate me from this Maya.

ikkanda nānā charāchara mokkeyum
en mahādevī nin līlakal niśchayam

mūrttikal mūvarum vārttum karalina
mārttya nāmi vanennum namikkyunnu

O Supreme Power, all these various mobile and immoblie things are surely Thy own Play (Lila). Mankind bows always to Thy Feet which are adored by the Three Gods (Brahma, Vishnu, Maheśvara).

ENNUTE JĪVITA

Vol. 10, B-2

ennute jīvita nauka bhavābdiyil
munkukayā namme muttum
maya valartum kodumkāttu rukshama
yutukayā nente chutum.

O Mother, my boat is sinking here in the ocean of this world. Fiercely the hurricane of delusion rages on every side.

chandikal āru vikārangal anende
tandu vali kārayullor
chukkān pidī chidān pādava mattava
nānen mana karna dhāran

Clumsy is my helmsman, the mind...
Stubborn my six oarsmen, the passions.

kāniyum kārunya hīna mikātilen
tonitā kerukayāyi
toniyil nin ayo bhaktitan pangāyam
vīnu kandīchadum poyi

Into a merciless wind I sailed my boat and now it is sinking...split is the rudder of devotion.

vishvāsamāyi ullo otupāyi ulladu
mikkadum jīr nīchu poyi
vallati lulloru villa lattilute
vellam kareyukayāyi

Tattered is the sail of faith...into my boat the waters are pouring.

entini che entu nyān inī nī vegam
chollita renammen amme
kurirul kūmbāra mān ende chutilum
nyān adilāndu po mumbe
ammatan tan tiru nāmamam kayyili
pon makal keti pidīkkum

Tell me, what shall I do? For with my failing eyes alas, nothing but darkness do I see. Here in the waves I will swim, O Mother, and cling to the raft of Thy Name.

MŪKA GĀNAM

Vol. 10, B-3

mūka gānam pātivarum
śoka mānasa śalabhangale
ningala nargga divya devālayam
pūkuva tinnu varāmo

O bees of sad feelings, melodies without words, won't you come to the Divine Abode of Mother?

pūri talangalil aralukalāyi
talayuka yende iniyum
bhūmiyil umayāl udayam chevatum
ariyaru tāyo iniyum

No more have we to wander on the dusty roads of this earth. Know that the Divine Mother has come to earth.

poya vasantattin pūvukal chūtiya
puti oru devata vannu
poya dinangal pokilum ininām
povuka divya talattil

Along with the flowers of spring has come this Goddess. The days gone are gone forever...Now let us go to this Divine Abode.

nāda kutūhala nūtana hridayam
tūkitu mātma rasattāl
deha manassukal dehikalalennu
otuka jñāna padattāl

Let us fill our hearts with the new words of wisdom and full with the Bliss of the Self exclaim that the body-mind complex is never That.

ĀRUTE MAKKAL NYANGAL

Vol. 11, A-1

ārute makkal nyangal amme
ārute makkal nyangal
entinu venti yitā
ī janmam nyangalku tannū

Whose children are we, Mother? Whose children are we? What for is this birth which Thou hast given to us?

āroru millātta nyān
ārennūchollittarū
ānanda lokattil ārātitān
āromale nī varū

I have no one to call my own. Tell me who I am, that I may dance in bliss. O Blissful One, come, come.

antima yātrayil nī ā
krityam nirvahicchu
ānanda lokattil ārātitān
ānandamāyi nī varū

O Blissful Mother, when is the final journey? That I may dance in bliss, O Blissful One, come, come.

NĀRĀYANA HARI

Vol. 11, A-2

nārāyana hari nārāyana hari
nārāyana hari nārāyana
satchidānanda ghana nārāyana
achyutānanda govinda nārāyana

śrī krishna krishna sakha nārāyana
kamala patrāksha adhokshaja nārāyana
nandagopa kumāra nārāyana
rādhikā ramana govinda nārāyana

krishna yagnyeśvara nārāyana
satyabhāma vinodaka nārāyana
keśika kamsaripu nārāyana
rādhikā ramana govinda nārāyana

krishna karunākara nārāyana
krishna dāmodar achyuta nārāyana
krishna nara kāntaka nārāyana
rādhikā ramana govinda nārāyana

śrī krishna gopāla nārāyana
bala subhadra sodara nārāyana
śyāma mangalānga nārāyana
rādhikā ramana govinda nārāyana

śri krishna kalpataru nārāyana
tirtha pāda karunārnava nārāyana
rāsotsava priya nārāyana
rādhika ramana govinda nārāyana

kamala lochana krishna nārāyana
loka ranjaka rakshaka nārāyana
kaumoda śrīdhara nārāyana
rādhikā ramana govinda nārāyana

govardhanodhara nārāyana
nara kāntaka narottama nārāyana
murahara mukunda nārāyana
rādhikā ramana govinda nārāyana

gopi jana priya nārāyana
gopa gopi janeśvara nārāyana
govatsa pālaka nārāyana
rādhikā ramana govinda nārāyana

devaki nandana nārāyana krishna
dīna jana vatsala nārāyana
āpadi rakshaka nārāyana
rādhikā ramana govinda nārāyana

dhara nīdhar achyuta nārāyana
krishna daityakula mardana nārāyana

gopāla kula tilaka nārāyana
rādhikā ramana govinda nārāyana

bhakti pravārtaka nārāyana
bhakta vāk paripālaka nārāyana
bhakti pradāyaka nārāyana
rādhikā ramana govinda nārāyana

gopika vallabha nārāyana
chakrapāni paramānanda nārāyana
kubja vinodaka nārāyana
rādhikā ramana govinda nārāyana

achyuta=Unshakable
adhokshaja=Whose vitality never flows downwards
āpadi rakshaka=Saviour from distress
bala subhadra sodara=Brother of Balarama and Subhadra
bhakta vāk paripālaka=Who fulfills the devotees' words
bhakti pradāyaka=Giver of devotion
bhakti pravārtaka=Who establishes the cult of devotion
chakrapani=Who holds the discus in His hand
daitya kula mardana=Destroyer of the demon clan
devaki nandana=Son of Devaki
dhara nīdhara=Who carried the Earth (as Varaha)
dāmodara=Who was bound by a rope around the waist
dīna jana vatsala=Affectionate to the afflicted
gopi jana priya=Beloved of the gopis
gopāla kula tilaka= King of the clan of the cowherds
govardhanodhara=Who bears the Govardhana Hill on His hand
govinda=Lord of the cows
gopa gopī janeśvara=Lord of the Gopas and Gopis

gopika vallabha=Lord of the Gopis
govatsa pālaka=Protector of the cows
hari=Remover of mankind's problems
kalpataru=Celestial wish-fulfilling tree
kamala lochana=Lotus-eyed One
kamala patrāksha=Having eyes like lotus petals
karunākara=Compassionate One
karunārnava=Ocean of Mercy
kaumoda śrīdhara=Who carries Sri (Goddess Lakshmi) and the weapon Kaumoda
keśika kamsaripu=Enemy of Kesi and Kamsa
krishna saka=Friend of Arjuna
kubja vinodaka=Who blessed the damsel Kubja
loka ranjaka rakshaka=Delighter and Protector of the world
mangalānga=Of auspicious limbs
mukunda=Giver of Liberation
murahara=Destroyer of the demon Mura
nandagopa kumāra=Son of the cowherd Nanda
narakāntaka=Destroyer of the demon Naraka
narottama=The Foremost Person
nārāyana=The Goal of mankind
paramānanda=Supreme Bliss Itself
rādhikā ramana=Delighter of Radha
rāsotsava priya=Lover of the Rasa Dance
satchidānanda ghana=Dense Existence-Awareness-Bliss Absolute
satyabhāma vinodaka=Who blesses Satyabhama
tirtha pāda=Of Holy Feet
yagneśvara=Lord of sacrifices

AMME KANNU TURAKŪLE

Vol. 11, A-3

amme kannu turakūle
andhata mātān varikille
āyiramāyiram akhanda nāmangal
ādaravāyi nyān chollīdām

O Mother, won't Thou open Thy eyes and come to remove the darkness? I will repeat Thy innumerable Names again and again.

ajñānikalute lokamitil
ajñata māttān mattāru
vijñānattin porulalle nī viśva mahāmayi yamme

In this ignorant world who else is there but Thee to remove the ignorance? Thou art the Essence of Knowledge and the Power behind this Universe.

bhakta priyayām rakteśvari nin bhaktan māril kaniyille
tripādattil namikyām nyangal trikkan pārkukayille

Thou art dear to the devotees and art their very life blood. Won't Thou graciously glance at us who always bow down to Thy Feet?

saptarshikalum nin nomal sūktam pādi nadanille
tapta manaskar nyangal vilippū śaktimayī
nī varu kille

The Seven Sages are ever engaged in singing Thy praises and now we afflicted ones are calling to Thee. Won't Thou come?

ĀRIKULLIL

Vol. 11, A-4

āri kullil dinakaran maranyu
anayunna pakalin tengaluyarnu
viśvaśilpiyute vikritikalalle
vishāda mentinu nali nangale

The sun has set in the western ocean and the day has started its lament. It is but the play of the Universal Architect so why should you, O closing lotuses, be dejected?

akhilānda rājande vinoda rangam
ī lokam śoka pūrnam
kalimara pāvayāyi nyānum karayuvān
kannunīr illātta śilayāyi

This world, full of misery and sorrow, is but a drama of God and I, the onlooker, am but a wooden puppet in His hands having no tears to shed.

verpātin vedana ullil otukki
tīnālamāyi eriyunnu...en manam tīnālamāyi eriyunnu
tīrā dukha katalin natuvil
tīram kānnāt alayunnu

Like a flame my mind is burning up in separation from Thee. In this ocean of grief I am getting tossed about unable to find the shore.

KANNATACCHĀLUM

Vol. 11, B-1

kannatacchālum turanālum ennaka
kannil udepporum ende amma

Eyes open or closed, my Mother ever resides in my eyes.

kārunya pūram churattum katākshamo
tāreyum vāri punarnnu gāddam
snehābhishekatil ātmā valiyikyum
āhlāda sindhuvān ende amma

With glances pouring forth compassion She hugs one and all. Melting the heart with a shower of love, my Mother is indeed an Ocean of Joy.

taskara nākatte mushkara nākatte
tan munnil amme kyaruma makkal
nindikilum abhivandhikilum prema
nishyandhi yānennum ende amma

A robber or a tyrant, in front of Mother, both are Her darling children. Whether despised or adored, Love always streams forth from Mother.

chetta mātateyum viśveśa śaktitan
tittūram eki anūgrahikkyān
vyāsande mannin undinum karutenna
vāstava mudrayā nende amma

In the lowly place of a poor hut the strength behind the whole universe can manifest. Illustrative of this fact is Mother's life befitting a descendant of the great sage Vyasa.

jāti kuśumbinde nātānu jātiye
pūjichu pūjichu mulluvāri
innumā mullil madikyunna jātiye
vellunna snehamā nende amma

A land of caste rivalries where caste has been worshipped endlessly, transcending even this enraging thorn of caste is my Mother's love.

kanninne kānuvān āvilla kanninā
kannin pratichāya tanne kānām
daivatte kānuvān ākātta kanninum
daivatin chāyayā nende amma

Though the taste of sweetness is enjoyed by the tongue, that sense is not perfect. Perfect sweetness is the love of God and the sense to enjoy that is had through my Mother.

KARUNANĪR KATALE

Vol. 11, B-2

karunanīr katale nin gati māri orukukil
śaranam verini yārammā ammā
śaranam verini yārammā

The Sea of Compassion art Thou and if Thou art not compassionate to me, who else is there to give me refuge?

pativāyen hridayam nin varavum kātirunnittum
phala minnum pari tāpamo ammā
phala minnum pari tāpamo

My heart keeps on waiting for Thee.
Will this day also be lost in vain, O Mother?
Will this day also be lost in vain?

unarvinde salilattāl tarukiyen hridayattin
tanu bhāva gati māttumo
marakalku mappuram maruvum nin mriduhāsa
prabhayil nyān vilayīkuvān yī
nara janmam vijayikuvān

In order that this human birth be fruitful through merging in the transcendent Light of Thy soft smile, remove my body-consciousness by bathing me in the cool water of Awakening.

oru nokku kanikānān kariyāte kālattin
gatiyil nyān vira mikyukil
karuna rasam nī vritha chuma kunnatāyi
parayumī jana kotikal tammil
parayu mī jana kotikal

If, in the course of time, I vanish devoid of Thy Vision, O compassionate Mother, the coming generations will conclude that Thy compassion is indeed of no avail.

MANNĀYI MARAYUM

Vol. 11, B-3

mannāyi marayum manushyan iniyum
kunyāyi valarum mahiyil

Man dies and disappears as dust but again takes birth on this earth and grows up.

janmam pala vidha punyam chetavan
vinnitil ettum vidhi pol vīndum
mannitil ettum vidhi pol

If he does good actions he may attain to a higher status and then return to earth again.

jarayum narayum pakarum janatati
alayum vyādhi kaladhikam
punar iniyum vidhi yitu polenkil
janana mitentinu manujā ninnute
vikritikal entinu manujā

In life one must go through disease and old age. O man[illegible] birth again and again worth having? What for all these evi[illegible] cies?

pāpam cheyi toru pāmara nenkilum
pārmana linnalayāte
pārinutayon āren ariyukil
pāpa bhayam poyi marayum avanum
ānandābdhiyil ārum

A person might have committed so many evil deeds but if he knows Who is there behind this world then all his bad tendencies will certainly be removed and he will be immersed in the Ocean of Bliss.

MŪKA HRIDAYA

Vol. 11, B-4

mūka hridaya vipañchikayil
śoka rāga kunyolangal
tapta bāshpa dhārayil onnāyi
sapta rāga marāla morukki

In the veena of the silent heart the subtle melodies of sorrowful songs mingling with the flow of hot tears created a symphony of divine atmosphere.

pāloli kala mānyu karinyu
pāvakan parihāsamu tirttu
tārakangal nishedhātma kamāyi
tānu kondu paranyu tutangi

The moon has faded away and the flame of the lamp only casts a shadow of scorn. The stars, as if coming down, have started uttering:

yī
latte
il

our hands. Why do you wish it to
ve of God and knowledge of
Truth, become one with That."

OMKĀRA DIVYA PORULE, II

Vol. 12, A-1

omkara divya porule varū
omana makkale vegam
omanayāyi valar nāmayangal nīkki
omkāra vastuvāyi tīru

Come quickly darling children, you who are the Divine Essence of OM. Removing all sorrow, grow as endearing ones and become one with the sacred syllable OM.

mokshatil āsa yundenkil makkal
svārtatā bhāvam tyajikkyū
dīna janatinte tengal dhvanikale
kātuttu kelkkān śramikkyu

Children, if you are desirous of attaining Liberation give up selfishness. Try to listen to the sorrows of the afflicted.

amma tan omal kitāngal makkal
amma chollum morikelkū
ningal āren nonnu ningal ariyukil
ningalil untamma yennum

Mother's dear children! Heed Mother's words. When you realise who you are, then you will know that Mother has always been within you.

chetassil pontum vichāram makkal
nerittu kānān padikkyū
pontunna chintakal chīnti kalañātma
chintayāl chittam telikkyū

Children, learn to observe the thoughts that rise in your mind. Dispelling them, purify the mind with thoughts of the Self.

chintāpa ratvam vediñu makkal
anta rātmāvil charikkyū
bhogam bhujichāsa tīrumen ārume
pūti vichāri chitenda

Give up the habit of brooding and look into your inner self. Do not vainly hope that by gratifying the senses one can eventually become dispassionate.

vyartatā bodham valarttum chintā
grastatayi kantyam varuttū
payitruka sambattil sambannarāyi makkal
pārinna nartham keduttū

Break the chain of thoughts that perpetuate the sense of futility. Extinguish the evils of the world arming yourselves with the fire of our rich heritage.

omana makkale ningal amma
otunna tattvam grahichu
jīvitā yodhanam dīramāyi cheyyukil
jīvante satgati nedām

If you fight the battle of life bravely after understanding Mother's teachings, you can reach the Great Goal destined for all souls.

sarvāgama tinte sāram orttāl
ayikama tyatin ninādam
sārattil ātma svarūpa mānāru
mennā veda sāram grahikkyū

The call to Unity is the message of all scriptures which declare that everyone is that One Self. Understand that everyone is the Self only, which is the Essence of the Vedic teaching.

oro manal tari polum sadā
samvadikyunnun dī satyam
svastha chitta tinu kelkkāma tin svanam
susthirātmā vinte śabdam

Even the grains of sand are ever declaring this Truth. The quiescent mind can hear that Voice, the Voice of the Unmoving Self.

ārdrata venam manassil bhakti
bhāsura tayikatu mukhyam
vighnangal ellām vilopam varum jīvan
mukti katonne sahāyam

Softness (fluidity or transparency) of mind is a prerequisite for gaining devotion to God. Gaining that, all obstacles will be removed resulting in the Liberation of the soul.

mumpokke nammal keteshtam kāttil
svachanda dhyānam nadattām
kātellām vetti teli chinnu martyante
chetassu kātāyi māri

In olden days we could meditate undisturbed in the forests. Now we have destroyed the forests outside and made a forest of our mind.

annatte vanya mrigangal nammo
tonnichu kūttayi karinyu
innatte vanya mrigangale polum nām
vellunnu nirdaya vāyipil

In those days, wild animals lived peacefully with the sages. Today, man is even more merciless than wild animals.

poya kālangalil ninnum ere
sthūla māni natte lokam
lakshya meten narinyi kālam nishtayil
śraddha venam mukti netān

The world today is far more materialistic and extroverted than in those days. Hence, we must ever be aware of our goal and vigilant in our sadhana in order to attain Liberation.

ātmāsaya tinu vendi venam
āśrama jīvitam tedān
āśramam sākshāt karippa talla lakshyam
ātmasākshātkāra mallo

One should lead an ashram life in search of the Self alone. The Goal is not realising an ashram but rather realising the Self.

buddhi kondettān prayāsam marttya
yukti kondettān prayāsam
nirmala hrittil teliyum pakal pol
prapañcha sāram makkal orkkū

The Truth is difficult to know through the intellect or through reasoning. But remember, my children, that in the pure heart the Essence of the world will shine as bright as day.

vāstavam viśmari kolla makkal
āścharyam kandu nilkolla
sachidānandam vinashtam varum mrityu
tottu pinpe yunda torkkū

Forget not the Truth. Be not fascinated on seeing the wonders of this world. Remember that if you miss the Existence-Awareness-Bliss (Satchidananda) Death will be just behind you.

pontāraka pūkkal makkal mannil
minnitil angana mennum
ningal tan jīvitam kandu venam lokam
tin makalkayi vittu vārān

Children, you are golden star-like flowers, you should shine in this world. Seeing your life, the world should abandon its evil ways.

pañchendriya tin pitiyil pettu
vañchita rākolla makkal
pañchendriyangal tan anchinam vastukkal
chinta cheyitā śakti nīkkū

Do not be deceived by the five senses, my children, contemplate on the Truth destroying the passions that arise in your mind through those very senses.

satyāva bodham sphurikkyum neram
ikān matellām nirartham
bhittimel tūngunna chitrangal ennapol
chittil trasippūprapañcham

When the Truth shines in your consciousness, all this that is seen here becomes meaningless. The Universe will be known to be like a picture on a wall.

neruttu pokuka makkal daiva
snehattin tīrtha tilāyikayi
ā mahā snehārnavatil ninnā volam
āchami chāyatāyi tīrām

Children, go directly to the pond of God's Love. Drink to your heart's content from that Ocean of Love.

mārki tala rolla makkal sarva
sāhodaryattvam pularttū
ammaye āśrayi chetunna makkale
amma vetiyu killorkkū

Have a fraternal feeling for each other. Try not to feel tired, my children. Remember, Mother will not forsake a child who takes refuge in Her.

snehattin kaikal korukkūmakkal
tyāgattin mantram japikkyū
gñanattin dīpam telichu ninnī loka
śokattin kūrirul nīkkū

Join your hands in love. Repeat the mantra of 'tyaga' (renunciation), light the lamp of Knowledge and dispel the darkness of the world.

anga kalattalla daivam sadā
tanna nayattunda kattum
engum nirañum tanullil teliñum
ninnellām nadattu natīśan

God is not far away. He is ever near you, nay, within you. Filling everywhere and shining within, all is done by Him alone.

nālana tuttān yerinyu daiva
prīti mohikkyunnu marttyan
ī prapañcha tinte ādhāra rūpanā
nālana tuttentu cheyivān

People seek His pleasure throwing a penny at His Feet. What is a penny to the Lord of this world?

daiva sampat āni tellām nammal
kaiyyata kunnatu maudyam
daiva prītikyāyi nam nalkum dhanangalum
daivattin svanta mānorkkil

Everything is the property of God. It is foolish of us to make it our own out of selfishness. Remember that the money we offer to HIm is His only.

arkkannu kannu kandītān nammal
kaittiri kāttenta tundo
daivattin svanta dhanatte yetuttu nām
daivattin ekenta tundo

Need we light a candle to enable the Sun to see? Why should we give to God that which is already His?

daiva sahāyam labhippān makkal
sarvam samarpikyūbhaktyā
oronnu mātma svabhāvam pulartunna
tānennu kānān śramīkkyū

Surrender everything with devotion to God that you may gain His help. Try to understand that everything is of the Self, nay, the Self Itself.

devatā bhāvam katannu makkal
devadevesa nil cherū
jīvante yādima sthānatte bodhichu
bodha svarūpamāyi tīrū

Go beyond the worship of deities and merge in the Supreme Being. Realising the basic Source of all souls, be that Reality Itself.

tālam pirayikyunna jīvan nere
tārottu porunnu vīndum
vaividhya bhāvam vetiyāyikil makkale
poyalla śokam timarkkūm

The soul that plays the discordant note falls down. Unless you give up the sense of multiplicity, you cannot escape pain.

jīvante pūrna svarūpam śuddha
bodha mānen nariyumbol
pokānu milla varānu milla nyanum
tānu millellām samatvam

When the True Form of the individual soul is known to be Pure Consciousness, then there is nowhere to go and no place from where to come. Nor is there any difference between oneself and others. Then everything becomes One Equality.

jīvante jīvattva bhāvam vittu
mārā tirikkyum varekyum
chetassil pūjichu dhyānikyanam
svasvarūpamen ortishta rūpam

However, until one sheds the sense of individuality one must worship the Lord and meditate on the Divine Form that one likes realising that Form to be one's own Self.

nirvyāja pūrvam bhajichāl ārkum
nirvāna saukhyam labhikyum
viśva visāl āntarangatil īśvaran
nityānu vartti tān allo

By worshipping God wholeheartedly, one could gain the Bliss of Liberation. Then the Universal Being would become one's Eternal Servant.

snehi chitendavar makkal tammil
krodhichu poko lorālum
pāril parasparam snehichu jīvichu
jīvante bandhanam nīkkū

Children, you should all love one another. None should get angry and break away. Living in this world loving each other, remove the shackles binding the soul.

sarva dukhangalum nalkkūmakkal
sarveśvaran tante kālkkal
sarvajñanam sarva sākshiyum ningale
sarvadā samtripta rākum

Children, offer all your sorrows at the Feet of the Lord of All. The Omnipotent, All-witnessing Lord will satisfy all your desires.

CHILANKA KETTI

Vol. 12, B-1

chilanka ketti oti oti vāyo
ende tāmara kannā āti āti vāyo

ninde piñju pādam teti teti nyangal
ninde divya nāmam pāti pāti vannen

Tying on Thy anklets, come running, O my lotus-eyed One, come dancing. Searching for Thy tender Feet, we have come singing Thy Divine Name.

devaki nandana rādhā jīvana keśavā hare mādhavā
pūtana mardana pāpavināśana keśavā hare mādhavā
gokula bālane oti vāyo
gopāla bālane āti vāyo

O Devaki's Son, Radha's Life, Kesava, Hare, Madhava (Names of Krishna) Slayer of Putana, Destroyer of sins, O Child of Gokula, come running, O Cowherd Boy, come dancing.

kamsa vimardana kāliya narttana keśavā hare mādhavā
āśrita vatsala āpat bhāndhava keśavā hare mādhavā
omkāra nādame oti vāyo
ānanda gītame āti vāyo

Slayer of Kamsa, Thou who danced on the serpent Kaliya, Kesava, Hare, Madhava. Affectionate to refugees, Protector of those in danger, O Embodiment of OM, come running, O blissful Melody, come dancing.

pāndava rakshaka pāpa vināśana keśavā hare mādhava
arjuna rakshaka anjana nāśaka keśavā hare mādhava
gītāmritame oti vāyo
hridayānandame āti vāyo

O Protector of the Pandavas, Destroyer of Sins, Kesava, Hare, Madhava, O Protector of Arjuna, Destroyer of ignorance, Kesava, Hare, Madhava, O Nectar of Gita, come running, O Bliss of the heart, come dancing!

NIN ORMAKAL

Vol. 12, B-2

nin ormakal mātram en manassil
en nennum mottittuyarnnu nilppū
amme nin ājñakya dhīna nākum
enne nī ormi chitātta tente

O Mother, memories of Thee are always sprouting in my mind. Why art Thou not remembering me, Thy bondslave, ever at Thy beck and call?

vānilum mannilum vānor puriyilum
teti nyān tengal dhvani kalumāyi
nūtana dehangal nūrunūr āyiram
ī vidham pārāyi korinyu munnam

With sorrowful cries I searched for Thee in the sky, on the earth and in all the dwelling places of man. In this way I have taken hundreds and thousands of bodies (births).

kārunya molunna nin nayana tinte
lāvanya leśam tarātta tente
ven chandrika prabhāpūram parattum
tūmandahāsam vitarātta tente

Why art Thou not even glancing at me with Thy beautiful eyes full of compassion? Why is Thy charming smile, which spreads the lustre and glory of moonlight, not shining?

ORU NĀLIL NYĀN EN

Vol. 12, B-3

oru nālil nyān en kannane kānum
oru gāna mādhuri kelkkum

omana chundukalil ota kuralumāyi
āromal kannante munnil varum

Some day I will see Kanna (Krishna) and hear His melodious singing. With the flute gently pressed against His lovely lips, my darling Krishna will come before me.

annende janmam saphalamākum
annu nyān ānanda magna nākum
unmatta bhakti tan uttunga sīmayil
ninnu nyān ānanda nritta mātum

On that day my life's purpose will be fulfilled and I will be immersed in Bliss. Standing on the summit of intoxicating devotion, blissfully I will dance in Divine Bliss.

ī jīva rāśikal kādhāramāyiyullo
rīśan alle jagat pālakane
īshalum kāla vilamba menye
īśvarā ninne nyān kantitatte

O Sustainer of the Universe, art Thou not the Lord who is the Substratum of all these beings? O God, let me see Thee without even a moments delay.

KARĀRAVINDENA

Vol. 12, B-4

karāravindena padāravindam
mukhāra vinde vini veśayantam
vadasya patrasya pute śayānam
bālam mukundam manasā smarāmi

samhritya lokān vata patra madhye
śayāna madyanta vihīna rūpam

sarveśvaram sarva hitāvatāram
bālam mukundam manasā smarāmi

indivara śyāmala komalāngam
indrādi devārchita pāda padmam
santānakalpa druma māśritānām
bālam mukundam manasā smarāmi

lambālakam lambita hāra yashtim
śringāra līlānkita danta panktim
bimbādharam chāru viśāla netram
bālam mukundam manasā smarāmi

kālinda jānta sthita kāliyanya
phanāgra range natana priyantam
tat pucha hastam saradintu vaktram
bālam mukundam manasā smarāmi

SAMSĀRA DUKHA SAMANAM

Vol. 13, A-1

samsāra dukha samanam cheyum
anputta loka jananī
nin divya hasta tannalā
nennum ennum namukora bhayam

O Mother of the World, Dispeller of the sorrows of transmigration, the shelter of Thy blessed Hand is the only refuge for us.

andhatva marnnu maruvum jīva
vrindattin amba śaranam
āpatti lārkku mabhayam amba
nin pāda patma smaranam

Thou art the refuge of the blind and lost souls. The rememberance of Thy Lotus Feet protects all from danger.

pāram bhramichu hridayam ghora
timira tilāndu valayum
ī dustitiku śamanam amba
nin nāma rūpa mananam

For those deluded ones who wallow in the dense darkness, meditation on Thy Name and Form is the only solution for their wretched state.

samdīpta lola miriyāl ennum
en mānasatte yuriyū
nin pādapatma manayān karu
vatonne namukku jananī

Cast a glance with Thy beautiful glowing eyes on my mind. O Mother, Thy Grace is the only means for reaching Thy Lotus Feet.

ANGALLĀTI

Vol. 13, A-2

angallāti vanārunda bhayam
kannā karalil kana leriyunnu
kannan kaniyukil karuti kaniyukil
karalyil vyasa namitente yiniyum

O Kanna, I have no other shelter than Thee. My heart is burning. If only Thou had showed mercy towards me and blessed me this grief would not have come to me.

andhata tīrkkum ambuja nayanan
anpiyalāyi kati nentoru bandham

chintāmalar talirennum nin pada
chentāmara talir tarukayalle

O Lotus-eyed One, Dispeller of darkness, why is it that Thou are not kind to me? Aren't my thoughts ever on Thy Lotus Feet?

chandrika sītala manjula hāsa
muntiri nīril muruki chenne
kannā kanivin pīyūshattāl
vannen karalin danthamorikkū

O Kanna, put an end to this grief by bathing me in the moonlight of Thy smile and the nectar of Thy compassion.

AMMA NIN RŪPAM

Vol. 13, A-3

ammā nin rūpam ennullil teli yename
nin darśanam nalkīduvān ammā nī kaniyename

Mother, let Thy Form become clear in my mind. Be compassionate and give the Vision of Thy Form.

satyam marañu nilkunnu nin māyayāl ambike
irulil tappi tadayunnu andhanāyi nyān kālike
mohavum rāga dveshavum enne marddi kyunnu
vari kāttuvān gati yekuvān ammā nī kaniyename

Truth lies concealed by Thy deluding power, O Ambika! And blinded, I grope in the dark, Destroyer of ignorance! Delusion, likes and dislikes torment me! Mother, kindly show the way and take me to my Goal.

tanayande kannīru kandālum mātru hridayam aliyukille
āroru millāta paitali nāyi amme nin kripa choriyukille

ātma dāham tīrkuvān ende amāntam amme
sāyūjyam nalkīduvān ammā nī kaniyename

Though seeing Thy son's tears, why doesn't Thy maternal heart melt? Will Thou not show compassion to a child who has no one, O Mother? Why delay in quenching my thirst for the Self, O Mother? Be compassionate and grant Eternal Union with Thee, O Mother.

BRAHMĀNDA PAKSHIKAL

Vol. 13, A-4

brahmānda pakshikal vannu chekerunna
pukarārnna jñanam drumam nī amme
enne arinyu nyān ninnil etum vare
nin tanalil nī valarttu enne
nin tanalil nī valarttu

O Mother, Thou art that glorious Tree of Knowledge into which galaxies, like birds, enter. Until I reach Thee by knowing my Self, make me grow under Thy shade, make me grow under Thy shade...

nīla vānam tava śirśa mennotunnu
bhūmi trichevati yennum amme
sarvānta rikshavum nin udalena torttum
vandippu nyān parāśakte bhaktya
vandippu nyān parāśakte bhaktya

O Mother of Supreme Power, I worship Thee knowing that this blue sky is Thy head, this vast earth is Thy Feet, and all the atmosphere is Thy body...

nānā matangalum vartum prabhāvame
nālu vedārtha sāram nī amme
nāma rūpangal layikyunna dhāmame

nyān namikyunnu vinītam ninne
nyān namikyunnu vinītam ninne

O Mother, I prostrate before Thee in all humility, Thou Who art glorified by all religions, Who art the Essence of the four Vedas and the Abode into which all names and forms dissolve...

AMBĀ BHAVĀNI JAYA

Vol. 13, A-5

ambā bhavāni jaya jagadambe
ambā bhavāni jaya jagadambe
ambā bhavāni jaya jagadambe
ambā bhavāni jaya jagadambe

Victory to the Mother, Consort of Bhava (Lord Śiva), Mother of the Universe!

HE AMBA

Vol. 13, B-1

he amba he amba he amba bol
īśvara sata chita ānanda bol
sāmba sadāśiva sāmba sadāśiva sāmba sadāśiva bol
pālaka preraka satapati bol
ambā ambā jaya jagadambā
akhilāndeśvari jaya jagadambā

Say "O Mother, O Mother, O Mother',
Say "Lord, Existence, Awareness, Bliss Absolute',
Say 'Eternally Auspicious One',
Say 'Protector, Inspirer and Lord of all'...
Hail to Mother, the Universal Mother,
Hail to the Mother of the entire Universe!

TĀYE TAVA TANAYARIL

Vol. 13. B- 2

tāye tava tanayaril
kārunya melāykayāl
tāpam hridi valarunnu
tārunya rūpāngane

O ever youthful Mother, because Thou are not showering mercy on Thy children, grief is intensifying in their hearts.

megham keri divākara prabhaye
mūtum kanakke napol
mohattāl vīnārān vitalle
tārunya rūpāngane

O ever youthful Mother, allow me not to fail and sink down due to delusion like the sun that gets covered by clouds.

tārum nīrum taruvum akhila
jīva jālangalum
nin māyayen ariyunnu nyān
tārunya rūpāngane

O ever youthful One, I know that flowers, water, trees and all living beings are Thy Maya.

HRIDAYA PUSHPAME

Vol. 13, B-3

hridaya pushpame parayūnin
nayanam nananya jalametu
dukha bhāshpamo ānanda bhāshpamo
teno sneha rasamo

Tell me, O flower of my heart, with what water are your eyes moistened? Is it tears of sorrow or tears of joy or honey or is it the juice of Love Itself?

anubhūti kalude madhura smritiyāl
ākattār tingiyo ramrito
parayūnayanam nanayān chernna
vikāram mānasa malare

Or is it due to the ambrosia that oozes from the sweet remembrance of most joyful divine experiences? Tell me, O flower of my mind, what is that emotion which makes your eyes moist?

āśa naśikāyikil kleśam iyanītām
kleśa manassennāl bāshpamiya nītām
svātma vichāratāl svartatta poyi ennāl
ātmānandatil bāshpakanam tūkām

If desires are not exhausted there will be sorrow, the sorrowful mind will be the cause for shedding tears. But if, by the enquiry into the Self, selfishness is eradicated, one can shed tears of the bliss of the Self.

PRATILOMA ŚAKTITAN

Vol. 13, B-4

pratiloma śaktitan kari niral mūtiyen
hridaya kavātam atayunnuvo amme
vijaya pratīkshatan chirakku talarninnu
vila kettatāyi tīrnnuvo mama janmam
vila kettatāyi tīrnnuvo

The doors of my heart are being closed by the shadows cast by adverse forces. O Mother, the wings of hopes of victory having become tired, life has become worthless.

paramārtha mariyāttorari vendinu ninde
padatāril anayātta vār ventinu
utalaham perukunna mati entinu ninde
arakāsvadi kyātta miri yendinu amme
arakāsvadi kyātta miri yendinu

Of what use is that knowledge which does not reveal the Ultimate Truth? Of what use is that life which does not take one to Thy Lotus Feet? What for is the intellect which causes one to feel that the body is oneself? In vain are those eyes that cannot enjoy Thy beauty.

irulil nin ātmāvu telivuttuyarnnu nin
anavadya kāntiyil vilayikuvān amme
mātru snehattinde amrita raśmikal ende
hridayattil viriyikummo hrittil
putuvenma viriyikummo

Will the rays of Thy motherly love bring new light to my heart so that this darkened soul of mine will merge in Thy brilliant, spotless Beauty?

CHĀMUNDAYE KĀLI MĀ

Vol. 13, B-5

chāmundāye kāli mā kāli mā kāli mā
chāmundāye kāli mā kāli mā kāli mā

O Goddess Chamundi
O Mother Kali...

AMME YENNU LORU

Vol. 14, A-1

amme yennu loru nāma morttīdave
romānja mākunna tende

amma ennamma ī chintayil innu nyān
yellām marakkunna tende

Why is it that my hairs stand on end when I happen to remember the word 'Amma'? Why am I forgetting everything else when I think of Mother, my Mother?

dāhavum illa visappu millinnaho
snānādiyum vittupoyi
nālum marannu poyi rāvum marannu poyi
ammayil ellām marannu

Thirst and hunger have left me. I have also forgotten my daily bath. I know not what is the day or date. I have forgotten everything in the thought of Mother.

nīlām budhiyilum nīlām budattilum
svetāmbaratilum nokki
kambita gātravumāyi nilkkumen manam
tengi pitakkyunna tende

What is my mind pining for and why is my body trembling when I look at the blue sea, the blue clouds and the white sky?

ammaye kānnātto rādhiyām bhāskaran
katti jvalichu nilkkumbol
ikkotum venalil torāte kannukal
pemāri peyunna tende

How is it that water gushes from my eyes when the sun of the agony of not being able to see Mother is burning intensely in the hot summer?

omkāratin porul omana makkale
omkāra māyittu tīrū

ammatan tenmori yorttorttu nilkkumen
ātmāvilun mādamende

'O my darling child, the essence of OM, become one with OM'. My soul is becoming ecstatic when I remember these words of Mother.

nīrum manassukal kāsvāsa dāyakam
ammatan mohana rūpam
ennini kanditum ennamma vannitum
ennili nonne vichāram

Mother's sweet form is a solace to suffering minds. Now my only thought is when will I see Her again...when will Mother come to me?

TAVA SANNIDHĀNATTIL

Vol. 14, A-2

tava sannidhānattil manatār arppichu
tapassu cheyunnu nyān aniśamamme
anaśvara rūpinī samasta lokeśvarī
anugrahikuka enne nī amme
anugrahikuka enne nī

Day and night I am doing penance, my mind surrendered at Thy Feet. O Goddess Eternal, Goddess of all the worlds, bless me, O Mother, bless me.

surajana pari pūjita nī dina
jana mānasattinu tanalum nī
tirunāma bhajanam cheythunarum śuddha
hridayattil nira jñānam nī
mama jananī jaya jananī
jaya jaya jananī jaya jaya jananī

Thou art the One worshipped by the gods as well as the Shelter for distressed hearts. In the hearts awakened and purified by the singing of Thy praises, Thou rise as the Knowledge Supreme.
Victory to Mother...Victory to my Mother,
Victory to the Mother of the Universe!

nigamāgamam pātum porul nī nityam
munijanam tetum nidhi nī
pranavā varttana tinde layanilayam nī
mana vacha sotungunno ritavum nī
mama jananī jaya jananī
jaya jaya jananī jaya jaya jananī

Thou art the Truth that the Vedas and Sastras sing of and the Treasure ever sought by ascetics. It is in Thee that the vibration of OM dissolves, speech and mind lose themselves in Thee.
Oh my Mother...Victory to Mother, Victory to Mother...Victory to the Mother of the Universe!

KĀTTINU KĀTĀYI

Vol. 14, A-3

kātinnu kātāyi manassin manassāyi
kanninnu kannāyi vilasunno ramme
prānannu prānan nī tanne yallo
jīvannu jīvan ninnun mayallo

O Mother who shines as the Ear of the ear, Mind of the mind, and Eye of the eye, Thou art the Life of life and Thy Being is the Life of the living.

ātmā vinātmā valakal korāri
vidyāmritattin amritayor amme
amritāt mamutte ānanda satte
śrī mahāmāye brahmavum nīye

As the ocean is to the waves, Thou art the Soul of souls. Thou art the Nectar of the nectar of knowledge, O Mother. The Pearl of the Immortal Self art Thou and the Essence of Bliss. Thou art the Great Maya (Illusion) and the Absolute Itself.

kannangu pokā manavum chalikkyā
vākkangu mūkam nin munnil amme
kandennu kandon kandilla ninne
buddhikyum mele mevum maheśi

Neither can the eyes reach Thee nor the mind grasp Thee. Words are hushed in Thy Presence, O Mother. Those who say they have seen Thee have not really done so, as Thou, O Great Goddess, art beyond the intellect.

sūryan jvalikkā svayam chandra tāram
amme nin tejassil ellām jvalikkum
dhīran orālī vivekātma bodhāl
param tatva viśrānti mārgam gamikkum

The sun, moon and stars shine not of themselves but are illumined by Thy Brilliance. Through discrimination the courageous one alone can tread on the path to the Abode of Eternal Peace, the Supreme Truth.

HRĪM KĀLI

Vol. 14, A-4

hrīm kāli mahākāli amme amritānandamayi
bhava tārinī avatārinī
karunāmayī ānandamayī
amme amritānandamayi

O Goddess Kali identified with the sound 'Hrim', the Great Kali, Mother Amritanandamayi, who takes one across the Ocean of Becoming, an Incarnation of Compassion and Bliss, Mother Amritanandamayi.

ādiyil ennamma tāmara kannanāyi
pinne kālitan sākshāt svarūpamāyi
kāli śāntamayi lalitāmbikayāyi
makkal kammayāyi bhaktarka bhayamāyi
dāsānu dāsiyāyi yatiku guruvāyi
atiyanu sarvam nī amme bhagavatī
karunāmayī ānandamayī
amme amritānandamayī

In the beginning my Mother became the Lotus-eyed One. Then She became Kali, Her actual Form. Kali became peaceful becoming Lalitambika, the Mother for Her children. She became the Refuge for the devotees, the Servant of servants, the Guru for ascetics, and everything for lowly me...O Mother Bhagavati, gracious Amritanandamayi.

kanni nānandam nin krishna bhāvam
karalinnu kulirekum nin devi bhāvam
kanninnum kannāya kankanta devate
arinyum ariyāteyum cheyta pirakale
poruttu kātukolkamme bhagavatī
karunāmayī ānandamayī
amme amritānandamayī

Thy mood as Krishna is a delight to the eyes, Thy mood as Devi soothes the heart, O Goddess in a visible form, Eye of my eyes. For wrongs done knowingly or unknowingly, forgive and protect me, O Mother Bhagavati, Amritanandamayi.

JAYA AMBE

Vol. 14, B-1

jai ambe jagadambe
mātā bhavānī jai ambe

Hail to the World Mother
Hail to Mother Bhavāni (Consort of Śiva)!

dukha vināśini durga jai jai
kāla vināśini kāli jai jai

Hail to the Destroyer of misery, Durga!
Hail to the Destroyer of Death, Kali!

umā ramā brahmānī jai jai
rādhā rukminī sītā jai jai

Hail to Parvati, Lakshmi and Sarasvati!
Hail to Radha, Rukmini and Sita!

KARUNATAN KATAMIRI

Vol. 14, B-2

karunatan katamiri katāksham tarane
tarasā mana sukham anayān
jananī tava trikaral atiyatiyen
toru tītunna katāril

O Mother, kindly cast a compassionate glance at me that I may attain peace of mind. I am adoring Thy Holy Feet in the inner flower of my mind.

ara lallakal paripūrita mānen
akatāril pakalira vellām
avanīpati nī yivanil kaniyū
anutāpāphaha śubhade

Day and night waves of sorrow are rising in my mind and overwhelming it. O Mother, Thou art the Ruler of the Earth, Destroyer of sorrow and Giver of good. Therefore, show mercy on me.

nala motu tava pada malaratikandu
torānita tarane jananī
karunā mirimuna patiyana mivanil
paramānandam nirayān

Mother, give me a chance to adore Thy flower-like Feet. May Thy look of compassion fall on me that I may become filled with bliss.

dīnata pāram perukum manassil
premāmrita kanam nī choriyū
ānanda kulir āriyilen manam
nīntān nīrātītān

Kindly shower the nectar-like drops of Thy Pure Love on my miserable and helpless mind. By doing so, I can bathe and swim in the cool waters of the Ocean of Bliss.

AMMA TAN NĀMAM

Vol. 14, B-3

ammatan nāmam kelkumbol kannīr
pohikkum kannukal nalku amme

Give me, O Mother, those eyes which shed tears when Thy Name is heard.

ammaye orkanam prānan pokumbol
kāyi kūpi amme nārāyana ennu
villikkum sanmanam nalku amme

I want to remember Thee, Mother, when my life departs. Give me a mind which cries, "Amme Narayana" with folded hands.

prānan pokumbol ammaye orkuvān
nityam ammaye smarikkenam

ellām ammatan rūpamāyi kanenam
kanninum kannāya entammaye ullil
kānuvān ulkan eku amme

If one wants to remember Mother when life departs, one must constantly think of Her and see all as so many forms of Her. O my Mother, give me the inner eye to see Thee, the Eye of my eyes.

ananta mām ennaṃmaye ennil
nin anyamāyi kandāl sadgati yilla
dvaita bhāvam pokate śāntiyilla
tattvatil bhakti undākuvān ammatan
padāravindatil pranāmikkyunnu

If I see Thee, my Mother, the Infinite, as different from my Self, then I do not gain the true end. There can be no peace if the feeling of duality persists. In order to get devotion to the Ideal, the Supreme that Mother represents, I prostrate at Her Lotus Feet.

ullil amma teliyumbol bāhya prapañcham
svapnampol mānyu pokum
ende ammayil appol nyān layikkyum
brahma satyam jagan mithya
ennā vākyam ennil appol vyaktamākum

When Mother shines clearly within, this external world will dissolve like a dream. Then will I merge in my Mother and the meaning of the statement, "Brahman is Truth, the world is unreal" will become clear.

AMMA YENNULLORĀ

Vol. 14, B-4

amma yennullorā tenmorikkokumo
pinnulla nekāyiram padangal

undo manushyande chintakku tanguvān
nin sneha mandalam vittoretam

Do thousands of other words have the flavour and beauty of the sweet word 'Amma'? Is there any other place for one's thoughts to revel except in the sphere of Thy Love?

ekānta rāvinde tīratta layumī
yerayām enne nī yorttitāyikil
tīrā vyathakalku vārān niyuktamāyi
tīrumen mānaso dyānarangam

O Mother, if Thou dost not remember this helpless one who resides on the banks of lonely, silent nights, this garden of the mind will become the residence of endless misery.

ARATI

Vol. 14, B-5

om jaya jaya jagajanani vande amritānandamayi
mangala ārati mātā bhavāni amritānandamayi
mātā amritanandamayi

Victory to the Mother of the Universe. Obeisance to Thee Amritanandamayi. Most auspicious arathi to Thee, Mother Bhavani.

janamana niga śukhadāyini mātā amritānandamayi
mangala kārini vande janani amritānandamayi
mātā amritānandamayi

Adorations to the Giver of real happiness to the people, the Giver of all good things.

sakalāgama niga mādishu charite amritānandamayi
nikhilāmaya hara janani vande amritānandamayi
mātā amritānandamayi

Thou art the One glorified in the Vedas and Sastras. Adorations to Thee who destroys all unhappiness.

prema rasāmrita varshini mātā amritānandamayi
prema bhakti sandāyini mātā amritānandamayi
mātā amritānandamayi

Thou pourest forth the nectar of Love, O Giver of unconditional Love.

sama dama dāyini manalaya kārini amritānandamayi
satatam mama hridi vasatām devi amritānandamayi
mātā amritānandamayi

Thou art the Giver of inner and outer control. O Thou who dissolves the mind, O Devi, kindly reside always in my heart.

patito dhāra nirantara hridaye amritānandamayi
paramahamsa pada nilaye devi amritānandamayi
mātā amritānandamayi

In Thy heart Thy aim is to lift the fallen ones. Establised Thou art in the state of a Paramahamsa (Realised Soul).

he janani jani marana nivārini amritānandamayi
he srita jana paripālini jayatām amritānandamayi
mātā amritānandamayi

O Mother, who saves one from the cycle of birth and death, who fosters all those who seek Thy protection.

surajana pūjita jaya jagadambe amritānandamayi
sahaja samādhi sudanye devi amritānandamayi
mātā amritānandamayi

Thou art the One worshipped by the gods, fulfilled and established in the Natural State of samadhi...

ŚAKTĪ MAHĀDEVĪ

Vol. 15, A-1

śaktī mahādevī bhakti gamye namaskāram
vitte ekasatte pūrna chitte namaskāram

Salutations to Sakti (Divine Energy), the Great Goddess, Who is accessible through devotion. Salutations to the Seed, the One Truth, the Infinite and Perfect Awareness.

kāmeśa vāmākshi kāmade
kāttarulīdenam nyangale
sarva charācharattil vilangumen sarveśvarī kamale

Protect us, O Thou who art the left eye of Lord Śiva, Who fulfills all desires, Who shines through all animate and inanimate objects, O my Kamala (Lotus), Ruler of all.

vinnavar nāthayāyi yamararkku
dandamorikkyu mamme
pālāri nātha neyum pālikkyunna
pāvanī padmasthite

Thou, the Goddess of the celestials, protects them from all sorrows. Thou, the Pure One, protects even the Lord of the Ocean of Milk (Vishnu).

apparameshti krityam vahippatum
vishtape nin katāksham
brahmānda bījakattre namāyaham
brāhmī sarasvatiye

The Creator does His work due to Thy glance. Salutations to Thee who came forth from Brahmā (the Creator) as Sarasvati, who is the Seed of the entire Universe.

srishti sthiti vināśājnyākari
ashtāham kāranāśe
vīnānāda priyayiko ninam
priyam krodham varunneram

Creation, sustenance and destruction take place at Thy command, O destroyer of the eight-faceted ego. The One who is fond of the sound of the veena is also fond of blood when angry.

vedavum brahmavum nī ellā
jīvanum mokshavum nī

Thou art the Veda, the Absolute, living beings and Release too.

AMME ULAKAM

Vol. 15, A-2

amme ulakam avitutte kāyivasam
chemme veru moru bhrāntālayam
nin sneha mākave varnni pāninne nī
kengane sādhya mākum devī
engene sādhya mākum

O Mother, this universe of Thine is verily a madhouse. O Divine Mother, it is impossible for me to describe Thy Divine Love.

ninnomal kāyikal konden chitta tārinkal
prema rasa modi nī dinavum
dehātma bodhattāl erum ahammati
nīki unmādam ekūninte bhakti unmāda meku

Please feed me daily with Thy own beautiful hand the nectar of love and thus remove my pride arising from the identification of the Selfwith the body and make me infatuated with that love.

kāli yennotumbol ennayanam sadā
kannīr porikku menkil chutu
kannīr porikku menkil
āgama kātale veda vedāngangal
apradhānangal allo atu buddhikyu mātram allo

O Mother, the Inner Core of the Scriptures, if my eyes should shed tears of devotion when I utter the Name of Kali, then all the Scriptures would become secondary things fit only for the intellect.

ATULYA TAYUTE

Vol. 15, A-3

atulyatayute ananyatayute
sumanta hāsa mukhī sumanta hāsa mukhī
varūdayāmayī viśva janeśvarī
viśuddha śālini nī viśuddha śālini nī

O Mother, whose incomparable smiling face expresses the truth of Oneness, O Embodiment of Compassion, Goddess ruling over all the people of the world, most pure and graceful One, come.

avarna nīya dayā hridayattil
amūlya raśmiyumāyi
varūvaram tarūmahāndhakāram
ketānivan matiyil

O Mother, come with the priceless rays radiating from Thy compassionate heart, come bless me that the great darkness enveloping my mind may be dispelled.

anāthare kani vārnu tunakkyum
amrita svarūpini nin
avikala ramya saroruha hridaya
kripā rasam tarane

O Thou, the Embodiment of Immortal Sweetness, the One who looks after the forlorn and helpless, Thy heart melting at their sight, O Mother, give me the water of Grace from Thy heart-lake which is wholesome, taintless, and lovely.

tarunnu kanmasha mānasa mambayil
ādara pūrva mivan
arinyu nalkanam ananta śānti
amānta merā tivanil

This daughter of Thine offers her sinful and impure heart to Thee with deep feeling. Even though knowing my faults, still Thou should grant me that unequalled peace without delay.

ATBHUTA CHARITRE

Vol. 15, B-1

atbhuta charitre amara vandite
tvat pada bhaktikāyi kelpu nalkane
andhatayāl cheta karmangal ārtta
bandhuvām ninnilitā arpikkyunnen
akshamayāl chonna jalpana mokkeyum
ikshiti nāthe kshamikkane

O Thou to whom the celestials bow down, whose tale is wonderful, grant us the strength to be devoted to Thy Feet. We offer Thee all our actions done in the darkness of ignorance, O Protector of the distressed. Forgive us for all our impatient utterances, Ruler of the Universe.

phulla bāla ravikatir polambike
ulla sichitena mende hrittate
tellu bheda buddhi tannitāte nī
tulya bhāva bodhame kitename

O Mother, please shine in my heart like the rising sun at dawn and give me a mind having equal vision devoid of the differentiating intellect.

sarva karma punya pāpa kārinī
sarva bandha bhedinī maheśvarī
sarva tattva sāra mukta pātayil
dharmma mūla pādaraksha yekane

O Great Goddess, the Cause of all actions both sinful and virtuous, the Liberator from all bondage, give me the protecting sandals (shoes) of basic virtues on the path of Release, the essence of all principles.

UTTAMA PREMATIN

Vol. 15, B-2

uttama prematin paryāya māyidum
śāśvata sneha pradāna mutte
pāvana vātsalyam ekunna pāvani
pādatil kannīrāl archi chīdām

Thou art the Embodiment of the Highest Love, O Giver of Eternal Love. O Pure One who gives pure affection, I worship Thy Feet with my tears.

bhāvana kapuram yengo vilasunna
satya svarūpatin tenmorikal
karna manohara mā vachanangalāl
kātum hridayavum śāntamāyi

Hearing the nectarean, joy giving words of the Embodiment of Truth who abides beyond where thought can reach, my heart, eyes and ears have become tranquil and quiet.

ā kripa varnikyān āvatil ārkume
ā sneham vākal paravatallā
ā premam yengane nyān ura chīduvān
kannīrāl vīndum nami chīdunnen

That love can be described by none. It is beyond words. Then how can I hope to speak about it? I can only bow down again and again with tears in my eyes.

ĀDIYIL PARAMEŚVARIYE

Vol. 15, B-3

ādiyil parameśvari ye
akhila loka janani ye
āru milla gati yenikku
amma yallā tīyu lakinkal

O Primal Supreme Goddess, O Mother of all the worlds, I have no goal in this world other than Mother.

pālikyunnu mūnnu lokangal
nīla vāri jalocha nayamma
māla kattu kale kama lālaye
mūla kārinī māye manohare

Mother, of beautiful eyes like the petals of a blue lotus, preserves the three worlds. O Dweller in the lotus, Maya, O Beautiful One, the Source of everything, rid me of all sorrows.

kāttu kollana menne kripāmayī
ārtti nāśinī samsāra tārinī

bhakti mukti pradāyinī yambike
kīrtti rūpinī kārttyāyanī namo

Protect me, O Gracious One, O Destroyer of greed, who takes one across the tract of transmigration. O Mother, giver of devotion and liberation, O Far-famed One, Katyayani, I bow to Thee.

vishtape sarva buddhiyum vidyayum
tushti pushtiyum srishtiyum nī tanne
ishta sādhike dhārshtya makattiyen
klishtata povān chitte vasikkanam

O Goddess of the earth who art Wisdom and Knowledge, delight, nourishment and creation are Thee only. O Fulfiller of desires, ridding me of pride, dwell in my mind in order to remove my distress.

AMME BHAGAVATI KĀLIMĀTE

Vol. 16, A-1

amme bhagavatī kāli māte
ninne nyān innu pidichu tinnum
onni valotunnu amma nī kel
gandāndha mulla piraviyāne

O Mother, Supreme Goddess Kali, today I will catch hold of You and devour You! Hear what I am saying! I was born under the star of death!

gandāndha yogam piranna pillā
tallaye tinnunna pillayāne
onnukil enne nī tinnidenam
allāyikil innu nyān ninne tinnum

A child born under such a planetary conjunction devours it's own mother. So, either You eat me or I will eat You today itself!

randile tengilu monnarinye
mindātini melil nyān adangū
kayyum mukharu matennu vendā
meyyilu māke kari puranden

I am not going to keep quiet unless I know of Your choice. As You are black, that blackness will rub off all over my body.

kolum kayarumāyi vannu kālan
chāle kāyarittu chutti dumbol
melāke melle urin yudan nyān
kālan mukhattu kari puratum

When Kala, Lord of Death, comes with the rope and rod and tries to catch me in His noose, I will smear the black ash from my body onto His face!

kāliye yullilotu kiyol nyān
kālende kāyyil kurungu menno
kālitan nāmam japichu kondū
kālende nere nyān goshti kāttum

How can I, who have contained Kali within me, be caught in the hand of Death? Chanting the Name of 'Kali', I will mock at Kāla (Death)!

AMMAYIL MĀNASAM

Vol. 16, A-2

ammayil mānasam chernnu ende
jīvitam dhanyamāyi tīrnnu amme
jīvitam dhanyamāyi tīrnnu

My mind is immersed in Mother.
O Mother, my life has become fulfilled.

ninnil nin nanyamāyi tonnunna tonnilum
tangunnattil ende ullam amme

O Mother, my mind is not staying in anything other than Thee.

mohamengu rāga dveshamengu innu
svanta mākkan onnum illayengil
kshanam māri marayumi dukha bhūvil

Where is desire and where is attraction or aversion if there is nothing worthwhile to make ones own on this sad earth which changes and vanishes all too sudden?

bhogatti nāyere kannīr chorinya nyān
amme ninne kāyi tinnu keram
prema sāgaram kannīral nyān rachikkām

O Mother, I, who have shed many tears for worldly enjoyments, will today cry for Thee. With tears I will create an ocean of love.

nirmala premamen ammayil mātramāyi
bandhichu badhanāyi ammayil nyān
aho bandhanam muktiyāyi tīrnnu venno

I have become bound to Mother. Binding my pure love to Her, O wonder! my bondage has become salvation!

amma mātram enikkamma mātram ennum
ā prema rāsitan nāsa mātram
ende ātmavin mantramāye tirnnu vallo
ende ātmavin mantramāye tirnnu allo

I have only Mother. I want Mother and the rays of Her Love. This has become the sole mantra of my soul.

ŚRI RĀMACHANDRA

Vol. 16, A-3

śrī rāmachandra raghu rāmachandra
prabhu rāmachandra bhagavān
śrī dhanya dhanya sītābhirāma
sukritātma rūpa rāma

O Sri Ramachandra, Thou of Raghu's dynasty, Lord Ramachandra, O God, the blessed and auspicious Beloved of Sita, whose Form is the very soul of the pious...

he jānaki ramana rāghava vimala
vīrya sūryakula jāta
he rāma rāma raghuvīra rāma
karunardra netra rāma
śrī rāma rāma...

O Delighter of Sita (Janaki), taintless One who was born in the dynasty of the Sun and glorified for His strength and bravery, O Rama, with eyes moistened by compassion...

he mouktikā bharana bhūshita bhuvana
soundaryātma jaya rāma
ānanda rūpa nigamānta sāra
nikhilātma rūpa rāma
śrī rāma rāma...

O Rama who wears ornaments of pearl, who is the Jewel of the world, Bliss Incarnate, the Quintessence of the Upanishads, the integral form of all souls...

ARUNA NIRAKATI

Vol. 16, A-4

aruna nira kati roliyil
amritorukum mori kalumāyi
adharattil puñjiri tūki
anayukille amme anayukille

Radiating rays of red hue and uttering sweet words, O Mother, won't Thou come with that beaming smile on Thy lips?

jananī jani marana tirayil
jīvitamām nauka kalanavadhi
niranirayāyi takarunnu nī
ninaka mūlam nī ninaka mūlam

O Mother, by Thy Will alone so many ships of lives are breaking one by one on the waves of birth and death.

kūrirul mayamāmen chittil
rāgādikal poruti varumpol
nī rāga kambikal mītti
choriyukille jñānam pakarukille

When emotions of attraction and repulsion fight within my mind filled with darkness, won't Thou pour out Knowledge while playing on the strings of Love?

maunattāl mandatayāyi
gānattāl garvvukal nīngi
dhyānattinu dhanyata yekān
tāmasam ente tāye tāmasam ente

Making me calm through silence, ridding me of pride through prayer, O Mother, why delay in making my meditation blessed?

abhaya prada māma pādum
akamalaril teliyunneram
ariyāttānanda nilāvu
pakaru kille śyāme patarukille

When Thy Feet that give refuge shine in the blossom of my heart, won't Thou inundate me with the moonlight of unknown Bliss, O Dark One?

DEVĪ BHAGAVATI

Vol. 16, B-1

devī bhagavatī śānti pūrne
bhāvuka rāśe śive namaste
rudrāniyāyum indrāniyāyum
buddhiyāyum sarva śaktiyāyum
atra jayikkyum agatikalkku
dhātriyām amme namo namaste

Salutations to Thee, Devi, illustrious and full of peace, Abode of prosperity and auspiciousness, Mother of the distressed. Victory to Thee as the Consort of Rudra (Śiva) and Indra, Thou being the intellect and all other powers.

bhūvilirikunna punyarūpe
bhūvināla jñāta vaishnavi nī
bhūvinullāndu sarvam natattum
devī parātmike te namaste

Thou abide on the earth in the form of virtue and Vaishnavi (Consort of Lord Vishnu), not understood by the earth. Salutations to Thee Devi, who art behind all actions which take place on earth and are beyond the soul.

prerana ullilirunnu nalkum
prerike devī śive namaste
devī varipol bhajikuvānen
dhyānatin amba karutu nalkū
tāye ripujana bādha mūlam
bhītiyerum nyangale kātukolka

Salutations to Thee, Devi, who art auspicious, the Inspirer, who prompts from within. Devi, my Mother, please strengthen my meditation so that I can worship Thee properly. O Mother, protect us from the fear of enemies' assaults.

KERUNNEN MĀNASAM AMMĀ

Vol. 16, B-2

kerunnen mānasam ammā kelkkān
kātille ninakken ammā ammā
kerunnen mānasam ammā

O Mother, my mind is crying. O my Mother, have Thou no ear to hear it?

pitayum hridaya vumāyi ninne teti
nātāke alannyu nyān ammā
en munnil varuvān entini tāmasam
entiha nyān cheyvū ammā ammā
entiha nyān cheyvu ammā

With an aching heart I have wandered all over the country in search of Thee. Why this delay to come before me? O Mother, what shall I do now?

aśaktanām ennotī alambhāvam kāttuvān
aparādham nyān entu chetu
chūtu kannīrāl nyān nin malaratikal
karukītām ennennum ammā ammā
karukītām ennennum ammā

What sin has this helpless weak one committed for Thee to show such indifference to me? O Mother, I will wash Thy flower-like Feet with my hot tears.

dussaha māmī prārabdha bhārattāl
kurayunnu nyān en ammā
talarumī atiyanu tāngu nalkituvān
tāmasam arute ammā ammā
tāmasam arute ammā

O Mother,I am getting tired of this unbearable burden of the fruits of past deeds. O Mother, be not late to give refuge to this humble servant of Thine who is getting utterly exhausted.

MADHURĀDHI PATE

Vol, 16. B-3

mathurādhi pate dvārakādhi pate
vaikuntha pate śrī rādhā pate
nanda nandanā krishna gopālā
mīrā ke prabhu giridhara bālā

O Lord of Madhura, Lord of Dvaraka, Lord of Vaikuntha, Radha's Lord, Son of Nanda, Krishna, Gopala, O Lord of Meera Bai, the Boy who upheld the mountain...

devakī nandanā he ghanaśyāmā
gopi manohara mangala dhāmā

kāliya nartana he nanda lālā
nācho nāchore bhayyā bānsurivālā

O Son of Devaki, of the complexion of a rain cloud, Enchanter of the Gopis' minds, Abode of auspiciousness, who danced on the serpent Kaliya's head, Nanda's Child, who dances with a flute in His hands...

sūrdas ke prabhu giridhārī
rādhākrishnā kunja vihāri
vasudeva nandana asura nikhandana
bhava bhaya bhanjana jagavandana

O upholder of the Hill (Govardhana), Lord of Surdas, Radha and Krishna, who play in the groves, Son of Vasudeva, killer of demons, Destroyer of the fear of becoming, to whom the world bows down...

mīrā ke prabhu giridhara nāgara
gopīkrishna kannayā
abhidenā tum tera darsan mere
krishna kannaya

O Lord of Meera, Giridhara, Beloved Child of the Gopis, let me have a glimpse of Thee now itself, my dear Child Krishna.

MAUNA GHANĀMRITAM

Vol. 16. B-4

mauna ghanāmrita śānti niketam
gautama manalaya sundara nilayam
bandhana nāśana kānti pūram
chintātīta nirāmaya tīram

The Abode of dense Silence, Eternal Peace and Beauty, in which was dissolved the mind of Gautama Buddha, the Effulgence that destroys bondage, the Shore of Bliss beyond the reach of thought.

santata samanila yarulum jñāna
antādikaluma kannoru dhāmam
chittavi kalpama kannānandam
śaktyā dhishtita chitghana deśam

The Knowledge that bestows perennial equanimity of mind, the Abode having no beginning or end, the Bliss experienced after the movements of the mind are hushed, the Seat of Power, the Region of dense Consciousness,

advaitāmrita satpada mekum
tattva masīpada lakshya svarūpam
anayānāyi nyān vembukayāyī
tvatkripa yallā tilloru mārggam

The Goal pointed to by statements like 'Thou art That', which grants the sweet eternal Non-dual State, there it is that I long to reach and there is no other way than Thy Grace.

DEVI ŚARANAM

Vol. 17, A-1

devī śaranam śaranam amme
devakal vārttunna divya mūrtte
devī śaranam śaranam amme
ādi parāśakti te namaste

Give me refuge, O Goddess, give me refuge, O Mother, O Thou whose divine form is being praised by the celestials. Salutations to Thee, the Primal Supreme Energy!

kalyāna kāriniyāyi sadā sā
kallyābhilāsha sandāyiniyāyi
siddhiyāyi mūla prakritiyāyi
varttikum amme torunnitā nyān

Salutations to Mother who is the Cause of all auspiciousness, Fulfiller of all desires, Perfection Itself,and the Source of Nature Herself.

srishti sthiti laya kāriniyāyi
dushta samsāra vimāthiniyāyi
sachit svarūpiniyāya devī
trichevatikku torunnitā nyān

Thou art the Cause of creation, sustenance and destruction. Thou art the Destroyer of the wicked. I bow to Thy Feet, Thou who art of the form of Pure Existence and Awareness..

nityayāyi sarvāvalam bayāyi
ardha mātrākshara sāramāyi
hrillekhayāyi jayi chītumamme
svarloka nāthe torunnitā nyān

Salutations to Thee, the Ruler of heaven, the Eternal and Substratum of all. Victory to Thee indicated by the sound 'OM' and by the sound 'Hrim'...

ninkal irikunnu viśvamellām
ninkal ninnellām udichitunnu
śankarī sandehamilla sarvam
ninkalallo vanno tungunnatum

The Universe has its existence in Thee and from Thee sprouts everything. O Giver of auspiciousness, there is no doubt that everything has its dissolution in Thee only.

tattvangal okkeyi nangumamme
satya svarūpini loka māte
engum niranyoru ninne yallā
tingu nyān kānmati lennu polum

O Mother of the Universe, Embodiment of Truth, all divergent principles find unity in Thee. Nothing appears before my sight other than Thee who pervades all.

amma dhukaitabha bādhanīki
amma viśvattin parappukātti
bhāvana kalkkum atīta mātre
tāvakamāya mahācharitram

O Mother, by ridding the world of the afflictions caused by the demons Madhu and Kaitabha, Thou revealed the expanse of the Universe. The great story of Thy doings is beyond the reach of imagination.

amba nin srishtiyil ulpetunna
brahmāndam etra yennārinnyum
kālttārina tavakūppi nyān onnarthichu
kollunnu bhakti pūrvam

O Mother, who can know the number of Universes created by Thee? Prostrating at Thy Feet, let me pray with devotion for just one thing...

tvannir malābhamāmī svarūpa
mennullil ennum vilangitenam
nin nāmamennu murukkarippā
nen nāvu tatparamāyi varenam

I pray that this pure, effulgent Form of Thine should shine forth within me forever and that my tongue should enjoy the taste of repeating Thy Name always.

nin pāda darśanamen mirikku
munpāyu varenname yennu mennum
ninne nirantara morttuvāru
menne nī yorkkannam dāsanāyi

Kindly let me have the sight of Thy Feet ever before my eyes. Consider me, who lives always in Thy remembrance, as Thy servant.

nī yumbayellā marinnyidunnol
peyan nyān pāmararkkagra gāmi
ninniccha yenten narinnyu cheyvān
pinne nyān engane śakti nākum

Mother, Thou art omniscient and I, a mad one, am the first among the ignorant. How am I to become capable of acting according to Thy Will even after knowing it?

kīrti gāyatri kamalakānti
mukti yomkāram svadhā virakti
nirguna mappol sagunamenna
lokeyum devī nī tanne yallā

O Devi, fame, the Gayatri mantra, the effulgence in the lotus, Liberation, OM, the offering, detachment, the Attributeless and That which has attributes, all is but Thee.

pūrnatinnam śangal jīvakoti
karnavattin tiramāla pole
ajjīva rāśiku mukti netān
sajjī karikunnu viśvamamba

The millions of living beings are parts of the Whole, like waves to the Ocean. This Universe is designed in such a way as to help all beings attain Liberation.

jīvan bhavati tāne narinyāl
kāyi vitum vyakti samsāra bandham
nannāyi natichotu kattuvesha
monnāyi vetiyum natan kanakke

When one comes to know that one's very life is naught but Thee, one will get detached from the world like an actor who takes off his costume at the end of a good performance.

lokeśi rāgādi mūla mundām
śokangal mithyābramanga lellām
pokki śaranam gamichorenne
kākkanam kāyitorām nin padābjam

O Ruler of the world, protect me who has taken refuge in Thee, by removing the sorrows and illusions arising out of attachment and aversion. I bow to Thy Feet!

AKALE AKALE

Vol. 17, A-2

akale akale yoru mani nādam
kelkunnu pranavamām śanku nādam
akale kānunna mala mukalil
tāyi karumāritan śrī kovil

From afar comes the sound of the ringing of a bell. Hear also the sound of the blowing of a conch. Yes, it is from the shrine of Mother Karumari1 on the top of yonder mountain.

manasoru kovil devitan ālayam
rāgādikalāl oru brāntālayam
idamillāteyen tāyi pinmāri
akale akannu poyitāyi karumāri

Mind is a temple, abode of the Divine Mother. But it has become a lunatic asylum due to passions like attraction and repulsion. Finding no place for Herself, Mother Karumari has gone away.

akale mani nādam murangunnū
manassine māriyamman vilikyunnu

The bell is ringing in the distance...
Mother Mariyamma is calling the mind...

tāyitannu sangītam tāye marannu nī
kāmini stuti pādum kāmākshi manase
kāmākshi ye bhajikkyu kāmam tyajichu nī
śāśvatānandam bhujikkyu manasse

It is the Divine Mother who gave the power to sing, but forgetting Mother, the mind is singing praises to the girlfriend. Give up desires and worship Mother Kamakshi, that you may enjoy lasting bliss.

akale mani nādam murangunnu
manassine māriyamman vilikyunnu

The bell is ringing in the distance...
Mother Mariyamman is calling the mind...

bhajikkyān kovilil ekantatayil
valarān pāyitalāyi entāyi madiyil
vara marulukayamme ninnil aliyān
nin amritānandam nitaram nukarān

Bless me to adore the Mother in a temple, in solitude, to grow up as a child in the lap of my Mother. Bless me that I may merge in Thee and drink forever the nectar of Thy Eternal Bliss.

kāmini kāñchanam akalenam
manassil māriyamman teliyenam

Bless me that lust and greed depart and Mother shines bright in the mind.

ŚRĪ CHAKRAM

Vol. 17, A-3

śrī chakramen oru chakra mundu atil
śrī vidya yen oru devi yundu
chakra svarūpiniyāya devi
loka chakram tirikunna śakti yāne

There is a mystic wheel named Sri Chakra. In it dwells the Goddess Sri Vidya. That Devi who is of the nature of motion, is the one Power that moves the wheel of the Universe.

simhavāha meri vanni rangārunde ā
hamsa vāhameri brahma śakti yākum
mūrtti trāyatte nayikyum ambe ninde
mūrti bheda rūpamalle kārttyāyanī

Sometimes She comes riding on a lion, sometimes manifesting as the Power of the Creator mounted on a swan (Saraswati). O Mother who leads and controls the divine Trinity (Brahma, Vishnu and Śiva), is not the Goddess Katyayani yet another of Thy forms?

durita nāśanārta mitā bhakta janangal ninde
darśanangal kandu vīnu vanangitunnū

These devotees pay obeisance to Thy forms, for the alleviation of their miseries.

manuja deham etra nindya menna satyam ī
māyā magnarām manushya rārariyunnū

O Mother, who among human beings captivated by Maya understands the truth that this human body is most despicable?

puli mukalileri lasikyumambe nin
pukalerum prabhāvumajña nengane vārttum

O Mother, who sports riding on a tiger, how can an ignorant one hope to extol Thy most exalted majesty?

MĀRĀ YADUKULA

Vol. 17, B-1

mārā yadukula hridayeśvara maramukil varnnā śrīdhara
taralita gānangal tarukiyu rakkum nin
viraluka levite tāmara kannā...mārā

O most charming One, Lord of the Yadavas' hearts, having the complexion of a rain cloud, who bears the Goddess Lakshmi on His chest, O lotus-eyed One, where are Thy fingers that caress soft songs to sleep?

vrindāvani kayil nanda kumāranāyi
vānaru lītunna tāmara kannā
vaishnava chaitanya cheto vikārattil
kelī natanam cheyitavane
ādiyu mantavum nīye devā
bhakta pārāyanā kāyi torunnen

O Thou who lived in Vrindavan as the Son of Nanda, who danced and played in the hearts of Lord Chaitanya and others, Thou art the beginning and end of everything. We join our palms in adoration to Thee who art bound to Thy devotees.

MALARUM MANAVUM

Vol. 17, B-2

malarum manavum verpedumo amme
madhuvum madhuravum verpedumo
rāpakal māri marayān maranālum
niśchayam ninne marakilla nyān

Will the flower and its fragrance ever separate? What about the honey and its sweetness? Even if day and night forget to alternate, I will never forget Thee.

etrayo nūta madyayangal ende yī
mugdha jīvanil nī eruti chertu
karunyame ninde kāladi vittoru
kālamorikkalum ekidolle

Thou hast added so many beautiful chapters to this life book of mine. O Embodiment of Compassion, never let there come a time when I am separated from Thy Feet. Allow not my memory to forsake Thee.

akaluvān akala millamme nī yende
akatāril adhivasi chenne
janmangalini yetra kariñjālu madiyane
adimalar sevaka nākkename
janma sāphalya mangeni kegenamme

There is no space to separate us for Thou abidest within me only. In all births to come, make me the worshipper of Thy Lotus Feet.

That would be the fulfillment of my life.

SKANDA JANANI

Vol. 17, B-3

skanda janani sankata harinī
amritānandamayi mama jananī
bhaya harinī bhava sāgara tarinī
amritānandam pakarūjananī

Mother of Skanda (Chief of the celestial army), Destroyer of sorrows, my Mother Amritanandamayi. Destroyer of fear, who takes one across the Ocean of Becoming, Please pour forth the Bliss Eternal...

jagajananī viśva vimohinī
amritānandamayi mama jananī
śaranam tāye śankaran jāye
mahāmāye kāttarulvāye

Thou art the Mother of the Universe, Enchantress of the World, O my Mother Amritanandamayi. Give us refuge, O Consort of Lord Śiva, protect us, O Great Power of Illusion.

ariyillamme nin nāvāhanam
ariyillame dhyānavum kriyayum
gatiyāyi nivan ekāvalambam
jananī nin tirupāda kamalam

I know not how to invoke Thee, I know not meditation or ceremonies. My only path and goal, O Mother, is Thy Holy Lotus Feet.

VINAYA MĀNASAM

Vol. 17, B-4

vinaya mānasam vyatha pūndu talarān
vidhi vanna kathayentaho jananī
chirakāla sankalpam viphalamāyi pokayo
mama janma vidhi pālinī jananī
tarumo nin pada darśanam

O Mother, what may be the reason that this humble heart of mine has been destined to languish under extreme grief? O Mother, Dispenser of my fate, will my long standing hopes finally prove in vain? Shall Thou not bless me with the darshan of Thy adorable Feet?

veru moru katalāsu pūvupolenne nī
vetiyunno veylettu talarunnu nyān
arakilla niramilla manamilla yenkilum
vinayattin arivillaho nin pāda
smaranāyi korari villaho

Art Thou forsaking me as a lifeless paper flower that is languishing under the heat of the sun? Though without beauty, color or fragrance, this flower is ever steady in its humility and the continued adoration of Thy Feet.

charitārtha nākatte nyān nin tirusneha
parilāla nāsvādanattāl
charanāra vindattin tanalā nenikennum
śaranam sadānandasindo jananī
mama janma sandānasindo

Mother, may I be blessed with the enjoyment of the caresses of Thy noble love. O Mother, the Ocean of Immortal Bliss, the shelter of Thy Lotus Feet is my refuge for all times...O Mother, Support of my life!

ICHĀMAYĪ

Vol. 17, B-5

ichā mayī yām nin ichapolallayo
viśvatilendum nada patamme
nī cheyyum karmangal oronnum mānushan
tan cheyvatennu tānorkkayallo

O Mother who is of the form of volition (will), everything in this Universe moves according to Thy wishes. Everything is really done by Thee but people consider themselves as the doers.

ānaye chertannil magna mākkunnatum
tāne nivarppatum nī tān allo
nin kripa yundengiletu mūdantanum
van mala kerān vishama mundo

Thou art the One who does and undoes, who casts the veil of ignorance and removes it as well. If Thy grace is there, a lame man feels no difficulty in climbing over a mountain.

brahmapadam chilarkekī dumammatan
chummā chilare valicheriyum
nyān yantram nī yantri nyān ratham nī rathī
nyān griham nī griha nāyikayum

The same Mother who bestows the Brahmic State to a few hurls others into darkness. I am the machine, Thou art the operator of the machine. I am the chariot and Thou art the Charioteer. I am the house and Thou art the Householder.

evan namamma yenne kondu cheyyikku
āvidhamellām nyān cheyvutāye
ichāmayi yām nin ichapol allayo
viśvatilendum nadappadamme

I shall act in whatever way Thou make me act. The whole Universe moves in tune to Thy wishes, O Thou whose very nature is volition.

OMKĀRA MENGUM

Vol. 18, A-1

omkāra mengum murangi tunnū
oro anuvilum mātoliyāyi
otuka chitta matakki nannāyi
om śakti om śakti om śakti om

The sound OM is ringing everywhere as an echo in every atom. With a peaceful mind, let us chant "Om Sakti."

valutāyi kānum prapañcha mellām
viravil vritāyen arinyitumbol
varavāyi ninne yariyu vānāyi
vara devate viśvavanda nīye

O Noble One who is adored by the Universe, we come to know Thee well when this Universe is understood to be worthless which so far was felt as great.

anapotti yorukunnu śoka bāshpam
tunayamba mātramāyi tīrnni tippol
vrana tuccha bhogam tyajicchivane
anikara meki yanugrahikyu

Tears of sorrow are overflowing and now Mother is the only support. With Thy beautiful hands, bless me who has given up the sorrowful and worthless worldly enjoyments.

kenivacha laukikā śakti yellām
panamoha jvālayil kettatangum

trinaval karikunnu yogi vrindam
kshana nera sukha mekum mriga jīvitam

All the deceitful worldly desires get destroyed in the flame of the infatuation for money. The animal life that provides us with momentary enjoyment is considered as worthless as grass by yogis.

bhava kānanāgni bhayannu vannu
bhaya bhanjinī nin padamananyu
bhava tārini nī vetinyu vennāl
bhuvanattil entināyi vānitenam

Getting frightened by the wild fire of transmigration, O Destroyer of fear, we have reached near Thy Feet. O Thou who takes us across this Ocean of Becoming, if Thou forsake me, what for should I live in this world?

mriti bhayamengo maranyu poyi
mrinmaya kāntiyil āśayum poyi
smara hara kānti kalarnna ninmeyi
smaranam nirantaramāyi varenam

The fear of death has gone. The desire for physical beauty is gone. Incessant must come the remembrance of Thy Form which shines with the Light of Śiva.

ullil niranyu kavinya dīpti
munnil teliyunna nāl varumbol
unmatta bhaktiyāl nin rūpa kāntiyil
onnāyi chernnu layikku mallo

When the overflowing inner light fills within and overflowing without, shines before me, I will merge in the beauty of Thy Form through the intoxication of devotion.

alavattu kānān koticha rūpam
arakellām onnāyuranyukūdi
atulita saundaryamāyi varunnū
alatallu nānanda bāshpa dhārā

This Form is what I longed to see most. All loveliness has crystallized and come as this unequalled beauty. And now the tears are overflowing...

OMKĀRA DIVYA PORULE-IV

Vol. 18, A-2, B-1

hrīmkāra mantram murakki sadā
pāyum purapol manassum
nīndoru kīdatte premātma sindhuvil
chernnangatāyi tīrnnidatte

Chanting the mantra 'Hrim', let the mind flow like a river towards the Ocean of Love and meet and and become one with It.

satyattin nervaritedūmakkal
nishkāma bhāvattilude
buddhiyum yuktiyum mangalettī dāte
mukti mārgattil charikkyū

Children, search for the straight road towards the Truth with a desireless attitude. Walk on the path of Liberation with a clear intellect and reason.

ullil velicham viriyān makkal
ullāl śramam cheyka nannāyi
ullunar nallāte yillātma śāntiye
nullatti lorkkanam makkal

Children, make intense internal effort for the dawning of the Inner Light. Remember, my children, that without the inner awakening, there is no peace of soul.

nishkāma bhāvārkka bhāsil svayam
vyaktamāyi kānām svarūpam
svāsthyam manassinnu sādhīppān santatam
svātma vichāram valarttū

One can clearly perceive one's Self in the sunlight of desirelessness. Always be engaged in self-enquiry to attain peace of mind.

chittam samāhitamākkūmakkal
chitsukham nedān śramikkyū
santāpa nāśavum śāntiyum kaivarān
svānta samatvam varuttū

Children, try to get peace of mind through integration of thought. In order to gain peace and put an end to sorrow, get established in internal equanimity.

kaipidi chamma nayikkām nīrum
kaivilang ellām arikkyām
samsāra vahniyil kāl varutīdāte
kaitannumārgam telikkyām

Mother will take your hand and lead you, removing your painful shackles. She will clear your path through the fire of worldly existence and support you lest you slip.

tatvārtha bodham valarttu makkal
sachidānandam smarikkyū
bhakti pūrvam manas ātmā vilarppichu
mukti lābham kaivarikkyū

Children, carefully nurture your reflection on the Supreme Principle and remember Existence-Awareness-Bliss. Gain Liberation by offering your mind with full devotion to the Self.

dūre vihāyasil engān tangum
daivatte yādarikkyenda
ammaye daivamen ārum karutenda
ningal ārānen nariyū

Respecting God sitting far away in heaven is not what is needed. Nor need one think that Mother is God. What is needed is to know who really you are.

āreyum snehikya sīlam janma
sīlamān amma kyatorkkū
poyyalla mujjanma bandha mundammayil
ettunna makkalku satyam

To love everyone is Mother's inborn nature. It is a truth that all the children who reach Mother have had their relationship with Her from the previous birth as well.

venna polullam telinyāl nannāyi
ulla tullattil teliyum
chinmoha nātmāvu narnnāl prapañchavum
sammoha nātmasvarūpam

When the mind is purified like butter (ghee), what is real will reflect as It is within. When the Self, now under the spell of the mind, is awakened, the entire universe becomes the beautiful form of the Self.

īśvar ājñāvidhe yatvam venam
ārkkum vipattāke nīngān

ātma viśvāsam ketuttukil makkale
vyartha tāśokam tarakkyum

To be free of danger, one should be obedient to the commands of God. Children, if you lose your self- confidence, a sorrowful sense of futility will flourish.

ammatan sāropadesam sravichantara
śuddhi varuttū
makkale ningalil nitya sāyujyattin
saddhanya lokam vilangum

Give attention to the essence of Mother's advice and cultivate internal purity. Then children, the Divine World of Eternal Bliss will shine forth within you.

munpottu pokān vitāte māya
pinpottu tallunnu namme
dehātma buddhi yil kālam karikkyunnu
śokam timarkkunnu hrittil

Maya, the Great Power of Illusion, is pushing us back from progressing (spiritually). We are spending our days in body-consciousness with a heart full of sorrow.

māyāpra lobham varikyāyi namme
bādhicho rāsā pisāchi
māyāndha kūpattil vīrttunnu hā kashtam
kālanno rūnākki namme

What a pity that the devil of desire, which affects us through illusory temptations, kicks us into the dark abyss of Maya (illusion), making us the food for the god of Death.

āsa pisāchin pidiyil pettāl
kashtam namukkātma nashtam
āsa vittīsanil āsavachāl mana
kleśangal ellām nasikkyum

If you get caught in the grip of the devil of desire, woe to you! for you will lose your soul. All worries will come to an end if only you give up your desires and keep your hopes in God alone.

ekānta dukha talarcha tīrān
ekātma bodham telikyū
ātmāvileka tvabodham talirkkumbol
tīrum bhayam śokamoham

To remove the weariness of loneliness, develop the awareness of the Oneness of the Soul. When that consciousness dawns, there ends fear, sorrow and illusion.

jīvande yudgatikyāyi venam
jīvippān nām bhūtalattil
oro niśvāsavum loka śāntikyulla
sneha sandesa mākatte

We should live on this earth for the upliftment of the soul. Let each breath of ours carry the message of peace to the world.

chitta viśuddhi varāyikil ārkkum
tatvārtha bodham varilla
tatvārtha bodham varāyikil varillārkkum
nisvārtha sevana sīlam

Without purity of mind, no one can grasp the subtle experience of Truth. And without that, the attitude of selfless service is impossible.

mantram manassāl japichum manam
ventārakam pol telichum
ārattil ārattil ārnetti yātmāvil
āmagnamāyi mukti netū

By incessant repetition of the mantra within, letting the mind shine like a star, and diving deep into the soul within, get Liberation.

āvatillātāvum munpe ātma
lābhattin ālākumakkal
tātan tanayanum tāyayum toranum
āru millantyattil bandhu

Before getting too old to do anything worthy, become capable of gaining your soul, my children. On your deathbed, your father, mother, wife and son will not be there to save you.

dhīrarāyi tīruvān makkal neril
dehātma bodham tyajikyū
tīyyil dahikkyunna deham allātmāvu
tīyinum tīyyānatorkkū

Be brave, my children, and give up body-consciousness. Remember that the soul cannot be burned by fire but is the Fire to even fire itself.

tyāgamānīmannin śakti loka
śānti yānīmannin siddhi
sneha mānī mannin ojassum vīryavum
jñānamān ātma chaitanyam

Renunciation is the real power on earth and world peace is the real achievement in this world. Love is the effulgence and vigour of this earth and knowledge its illumining soul.

śāntarāyi chintikya makkal irul
mārānoli vīsidenam
tyāgamen tānaten tennum dharikyanam
tyāgattilalo viśrānti

Children, please think it over peacefully; only light can remove darkness. Grasp what is meant by renunciation, for only in that there is complete rest.

venam viśvāsam vinayam ārkkum
venam manassin nadakkam
venam dayāvāyi puvenam nisvārthata
venam balam kshamā sīlam

One should have faith, humility, a disciplined mind, compassion, selflessness, strength and patience.

nānā matangalum namme eka
sārattilekyāyi nayippū
chitrakāran bhinnavar nangalāl navya
chitran telikyunna pole

All the different religions lead us to the same Principle. It is like a painter using different colors to paint a picture.

satru tābhāvam tyajikyūmakkal
mitra mānāru menorkkū
svantam sukham tyajichanyarkku santāpa
śāntikyu pāyam tirayū

Give up enmity, children, and remember that all are friends. Try to find out the means to relieve others of their sorrows even at the cost of your own comfort.

onnil ninnonnu millanyam ellām
onninde bhinna tābhāvam
anyane tannil ninnanyanāyi kānukil
tannil ninnum tānumanyan

Nothing is separate from the Unity of Existence. All are but diverse aspects of the same Truth. If you look upon someone as separate from yourself, you are but alienating yourself from yourself.

daiva tārādhana mākkūmakkal
cheyyunna karmangal ellām
daiva nishedhamāyi cheyyunna karmam tan
kaivilangāne nariyū

Children, make all of your actions into worship of God. Know that any action done against Him only binds you.

nirmala mānasarākku makkal
dharma sāram kandariyū
nūtana vastukal nedān durāsakal
eriyā lerum nirāsa

Children, make your mind pure and then understand the essence of dharma (righteousness). If you perpetuate the evil desire for ever new things, it will lead to disappointment.

ādaravāyi pode venam loka
jīvitam nām nayichīdān
ātmāvil sūkshmata venam manassil nin
āsakal verattu ponam

We should lead our life in this world with an attitude of reverence. Be watchful in spirit and root out desires from the mind.

tatvam grahikyunna buddhi bāhya
svattil bhramikkyilla tellum
chittum jadavum tiri chariyāttavar
chattapol jīvippu kashtam

The intellect which knows the Truth will not be swayed by external wealth. Those who cannot discriminate between the inert and the conscious are as good as dead.

chaitanya mātramānengum jadam
sādhu vallennāl namukku
sādhan ārambhattil venam valarchakkyāyi
chijjada bhāva vichāram

Even though the world is naught but Consciousness and matter does not matter at all, during the initial stages of spiritual practice, a discriminating intellect is needed to differentiate between the two for the sake of our growth.

veda vedāntangal ellām tannil
tāne teliyum pakalpol
dhyāna nilīnam vilangunna chetassil
jñānāmritam churannīdum

The Nectar of Knowledge will gush forth in the mind that is absorbed in meditation and the Vedas and Upanishads will shine forth of themselves from within as clear as daylight.

antarālam chuttunīri daiva
chinta cheytandata nīkkū
tannullin ullil ullātma svarūpanil
nannāyi samarppanam venam

Remove the darkness of ignorance by thinking of God with a burning heart. There should be total surrender to that One within in the form of one's own soul.

kārunya rūpan kaninyāl janma
sāphalyamā yennariyū
ātmārtha bhakti yodāśrayi kyunnavar
kīśvaran śāśvatānandam

Know that if the Compassionate One is pleased, your life will be fulfilled. For those who take refuge in Him with sincere devotion, God is for them the Eternal Bliss Itself.

RĀDHE GOVINDA GOPI

Vol. 18, B-2

rādhe govinda gopī gopāla
govinda gopāla he nandalālā
rādhe govinda gopī gopāla

mīrā ke nātha prabhu murali gopāla
govardhan odhāra gopāla bāla
rādhe govinda gopī gopāla

radhe=O Radha
govinda=Lord of the cows
gopī=Cowherd damsel
gopāla=Cowherd boy
nandalālā=Son of Nanda
mīrā ke nātha prabhu=Mira Bai's Lord
murali=Flute player
govardhan odhāra=who lifted up the Govardhana Hill
bāla=Boy

DAYĀ KARO MĀTĀ

Vol. 18, B-3

dayā karo mātā ambā
kripā karo janani
kripā karo mātā ambā
rakshā karo janani
kalyāna rūpini kāli kapālini
karunāmayi amba mām pāhi
om mātā om mātā om mātā ānandamayi

O Mother, have mercy. O Mother, save us. Auspiciousness incarnate, merciful One, Mother Kali who wears a garland of human skulls, protect us.

ABHAYAM ABHAYAM AMMA

abhayam abhayam amma amma (3 times)
ajñānikalām adiyangalil nī
aparādhangal porutida venum
ajñānikalām nyangalil ennum
kaniyename mahāmāye

O Mother, give refuge, give refuge. Forgive all the mistakes that this ignorant servant has committed. O Great Illusion, shower Thy mercy on this ignorant servant of Thine.

annapūrneśvarī akhilāndeśvarī
anādha rakshakī mahāmāye
annapūrneśvarī rājarājeśvarī
śaranam ekuka śaranam śaranam

O Annapurneśvari, Goddess of the Universe, Protectress of the miserable, O Great Illusion, Rajarajeśvari, grant us refuge.

ĀDI PARĀŚAKTĪ

ādi parā śaktī ādi parā śaktī
adhikal tirtarulu devi ādi parā śaktī

O Primal Supreme Power,
Please bless us, ridding us of distress.

nava yiru gunita karam devi
vāhanam oru simham
kamala dalam torumā kannukal
oru mridu hasakaram

O Goddess having 18 arms, whose mount is a lion, Thy eyes are worshipped even by the lotus petals, O Thou having a gentle smile.

oli chitarum vadanam devi
kyoru poleru gunam
gaja mriga madana taram kopam
ajanātikal bhajitam

Thou hast a radiant face and possess all the seven virtues in equal measure. Thy anger is like that of a mad elephant and Thou art worshipped by the Gods like Ajan.

tiriyuka mama hridi nī nityam
choriyuka sakala varam
karu tuka yagati yeyum varipol
akhilān deśvariye

O Goddess of the Universe, dance in my heart always, granting me all boons. Kindly take into consideration this suppliant.

ĀDI PURŪSHA

ādi purūsha ananta sayana
nāda svarūpa nara hari rūpa
hari nārāyana hari nārāyana
amme nārāyana lakshmī nārāyana

ādi purūsha=The First Person
ananta sayana=Who rests on the Serpent Ananta (Time)
nāda svarūpa=Whose nature is Sound (OM)
nara hari rūpa=Who manifested as a Man-Lion
hari=Savior of the distressed
nārāyana=Who rests on the Primal Waters
amme, lakshmī=The Goddess Mother Lakshmi

AKALATĀ KOVILIL

akalatā kovilil oru tiri prabha yennum
anayā tirunirunnū
irulil petturalunna manujarku vari kāttān
kanivarn nirunīrunnu amma
kanivarn nirunīrunnu

In a distant temple a wick was kept ever burning in order to guide the human beings groping in the darkness. In this way Mother had been showing Her compassion.

oru dina matu vari alayumpo renneyā
prabhāmayi mādi vilichū
tiru nata turnittā kālabha metu tente
nerukayil aniyichū nerukayil aniyichū

One day when I was wandering along that path, that Radiant One beckoned me with Her hand. Opening the sacred door and taking some holy ash, She smeared it on my forehead...

hari gīta svara moti tirumridu karataril
mayanguvān idamorukki
oru nava svapna men arikattu vannirunnadoru
satya murachetu...oru satya murachetu

Singing the songs of God, She made a place for me to sleep with Her own soft hands. A novel kind of dream came to me declaring a truth, declaring a truth:

karayunna tini yentinakhileśi tirupāda
tananyenna tarinyillayo
oru nedu verpumāyi unarnitā mukha padmam
telivode kanikantū..telivode kanikantū

"Why are you crying? Don't you know that you have reached near the Holy Feet of the Lord?" Waking with a sigh, I saw that Lotus Face clearly, I saw it clearly.

AMBA BHAVĀNI ŚĀRADE

amba bhavānī śārade
jagadamba bhavānī śārade

Mother, Consort of Bhava (Śiva), Goddess of Wisdom.

sāhītya rasa pāna sarasa ullāsinī
kavi jana bhūshinī kāma vilochanī

Drinker of the juice of Literature, possessing humour, Ornament of poets, Lotus-eyed One,

sringāra rasa pāna vāni girvāni
sarva veda rasa pāna sarasa ullāsinī

Who relishes the sentiment of love, Goddess of Sanskrit. Relishing the Essence of all the Vedas,

sangīta nāda prīya nāda tanūmayī
ratna hari śobhinī rājivalochanī

Lover of music whose body is Sound itself, shining Gem, Lotus-eyed One,

vāgme vachāli vāchāmagocharī
ulla lochanī ulla vānantanī

Source of speech yet unreachable through words, having beautiful eyes, Infinite,

hamsa lolanī sadā pāni
pani gana bhūshanī rishi gana sevitā

Ever playing in the minds of sages, adorned with serpents, served by the sages,

satchid ānandinī sādhu rakshinī
nandini ānandinī satchid ānandinī

Existence, Awareness, Bliss, Saviour of the saints, Blissful One, the Absolute Reality.

AMBĀ MĀTĀ

ambā mātā jagan mātā
vīra mātā satya prema mātā

O Divine Mother, Mother of the World, O Most Courageous Mother, Giver of Truth and Divine Love...

ambā mayī jagan mayī
vīra mayī satya prema mayī

O Thou Who art the Universe Itself, Courage, Truth and Divine Love Itself...

AMBĀ SAHITA

ambā sahita mahādeva
jagadambā sahita mahādeva
hara hara śankara mahādeva
girijā ramana sadāśiva

O Great God with the Mother, O Great God with the Mother of the World, the Destroyer, Auspicious Great God, born of the Mountain (Devi, Daughter of Himavan), the Sweet One, The Ever-Auspicious...

AMBIKE JAGADAMBIKE

ambike jagadambike
umā maheśvarī jagadambike
ambike mūkambike
ambā parameśvarī mūkambike

kadambarī ambā svethāmbarī
hari sodari ambā śiva śankarī
hari sodari ambā śiva śankarī

maheśvarī ambā jagadīśvarī
sarveśvarī akhila lokeśvarī
sarveśvarī akhila lokeśvarī

ambike=Mother
jagadambike=Mother of the Universe
umā maheśvarī=The Great Goddess Who dissolves the universe into Herself
parameśvarī=Supreme Goddess
mūkambike=Mother Goddess at Mukambika Temple
kadambarī=Who resides in a forest of Kadamba trees
svethāmbarī=Clothed in white
hari sodari=Sister of Lord Vishnu
śiva śankarī=Bestower of auspiciousness
maheśvarī=Great Goddess
jagadīśvarī=Creatress of the Universe
sarveśvarī=Goddess lording over all
akila lokeśvarī=Goddess of the entire universe

AMMA AMMA TĀYE

ammā ammā tāye
akhilāndeśvarī nīye
anna pūrneśvarī tāye
ādi parāśaktī nīye

O Mother, Mother, dear Divine Mother, Goddess of the Universe, Giver of food to all creatures, Thou art the Primal Supreme Power.

īm mān ilatil yellām
nadakutammā untan ādalīnāl

Everything in the world happens because of Your Divine Play

rakshikka vendum ammā ammammā
rakshikka vendum ammā
kutchiyil summakkamal kodi latcham
uyirgal endrāyi

Protect me Mother, O Mother, protect me...without conceiving in the womb, You have given birth to millions and millions of beings.

pakshi vāhananin sodari soundari
petra mudal unnai padi duven
pari pūrani hārani kārini nīye

O Sister of Lord Vishnu Who rides the bird Garuda, O Beautiful One, from birth itself I am singing Your glories. Thou art the Perfect One, Primordial Cause, the Destroyer...

lakshiyam enakku nīye ammā...ammā
lakshiyam enakku nīye
alakshiyam chethidāthe
jagadīśvari tāye bhuvaneśvarī nīye
katti katti enne nī ammā...ammā
katti katti enne nī kavalai padutha ennināl
kattiduvar yāro kāmākshi mīnākshi nī sākshi
rakshikka vendum ammā...

Thou art my life's Goal, O Mother. Ignore me not, O Goddess of the World. Thou art the Goddess Lalita, Ruler of the World. O Mother, if Thou throwest me into troubles again and again, who else is there to protect me? O Mother with the enchanting eyes, Thou art the Omnipresent witness of all.

ĀTMA RĀMA

ātma rāma ānanda ramana
achyuta keśava hari nārāyana

Delighter in the Self, Sweet Blissful One, Immovable Lord of the senses,

bhava bhaya harana vandita charana
raghu kula bhūshana rājiva lochana

Destroyer of the fear of Becoming, whose Feet are worthy of worship, Ornament of the clan of Raghu, of Lotus Eyes,

ādi nārāyana ānanta śayana
satchid ānanda satya nārāyana

Primal Lord reclining on the serpent Ananta, Lord of Truth Who is Existence, Awareness, Bliss...

ĀYIYE GURU MAHARĀNI

āyiye guru maharāni mātā amritānandamayi
jai jai jai maharāni mātā amritānandamayi

śaranam śaranam amma
abhayam abhayam amma

ayiye=Please come
guru maharāni=Queen among Realized Masters
saranam=Protect us
abhayam=Give us refuge

BHAGAVĀNE

bhagavāne...bhagavāne...
bhaktavatsalā bhagavāne

O Lord...O Lord...
O Lord Who art the Lover of the devotees

pāvana pūrūshā pāpa vināśana
pāpikal mātramāyi pāridattil

O Pure One, Destroyer of sin, there seem to be only sinners in this world.

nerāya mārgangal nalkuvān ārundu
nārayana nanma poyi maranyu

Who is there to show the correct path? O Narayana, virtue has disappeared.

satya dharmādikal nashtamāyi marttyaril
tattvangal etil mātram ottungi nilpū

Mankind has lost all senses of truth and righteousness and real spiritual truths exist only in pages of books.

kānuna tokkeyum kāpatya veshangal
kāttitūkannā dharmam vinte dukkū

All that is seen wears the vesture of hypocrisy. O Krishna, protect and revive righteousness.

BHAJAMANA RĀM

bhajamana rām bhajamana rām
pānduranga śrī ranga bhajamana rām

Worship Rama, worship Rama, worship Rama who is also Panduranga and Sri Ranga.

bhajamana keśava bhajamana mādhava
bhajamana yādava bhajamana rām

Worship Kesava and Madhava (names of Krishna)
worship Yadava (Krishna) and Rama

bhajamana govinda bhajamana mukunda
bhajamana giridhara bhajamana rām

Worship Govinda and Mukunda, worship also the One Who held the mountain on His hand and the Destroyer of the demon Mura.

bhajamana raghuvara bhajamana murahara
bhajamana ānanda bhajamana rām

Worship Raghuvara, worship Rama, worship Rama, worship Rama.

BOLO BOLO

bolo bolo sab mil bolo om nama śivāya
om nama śivaya om nama śivaya

Let everyone say "Om Nama Śivaya"

jūta jatā me gangā dhāri
trisūla dhāri damaru bajāve

The One Who bears the Ganges in His matted locks, who holds the trident and plays the damaru (drum)

dama dama dama dama damaru baje
gunj uthao om nama śivāya

Play the drum and loudly sing "Om Nama Śivaya."

CHANDRAŚEKARĀYA NAMA OM

chandra śekarāya nama om
gangādharāya nama om
om nama śivāya nama om
hara hara harāya nama om
śiva śiva śivāya nama om
parameśvarāya nama om

chandraśekara=Having the crescent moon on the forehead
gangādhara=Wears the Ganges River in His locks
hara=The Destroyer
śiva=The Auspicious One
parameśvara=Supreme Lord

CHITTA CHORA

chitta chora yaśoda ke bāl
nava nīta chora gopāl
gopāl gopāl gopāl gopāl
govardhana dhara gopāl

chitta chora=Stealer of the mind
yaśoda ke bāl=Mother Yashoda's Child
navanīta chora=Stealer of butter
gopāl=Cowherd boy
govardhana dhara=Holder of the Govardhana mountain

CHITTA VRINDĀVANAM

chitta vrindāvanam tannil ninnum
venu gānam pondunnida
mana mandiratile chinmurtitān
venu gāna priya mohanā
jagannātha yadu nandanā

The melodious sound of the flute is rising from the Vrindavan of my mind. O Deity in the temple of my mind, who abides in the form of Awareness, O Sweet Lover of flute music, Lord of the world, Son of Yadu...

mano vritti māyilukal antarange
nritta madi sarva kālam
chit pumane tanne sevikkyunnu

The peacocks of the pure mind are eternally dancing in the service of that Being.

kalavenu nisvanam kettuhā ñan
mugdha bhāva magnayāyi
gāna vilolane dhyānam cheyitu

On hearing that beautiful music of the flute, I entered into an ecstatic mood in deep meditation on that One who is fond of the flute.

hridaya kovil le pūjāri nyan
pūja yellām vismarichu
dhyāna nimagnāyai kattirunnu

Though I was the priest in the temple of the heart, I forgot all about the puja and was immersed in meditation.

chintā malar kondu pūja cheytū
ulkannināl māla chārti
ānanda bāshpābhishekam cheytū

I worshipped Him with the flowers of thought, garlanded Him with the garland of the inner eye, and gave the ceremonial bath with the tears of joy.

prema payasine gopālanāyi
rāga mākum mādhurya mittū
bhaktyā naivedyamayi kārcha vechu

With deep devotion I offered food to that Gopala after sweetening it with my love.

pragnya yākum bhringam vana mālitan
prema madhu āsvati pān
antarangatile ketti nokki

My consciousness in the form of a bee peeped into the mind in order to enjoy the nectar of love of the One who wears a garland of wild flowers.

venugopāla hridayeśvarā
bhakta priyā sarveśvarā
tannītuka vegam darśanam nī

O Venugopala, Lord of my heart, Lover of devotees, Supreme Lord of all, grant me Thy Vision soon.

DAŚARATHA NANDANA RĀMA

daśaratha nandana rāma
dayā sāgara rāma
daśa mukha mardana rāma
daitya kulāntaka rāma
lakshmana sevita rāma
sīta vallabha rāma
sundara rūpa rāma

dasaratha nandana=The Son of King Dasaratha
dayāsāgara=The Ocean of Compassion
dasa mukha mardana=Slayer of the ten-headed Ravana
daitya kulāntaka=Destroyer of the demon clan
lakshmana sevita=One who is served by Lakshmana
sīta vallabha=Beloved of Sita
sundara rūpa=Of beautiful Form

DHANYA DHANYE

dhanya dhanye jananī jaganmayī
brahma vādini chinmayī sanmayi
amme nin pāda padma parāgamen
karma mālinya mellām morikkane

O Blessed one, O World Mother, who speaks of the Absolute, O Pure Consciousness and Pure Existence. O Mother, may the fragrant dust of Thy Lotus Feet rid me of all impurities born of action.

kannukal kentor ānandam ambike
munnil minnum ī divya rūpāmritam
śarmade śubhe śārade śyāmale
sarvamangale pāhimām pāhimām

O Ambika, what a joy for my eyes is Thy divine ambrosial Form shining before me! O Giver of bliss, Auspicious One, Goddess of Wisdom, dark-colored One who art all-auspicious, protect me, protect me!

vāledu kilum veletu tītilum
vārnorukunna vātsalya dhāmame
parinānanda pīyusha dhārayāl
pārvanendu prabhāmayi kaitorām

Even though Thou may hold a sword or spear, Thou art still the abode of overflowing motherly love. O Giver of happiness to the world through bliss, O Thou with the radiance of the full moon, my salutations to Thee.

kāla kāla priyatame nirmale
kāmade devi sarva mantrātmike
kalitarumpol ulkarutekiyen
mālakattane mātāmriteśvarī

O Beloved of the Destroyer of Time (Śiva), Pure One, O Thou who grants one's desires, O Goddess, the Soul of all mantras, O Mother Amritanandamayi, deign to remove my sorrows imbuing me with strength when I falter.

DHIMIKI DHIMIKI

om dhimiki dhimiki dhim
dhimiki dhimiki dhim

nāche bholā nāth
nāche bholā nāth
mridanga bole śiva śiva śiva om
damaru bole hara hara hara om
vīna bole hari om hari om
nāche bholā nāth

DURGA BHAVĀNI MĀ

durga bhavāni mā
jaya jaya devi mā
kāli kapālini mā
jaya jaya devi mā
parama śivānī mā
jaya jaya devi mā
jagado dhārini mā
jaya jaya devi mā
durga bhavāni mā
jaya jaya devi mā

DURGE DURGE

durge durge durge jai jai mā
durge durge durge jai jai mā

karuna sāgari mā
kāli kapālini mā
jagado dhārini mā
jagadambe jai jai mā

Victory, victory to Mother Durga! O Mother, Ocean of Compassion, Mother Kali adorned with a garland of human skulls (representing the death of the ego), Uplifter of the world, victory to that Divine Mother of the Universe!

GANGĀDHARA HARA

gangādhara hara gangādhara hara
gangādhara hara gangādhara
paramaśiva śankara gangādhara
jaya jagadīśa mām raksha gangādhara

O Thou Who wears the Ganges River on His head, Destroyer of ignorance, Supreme Truth, Giver of auspiciousness, hail to that Lord of the Universe! Protect me, O Lord.

viśva bhava nāśaka gangādhara
viśvarūpa viśvātmaka gangādhara
viśveśa vikhyata gangādhara
jaya jagadīśa mām raksha gangādhara

O Śiva, Destroyer of the Ocean of Becoming, Universal Being and Soul of the Universe, far-famed Lord of the Universe, hail to that Universal Lord! Protect me O Śiva.

bhasmāngara kahara gangādhara
śaktinātha mrityunjaya gangādhara
śrī jagannivāsa śiva gangādhara
jaya jagadīśa mām raksha gangādhara

O Thou Who smears sacred ash all over Thy body,
Lord of all powers, Conqueror of Death, whose abode is the Universe, hail to the Universal Lord! Protect me, O Śiva!

śrī somanātha śiva gangādhara
dukha daridra bhaya nāśa gangādhara
parvati vallabha gangādhara
jaya jagadīśa mām raksha gangādhara

O Śiva residing in Somanath Temple, Annihilator of sorrow, poverty and fear, Beloved of Parvati, hail to that Lord of the Universe! Protect me, O Śiva.

varanāsi pura gangādhara
jaya kailāsa giri vāsa gangādhara
kedara rishikeśa gangādhara
jaya jagdīśa mām raksha gangādhara

O Śiva who resides in Varanasi, on Mt. Kailasa, in Kedaranath and Rishikesh, hail to that Lord of the Universe! Protect me, O Śiva.

jaya vaidyanātha śiva gangādhara
bhima śankara nāgeśa gangādhara
śri mallikārjuna gangādhara
jaya jagadīśa mām raksha gangādhara

Hail to the Lord at Vaidyanatha,
The Lord of serpents, Bhima Sankara,
The Lord Mallilkarjuna (of Srisaila Temple), hail to that Lord of the Universe! Protect me, O Gangadhara.

NB: The above are temples wherein the 12 sacred Śiva Lingas of India are installed.

GHANA ŚYĀMA SUNDARA

ghana śyāma sundara
bansīdhara he krishna kannayya
tū hi mere mām bapu bhaya

devakī nandana he parandhāma
dīna bāndava dvāraka nātha
rādhā hridaya vihāra hare krishna
muralī dharā madhusūdana
gopāla nā he gopāla nā

O Beautiful, Dark-colored One, O dear Krishna who holds the flute, Thou art my Mother, Father and Brother. Thou art the Son of Devaki and the Supreme Abode. Thou protect the afflicted and are Lord of Dvaraka. Thou art playing in Radha's heart and are the Holder of the flute, Destroyer of the demon Madhu.

GIRIDHĀRI JAI GIRIDHĀRI

giridhāri jai giridhāri
sugandha tulasi dala vanamāli
giridhāri jai giridhāri

Hail to He who lifted up the Hill (Govardhana). To He who wears a garland of fragrant basil leaves, hail to that Giridhari!

munijana sevita mādhava murahara
murali mohana giridhāri
gopi manohara giridhāri
gopa manohara giridhāri

To Him who is served by the sages, Beloved of Goddess Lakshmi, Destroyer of the demon Mura, the enchanting Flute Player, Giridhari, who the minds of the Gopis and Gopas enraptured, hail!

GOVARDHANA GIRIDHĀRI

govardhana giri dhāri
gopikā jana hridaya vihārī

gokula pālā līlā lolā
gān āmrita muralī rava dhārī

O Thou who lifted up Govardhana Hill, who plays in the hearts of the shepherd women, who protects Gokula and indulges in play, who bears the sweet sound of the flute...

kāliya mada bhaya damana natana
kāma nāśana kāmita phaladā
kinchana polum tāmasam arutini
kanja dalāyata lochana varunī...kannā...

Thou has danced on the snake Kaliya's head in order to dispel fear of him caused by his pride. O Thou who destroys desires and offers desired things, please do not delay even for a short time to come, O Thou with large eyes like lotus petals.

sañchita karma phala pradanām nin
pinchika polila kītum mānasam
pañcha hayangale bandhi chatiyan
nin chevatikalil amaruva tenno...kannā...

Thou art the One who gives the fruits of one's accumulated actions. My mind is shaking like a peacock feather while trying to control the five senses. O Krishna, when will I merge in Thy Feet?

madhura manohara mridula kalebara
māyā mohana mādhava mukundā
mīna dhvaja kaustubha vanamālī
mām pari pālaya trānana bhagavan

O Thou whose body is soft, sweet and enchanting. Beloved of the Goddess of Wealth, Bestower of Liberation, Enchanter through Maya who has the sign of the fish on His banner, O Thou who wears the Kaustubha gem and a garland of wild flowers, O Lord, please protect and save me.

GOVINDA KRISHNA JAI

govinda krishna jai gopāla krishna jai
gopāla bāla bāla rādhā krishna jai

krishna jai krishna jai krishna jai
krishna krishna krishna krishna jai

gopika māla hari pyāri mayi mīra mana vihāri
madana mohana murali dhāri krishna jai

krishna jai rāma krishna jai rādhā krishna jai
bāla krishna krishna krishna krishna jai

govinda=Lord of the cows
gopāla=cowherd
bāla=child
gopika māla hari pyāri=Beloved Lord of the Gopis
mayi mīra mana vihāri=Who plays in Mother Mira's mind
madana mohana=Enchanter of the mind
murali dhāri=Holding the flute

GOVINDA NĀRĀYANA

govinda nārāyana gopāla nārāyana
govinda govinda nārāyana
govinda gopāla nārāyana
govinda govinda nārāyana
hari govinda gopāla nārāyana
govinda ānanda nārāyana

HAMSA VĀHINI DEVI

hamsa vāhini devī
ambā sarasvatī

O Goddess who rides the swan,
Mother Saraswati (Goddess of Wisdom)...

akhila loka kala devī ambā sarasvatī
hamsa vāhini devī ambā sarasvati

Who is the Moon to the entire Universe...

sringa saila vāśini ambā sarasvatī
sangīta rasa vilāsini ambā sarasvatī

Who resides on the Sringeri Mountain...
Who plays in the bliss of music...

HARE KEŚAVA GOVINDA

hare keśava govinda vāsudeva jaganmaya
śiva śankara rudreśa nīlakantha trilochana

gopāla mukunda mādhava
gopa rakshaka dāmodara
gauripati śiva śiva hara
deva deva gangādhara
madhusūdana madanamohana
madhuvairi mangalākara
mahādeva maheśvara
mrityunjaya bhava bhaya hara

sīta nātha rādha nātha lakshmī nātha jagannātha
gangā nātha gauri nātha dīna nātha viśvanātha

hare=Lord Vishnu
keśava=Slayer of the demon Kesi
govinda=Lord of the cows (senses)
vāsudeva=Son of Vasudeva
jaganmaya=Pervading the Universe
śiva=Auspicious One
hara=The Destroyer
rudreśa=Lord of the Rudras
nīlakantha=Blue-throated Lord
trilochana=Having three eyes
gopāla=Protector of the cows
mukunda=Giver of Liberation
mādhava=Beloved of Goddess Lakshmi
goparakshaka=Protector of the cowherds
dāmodara=Who was bound around the waist with a rope
gauripati=Husband of Parvati
hara=Destroyer
deva deva=God of gods
gangādhara=Wearing the Ganges River on His head
madhusūdana=Slayer of the demon Madhu
madana mohana=Enchanter of the mind
madhuvairi=Foe of the demon Madhu
mangalākara=Giver of auspiciousness
mahādeva=Great God
maheśvara=Great Lord
mrityunjaya=Conqueror of death
bhavabhayahara=Destroyer of the fear of Becoming
sītā nātha=Lord of Sita
rādhānātha=Lord of Radha

gangānātha=Lord of Ganges
lakshmīnātha=Lord of Lakshmi
jagannātha=Lord of the universe
gaurinātha=Lord of Parvati
dīnanātha=Lord of the afflicted
viśvanātha=Lord of the Universe

HARE MURARE

hare murāre madhu kaita bhāre
govinda gopāla mukunda śaure

O Hari who slayed the demons Mura, Madhu and Kaitabha, Lord and Protector of the cows, Bestower of Liberation who is born in Surasena's dynasty...

ananta śrīdhara govinda keśava
mukunda mādhava nārāyana hare

O Infinite One bearing Goddess Lakshmi on Thy chest, Govinda, Slayer of Kesi, Bestower of Liberation, Beloved of Lakshmi who hovers over the Primeval Waters, O Hari...

devakī tanaya gopikā ramana
bhakta udharana trivikrama

Darling of Mother Devaki, Beloved ot the Gopis, Uplifter of the devotees, who took three strides to cover the entire Universe...

HE GIRIDHARA GOPĀLĀ

he giridhara gopālā (3 times)
mādhava murahara madhura manohara
giridhara gopāla

O Thou who holds the Hill, Protector of the cowherds, Beloved of Lakshmi, Destroyer of the demon Mura, Sweet One, Enchanter of the mind...

nanda kumāra sundarākāra
vrindāvana sañchāra
murali lola muni jana pāla
giridhara gopala

O Son of Nanda of Beautiful Form, who sports in Vrindavan, Player of the flute, Protector of the sages...

kaustubha dhāra mauktika hāra
rādhā hridaya vihāra
bhaktodhāra bāla gopāla

Thou who wears the Kaustubha gem and pearl necklace, who plays in Radha's heart, Uplifter of devotees, O Baby Krishna...

gopari pāla gopīlola
govardhan odhāra
nanda kumāra navanīta chora

Protector of the Gopas, who plays with the Gopis, Uplifter of the Govardhana Hill, Son of Nanda who steals butter...

HE MĀDHAVA

he mādhava yadu nandana
manamohana he madhusūdana
janārdhana rādhā jīvana
gopālanā gopī ranjana

O Beloved of Goddess Lakshmi, Son of the Yadu clan, Enchanter of the mind, Killer of the demon Madhu, Oppressor of the wicked, the very Life of Radha, Protector of the cows and Delighter of the Gopis...

INI ORU JANMAM

ini oru janmam ivane kola krishna
mati moha cheliyil kālitari vīrum
yekukil tava bhakta dāsānu dāsanāyi
kariyuvān ivanennum varamekanam

O Krishna, give me not another birth lest I fall into the deep quagmire of delusion. If Thou givest, then bestow the boon of taking birth as the servant of Thy servants forever.

tirunāmam manasinnu taravākanam krishna
tava pāda mālarennum telivākanam
sakalatum bhagavānte pratibhayāyi tonnanam
samanila avirāmam uravākanam

O Krishna, Thou should fill my mind with Thy Holy Name and reveal Thy Lotus Feet bright and clear therein. Keeping my mind ever equipoised, all should be felt to be Thy manifestation.

krishnā...karunā nidhe...torunnen ivan...
kaitorunnen kaitorunnen

O Krishna...Treasure of Compassion...I salute Thee with joined palms...I humbly salute Thee...

avaniyil upakāra pradamā kanam janmam
avināśa sukha dāna gati yākanam
anumati atinayi nī tarumengil anavadhi

nara janmam iniyum nī ivanu nalkū
krishnā...karunā nidhe...
torunnen ivan...kaitorunnen...kaitorunnen...

If I should get another birth, let it be beneficial to the world by giving the Imperishable Joy to others as well. If Thou allowest me that, then please give me any number of births as a human being. O Krishna...Treasure of Compassion...I salute Thee with joined palms...I humbly salute Thee...

ĪŚVARI JAGADĪŚVARI

īśvari jagadīśvari paripālaki karunākari
śāśvata mukti dāyaki
mama khedamokke orikkanne

O Goddess, Goddess of the Universe, Preserver and Giver of Grace and Eternal Liberation, please rid me of all my sorrows.

kleśa sampurnna mākumī loka
jīvita sukham kantu nyān
agniyil salabhangal viruvatu
pole yākki valayi kalle

I have seen the pleasures of this worldly life so full of afflictions; please do not make me suffer like the moths that fall into the fire.

āśa pāśatte munnil nirttiyum
kāla pāśatte pinnilum
ittu korttu kalippi kunnatu
kashta mallayo mātāve

Bound by the noose of desire in front and the noose of death at the back, O Mother, to play tying them together, isn't it a pity?

mośamām vari kātti tātennil
śāśvate kaniyenname
kleśa nāśini śokabhāram
akatti tenname mātāve

Without showing the wrong path, shed Thy Grace on me, O Eternal One. O Mother, Destroyer of misery, remove my burden of sorrow.

innu kanmatu nāle illaho
chinmayi ninte līlakal
ulla tinnoru nāśame illa
nāśa mullata naśvaram

What is seen today is not there tomorrow. O Pure Consciousness, this is Thy play. What really is, has no destruction. Anything destructible is transient.

marttya janma phalam varuttuvān
loka nāyaki kaitorām
loka nayaki sarva rūpini
kumpitunnu nyān nin pādam

O Mother of the World, for achieving the fruit of human birth, I pray with joined palms. O Goddess of the World, All-formed One, I bow at Thy Feet.

JAI JAI RĀMAKRISHNA

jai jai rāmakrishna hare
jai jai rāmakrishna hare

daśaratha nandana rāma namo
vasudeva nandana krishna namo

Salutations to Rama, Son of Dasaratha,
Salutations to Krishna, Son of Vasudeva.

kausalya tanaya rāma namo
devaki nandana krishna namo

Salutations to Rama, Son of Kausalya,
Salutations to Krishna, Son of Devaki.

ayodhya vāśi rāma namo
dvāraka vāśī krishna namo

Salutations to Rama, resident of Ayodhya,
Salutations to Krishna residing in Dvaraka.

sītā vallabha rāma namo
rādhā vallabha krishna namo

Salutation to Rama, Sita's Lord,
Salutations to Krishna, Radha's Lord.

rāvana mardana rāma namo
kamsa vimardana krishna namo

Salutations to Rama, killer of Ravana,
Salutations to Krishna, killer of Kamsa.

JAYA JAYA ĀRATI

jaya jaya ārati rāma tumāri
pīta vasana vayi jayanti mālā
śyāma bharana tanu nayano visāla

Hail! Hail! We do the auspicious waving of lights to Thee, O Rama. Thou hast yellow raiment, a garland of wild flowers, a body of dark hue and large eyes.

pīta makutā kasa saranga sohe
sīta rāmani rekha mana mohe
nārada śārada mangala gāve
hari hari he guna rāja gabhīra

Thy golden yellow crown, bow and its string all shine. Enchanting is Sita's beautiful form. Sage Narada and Goddess Sarasvati sing auspicious songs. Lord Hari is a virtuous, majestic king!

satrugna o jaya lakshmana bhārata
ārati karu kausalya mātā
sammukha charana sakhe hanuvīra
hari hari he guna rāja gambhīra
śri rāma jaya rāma jaya jaya rāma
jagadāti rāma jagateka rāma jānaki rāma

We are doing arati to Satrugna, Lakshmana, Bharata and Mother Kausalya. O friend Hanuman, Thou art in front of Rama's Feet. Lord Hari is a virtuous, majestic king! Victory to Sri Rama! Rama is the greatest in the world! He alone exists!

JAYA OM ŚRĪ MĀTĀ

jaya om śrī mātā mātā
jaya jaya jaganmātā
jaya om śrī mātā mātā
jaya jaya jagan mātā
jaya śiva ramani guru guha janani
jaya vanamana harini

Hail to the Mother, the Mother of the World! Hail to that Beautiful Woman with Śiva, the Mother of Lord Subrahmanya. Hail to the Destroyer of the forest of the mind!

JAYA RĀMA JĀNAKI RĀMA

jaya rāma jānaki rāma
jaya rāma sītā rāma
jaya rāma śrī raghu rāma
jaya rāma sītā rāma
jaya rāma sīta rāma
jaya rāma rāma rāma

JAI JAI JAI GANANẠYAKA

jai jai jai gana nāyaka
jai jai jai vigna nāśaka
gajavadana gauri nandana
gangādhara śiva śambo nandana

Hail to the Lord of Śiva's attendants! Hail to the Destroyer of obstacles! To the elephant-headed Son of Parvati, Son of Śiva, hail!

GOPI VALLABHA

gopi vallabha gopāla krishna
govardhana giri dhāri
rādhā mānasa rājīvalochana
kāyām pūvutal varnnā krishnā
kāyām pūvutal varnnā

O Gopala Krishna, Beloved of the Gopis, Uplifter of the Govardhana Hill, Lotus-eyed One in Radha's mind, Thy color is that of a blue lotus...

vrindāvana sanchāriyām krishnā
chen tāmara dala nayana
bandhama kattuka nanda kumāra
sundara bāla mukundā krishna
sundara bāla mukunda

O Krishna who moves about in Vrindavan, whose eyes are like the petals of a red lotus, O Son of Nanda, rid me of all bondage. O beautiful Child Krishna, Bestower of Liberation...

madhurādhi pate śrī krishna
sakalā maya hara devā
paritā pakanam tava pada dāsanil
abhayam nalkuka devā krishnā
abhayam nalkuka devā

O Sri Krishna, Lord of Mathura, who destroys all sorrow, deign to give refuge to the afflicted servants at Thy Feet.

KASTURI TILAKAM

kasturi tilakam lalāta bhalake
vaksha sthale kaustubham krishna

Krishna puts the vermillion mark on His forehead and wears the Kaustubha gem on His chest.

nasāgre nava mauthikam krishna
karatale venum kare kanganam

From Krishna's nostril hangs a pearl ring and in His hand is a flute with bracelets around His wrists.

sarvānge hari chandanam cha kalayan
kande cha muktāvali

Sandalwood paste is applied to all His limbs and there is a pearl necklace around His neck.

gopastrī pari veshtitito vijayate
gopāla chūdāmani krishna

Victory to that Krishna who is surrounded by the cowherd women and is the Crest Jewel of the cowherds!

KEŚAVA NĀRĀYANA

keśava nārāyana mādhava govinda
vishnu madhusūdana trivikrama vāmana
śrīdhara hrishikeśa padmanābha dāmodara
sankārshana vāsudeva pradyumna aniruddha
purushottama adhokshaja narasimhachyuta
janārdhana upendra hari śrī krishna

keśava=Slayer of the demon Kesi
nārāyana=Lord on the Primeval Waters
mādhava=Beloved of Goddess Lakshmi
govinda=Lord of the cows
vishnu=All-pervading Lord
madhusūdana=Slayer of the demon Madhu
trivikrama=Who covered the Universe in three strides
vāmana=Dwarf manifestation of Vishnu
śrīdhara=Who wears Lakshmi on His chest

hrishikeśa=Lord of the senses
padmanābha=Lotus-navelled
dāmodara=Who had a pestle tied to His waist
sankārshana=Brother of Sri Krishna
vāsudeva=Son of Vasudeva
pradyumna=Son of Sri Krishna
aniruddha=Grandson of Sri Krishna
purushottama=The Supreme Person
adhokshaja=Whose vital force never goes downwards
narasimha=Man-lion manifestation of Vishnu
achyuta=Unshakable
janārdhana=Oppressor of the wicked
upendra=Dwarf manifestation of Vishnu

KODĀNUKOTI

kodānukoti varshangalayi satyame
tetunnu ninne manushyan

O Truth Eternal, mankind is searching for Thee since millions and millions of years...

dhyāna nimagnarāyi nin divya dhārayil
ātmā vineche torukkān
ellām tyajichu rishīśvarar enniyāl
tirātta varsham tapas irunnu

The ancient sages, renouncing everything, performed endless years of austerities in order to make their self flow into Thy Divine Stream through meditation.

khoramāyi vīsum kotum kāttilum ninte
surya tejasulla kochu nālum

ati kalikkāt āngate nilkunnu
arkkum atukuvān kelperāte

Inaccessible to all, Thy infinitesimal Flame, glowing like the effulgence of the sun, stands still without dancing even in the fiercely blowing cyclone.

pushpa latakalum pūja murikalum
pūtten kotimara kshetrangalum
yetra yugangalāyi kāttirunnu ninne
yettātta dure aninunnum

Flowers, creepers, shrine rooms and temples with newly installed sacred pillars, all are waiting for Thee since aeons and aeons, but still Thou art inaccessibly distant.

KRISHNA KANNAYA

krishna kannaya krishna kannaya
nada vara nanda kumāra kannaya
vrindāvana ke bansi kannaya
rādhā mano hara rāsa rasaya
murali manohara krishna kannaya
śrī madhusūdana rādhe kannaya

krishna kannaya=Darling Krishna
nadavara=Dancing
nanda kumāra=Son of Nanda
vrindāvana ke bansi=Flute Player of Vrindavan
rādhā manohara=Enchanter of Radha's mind
rāsa rasaya=Relisher of the Rasa Dance
murali=Flute Player
śrī madhusūdana=Slayer of the demon Madhu

KRISHNA KRISHNA

krishna krishna mukunda janārdhana
krishna govinda nārāyana hare
achyutānanta govinda mādhavā
satchidānanda nārayana hare

O Krishna, Bestower of Liberation and Oppressor of the wicked, Lord of the cows, Saviour of the afflicted, Unshakable, Infinite, Beloved of Lakshmi, Existence, Awareness, Bliss Absolute...

krishna vāsudeva hare
krishna vāsudeva hare

garuda gamana kamsāre madhusūdana
madana gopāla nārāyana hare
murali krishna murāre mana mohana
nanda nandana nārayana hare

O Thou Who flies on Garuda, Slayer of Kamsa and the demon Madhu, Flute Player, Slayer of the demon Mura, Enchanter of the mind, Son of Nanda...

nārāyana nārāyana nārāyana nārāyana
nārāyana nārāyana nārāyana namo nārāyana

rāma rāma narasimha purushottama
rāghava rāma nārāyana hare
rāvanāre kodanda rāma raghuvarā
rākshasāntaka nārāyana hare

O Rama, the Supreme Person manifested as the Man-Lion, born in the clan of Raghu, Slayer of Ravana, Bearer of a bow, Destroyer of the demons, Narayana, Hari...

padmanābha parameśa sanātana
parama purusha nārāyana hare
pānduranga vithala purandara
pundari kāksha nārāyana hare

O Lotus-navelled One, Supreme Eternal Lord, the Supreme Person, Narayana, Hari, who is Panduranga Vithala in Pandarapur...

śrinivāsa aniruddha dharanīdhara
aprameyātma nārāyana hare
dinabandho bhagavanta dayā nidhe
devakī tanaya nārāyana hare

O Abode of the Goddess of Prosperity, Upholder of the earth, the Self beyond thought, Lover of the suffering ones, Treasure of Compassion, Darling of Devaki, Narayana Hari...

KRISHNA KRISHNA RĀDHĀ

krishna krishna rādhā krishna
govinda gopāla venu krishna
mohana krishna madhusūdana krishna
mana mohana krishna madhusūdana krishna
murāre krishna mukunda krishna

KRISHNA MUKUNDA

krishna mukunda murāri
jaya krishna mukunda murāri

rādhe govinda krishna mukunda
rādhe govinda krishna murāri

nandaya nanda rādhā govinda
rādhe govinda krishna mukunda

KUMBHODARA VARADĀ

kumbhodara varadā gajāmukha
sambhu kumāra ganapathi bhagavān
kumbhodara varadā

O Thou with a big belly, elephant-faced Giver of boons, Son of Śiva, Lord of the Ganas....

ainkara śambhava sankata harana
nalgati yaruluka śiva sadanā
anpiyalum miri patiyana matiyanil
śankara sūno kaniyename

O Thou with five hands bestowing boons, Destroyer of sorrows, Son of Śiva, bless us with Salvation. Thy kind glance must fall on me. O Son of Śiva, show Thy mercy.

ādināthane bhavanadi tarana
karunālaya maya śubhadā hare
ānandāmrita vighna vināyaka
kripa yarulītuka durita hare

O Primal Lord who has crossed the River of Becoming, Abode of mercy, Giver of auspiciousness, O Hari, Nectar of bliss, Destroyer of misery, show Thy compassion.

LAMBODARA PĀHIMĀM

lambodara pāhi mām
jagadamba sūtā raksha mām
jaya lambodara pāhi mām

Protect me, O pot-bellied One. Save me, O Son of the Universal Mother. Hail! Protect me, O pot-bellied One.

śaranāgata raksha mām
he karunānidhe pāhi mām

Give me refuge and save me. Protect me, O Treasure of Compassion.

śrī gananātha samraksha mām
nīja bhakti mudam dehi mām

O Lord of the Ganas, protect me. Give me the bliss of real devotion.

MĀDHAVA GOPAL

mādhava gopālā mana mohana gopāla
yaśoda ke bālā yadu nandana gopālā

O Beloved of Goddess Lakshmi, Enchanter of the mind, Son of Yashoda born in the clan of Yadu, O Protector of the cows...

bāla gopālā he giridhara gopālā
he giridhara gopālā
yadunandana gopālā

O Child Krishna, Holder of the Hill, born in the clan of Yadu...

MATHURĀDHIPATE

mathurādhipate dvarakā dhipate
vaikunta pate śrī rādhā pate
nanda nandanā krishna gopālā
mīra ke prabhu giridhara bālā

Lord of Mathura and Dvaraka (two cities where Sri Krishna lived), Lord of Vaikunta (Vishnu's Abode), Lord of Radha, Son of Nanda, cowherd Krishna, Lord of Mira Bhai (a lady saint of Rajasthan), O Child who held the Govardhana Hill on His hand...

devakī nandana he ghana śyāma
gopī manohara mangala dhāma
kāliya mārdana he nandalālā
nācho nāchore bhayya bhansūri vala

O Son of Devaki, Dark-colored One, Enchanter of the Gopis, Bestower of auspiciousness, Subduer of the serpent Kaliya, Child of Nanda, dance, do dance, O Brother Flute Player...

sūrdās ke prabhu giridhāri
rādhā krishnā kunja vihāri
vasudeva nandana āsura nikhandana
bhava bhāya bhanjana jagan vandana

O Lord of Saint Surdas, who lifted the Hill, Radha's Lord who resides in the heart, Son of Vasudeva, Destroyer of demons, Destroyer of the fear of transmigration, to whom the entire Universe bows down...

mīra ke prabhu giridhara nāgara
gopī krishna kanayyā

abhi dena tum tera darshan mera
krishna kannaya

O Mira's Lord, Uplifter of the Hill, Darling of the Gopis, be gracious and give Thy Darshan now, O my darling Krishna.

MANDAHĀSA

manda hāsa vadane manohari
mātā jagad jananī
mātā mātā mātā jagad jananī
mātā mātā mātā jagad jananī

jagad jananī śubha jananī
mātā jagad jananī
amba mātā jagad jananī

īśvarī ambā parameśvarī ambā
jagadīśvarī ambā parameśvarī ambā

mandahāsa vadane=Gently smiling face
manohari=Enchanting
jagad jananī=Mother of the world
śubha=Auspicious
īśvarī=Goddess
ambā=Mother
parameśvarī=Supreme Goddess
jagadīśvarī=World ruler

MANGALA ĀRATI

mangala ārati gopāla ki
kamala nayana ki yaśodā nandana ki

mangala rūpa śyāma sundara ki
mangala bhrikutī vāla ki
chatūr bhuja dās sadā mangala nidhi
pālita giridhara bāla ki

Auspicious waving of lights to the Protector of the Cows, to the Lotus-eyed One, Yashoda's Son, the Beautiful Dark One. O Thou with an auspicious Form and eyebrows, Thou, Lord Vishnu, art the ever-auspicious Treasure of this servant of Thine, O Protector and Uplifter of the Govardhana Hill.

MANO BUDDHYA

mano buddhyahankāra chittāni nāham
na cha śrotra jihve na cha khrāna netre
na cha vyoma bhūmir na tejo na vāyu
chidānanda rūpaha śivoham śivoham

I am neither the mind, intellect, ego nor memory; neither ears nor tongue nor the senses of smell and sight; nor am I ether, earth, fire, water or air; I am Pure Awareness-Bliss, I am Śiva! I am Śiva!

na cha prāna samnyo navai pañcha vāyu
navā sapta dhātur na vā pañcha kośaha
na vāk pāni pādam na cho pastha pāyu
chidānanda rūpaha śivoham śivoham

I am neither the life force nor the five vital airs; neither the body's seven elements nor its five sheaths; nor hands nor feet nor tongue, nor the organs of sex and voiding; I am Pure Awareness-Bliss, I am Śiva! I am Śiva!

na me dvesha rāgau na me lobha mohau
mado naiva me naiva mātsarya bhāvaha
na dharmo na chārtho na kāmo na moksha
chidānanda rūpaha śivoham śivoham

Neither loathing nor liking have I, neither greed nor delusion; no sense have I of ego or pride, neither religious merit nor wealth, neither enjoyment nor Liberation have I; I am Pure Awareness-Bliss, I am Śiva! I am Śiva!

na punyam na pāpam na saukhyam na dukham
na mantro na tīrtham na veda na yagnyaha
aham bhojanam naiva bhojyam na bhoktā
chidānanda rūpaha śivoham śivoham

Neither right nor wrong doing am I, neither pleasure nor pain; nor the mantra, nor the sacred place, the Vedas, the sacrifice; neither the act of eating, the eater, nor the food; I am Pure Awareness-Bliss I am Śiva! I am Śiva!

na mrityur na sankā na me jāti bhedaha
pitā naiva me naiva mātā cha janma
na bandhur na mitram guru naiva sishya
chidānanda rūpaha śivoham śivoham

Death or fear I have none, nor any distinction of caste; neither father nor mother nor even a birth have I; neither friend nor comrade, neither guru nor disciple; I am Pure Awareness-Bliss, I am Śiva! I am Śiva!

aham nirvikalpo nirākāra rūpo
vibhut vācha sarvatra sarvendriyānām
na chā sangato naiva muktirnna meya
chidānanda rūpaha śivoham śivoham

I have no form or fancy, the All-pervading am I; everywhere I exist, yet I am beyond the senses; neither salvation am I, nor anything that may be known; I am Pure Awareness-Bliss, I am Śiva! I am Śiva!

NANDA KUMĀRA

nanda kumāra gopāla
vrindāvana ke sundara bāla

O Son of Nanda, Protector of the cows, beautiful Child of Vrindavan...

mohana rādhe śyāma gopāla
mohana murali dhāri gopāla

O Enchanter of Radha, dark-colored Gopala, enchanting Flute Player...

govardhana giridhāri gopāla
gopī mānasa lolā gopāla

O Gopal who lifted up the Govardhana Hill, who plays in the Gopis' minds...

NANDALĀL

nandalāl nandalāl nandalāl yadu nandalāl
nandalālā navanīta chora
rādhā pyāre nandalāl
māyi mīrā manasa chora
hridaya vihārā nandalāl

O Son of Nanda, born in the Yadu clan, Stealer of butter, Beloved of Radha, who stole Mother Mira Bai's mind, that Son of Nanda who plays in the heart...

NANDALĀLĀ YADU

nandalālā yadu nandalālā
brindāvana govinda lālā
rādhā mādhava nandalālā
rādhā lola nandalālā

O Son of Nanda born in the Yadu clan, Lord of the cows in Brindavan, Beloved of the Goddess Lakshmi, who is dear to Radha, O Son of Nanda...

PARAMAŚIVA MĀM PĀHI

parama śiva mām pāhi
sadā śiva mām pāhi
śambho śiva mām pāhi
parama śiva mām pāhi

akshara linga mām pāhi
avyāya linga mām pāhi
ākāśa linga mām pāhi
ātmā linga mām pāhi

hara hara hara mām pāhi
hara hara hara hara hara hara mām pāhi
śiva śiva śiva śiva śiva śiva mām pāhi

parama śiva mām pāhi
amrita linga pāhi mām

advaya linga pāhi mām
chinmaya linga pāhi mām

O Supremely Auspicious One, protect me! O Ever-Auspicious One, protect me! O Śiva from whom everything manifests, protect me!

akshara=Indestructible
linga=Symbol for the absolute
avyāya=Which does not decay
ākāśa=Ether
ātmā=Self
hara=Destroyer
amrita=Immortal
advaya=Non-dual
chinmaya=Awareness absolute

PARĀŚAKTI

parāśakti paramjyoti
parāt pare rādhe devī

O Supreme Power, Supreme Light, O Supreme One, Divine Mother Radha...

jaya rādhe jaya rādhe
rāsa rāseśvari priya priya

Hail to Radha! O Goddess of the Rasa Play, Beloved of the Beloved...

jaya rādhe jaya rādhe
rādhe śyām rādhe śyām

Victory to Radha! O Radha and Krishna...

PRABHU MĪŚAM

prabhu mīśam anīśam asesha gunam
guna hīna mahīsha garā bhāranam
rana nirjīta durjaya daitya kulam
prana māmi śivam śiva kalpa tarum

giri rāja sutan jita vāma talam
tanu nindita rājita kodi vibhum
vidhi vishnu siror druta pāda yugam
prana māmi śivam śiva kalpa tarum

sasa lanjita ranjita san makutam
sasi lanjita sundara mukti padam
sura saivali nikruta bhūta jadam
prana māmi śivam śiva kalpa tarum

nayana traya bhūshita chāru mukham
mukha padma parājita kodi vibhum
vibhu khanda vimandita phala tadam
prana māmi śivam śiva kalpa tarum

sāmba śiva sāmba śiva
mahādeva sāmba śiva mahādeva sāmba śiva

mriga rāja niketana madi gurum
gara lasana madi visāla tadam
prama dadhi pa sevita ranjanakam
prana māmi śivam śiva kalpa tarum

śiva sambho śiva
hara hara hara hara sāmba śiva

makara dvaja matta madanga haram
kari chārmaka nāga vibodha karam
vara margana sūla visāla taram
prana māmi śivam śiva kalpa tarum

jagadud bhava pālana nāśa karam
vita śaiva siromani prishta param
priya mānava sādhu janaika gatim
pranamāmi śivam śiva kalpa tarum

anādam sudhīnam vibho viśva nātham
punar janma dukhāt parī trāhi śambho
smara kokila dukha samūha haram
prana māmi śivam śiva kalpa tarum

mahādeva mahādeva sāmba śiva
śambho mahādeva sāmba śiva
śambho mahādeva sāmba śiva
sāmba śiva sāmba śiva
hara hara sāmba śiva
śambho śiva sadā śiva

hara hara hara śambho śiva
hara śambho śiva
sāmba sadā śiva sāmba sadā śiva
samba sadā śiva sāmba śiva

karpūra gauram karunāvatāram
samsāra hāram bhūjagendra hāram

sadā vasantam hridayāravinde
bhavam bhavāni sahitam namāmi

śiva śiva sambho hara hara mahādeva
śiva śiva sambho hara hara mahādeva
hara hara mahādeva
hara hara mahādeva

RĀDHE ŚYĀMA

rādhe śyāma he khana śyāma
rādhā mādhava mangala dhāma
jaya jaya jaya he megha śyāma
megha śyāma megha śyāma
jaya jaya jaya vrindāvana dhāma

O Dark-colored Krishna with Radha, Beloved of Goddess Lakshmi, Abode of auspiciousness, hail to that cloud-colored One, who stays in Vrindavana...

rām nām sukha dāyi bhajore
rām nām ke do akshar me sab sukh śānti samāyire
rām prabhu ke charan me ākar
jīvan sabhal banavore

Worship the name of Rama, giver of bliss. The two syllables of 'Ra' and 'Ma' will give all bliss and peace. Fall at the Feet of Lord Rama and attain the fruition of Life.

RAGHU NANDANA

raghu nandana mama jīvana
śrī rām jai rām jai jai rām

raghu pate sīta pate daśarathe dayānidhe
rāma rāghava he sīta nāyaka
lokānātha rāghava
śrī rām jai rām jai jai rām

O Son of Raghu, my very life! Lakshmi's Lord, victory to Ram, victory to Ram, victory to Ram! O Lord of Raghu's dynasty, Lord of Sita, Son of Dasaratha, Treasure of Compassion! O Rama Raghava, Lord of Sita, Lord of the Universe, Raghava, victory to Ram!

RĀJA RĀMA

rāja rāma rāma rāma
sītā rāma sītā rāma
kodanda rāma rāma rāma
sītā rāma rāma rāma

tāraka nāma rāma rāma
sītā rāma rāma rāma
rāma rāma rāma rāma

kodanda rāma kodanda rāma
kodanda rāma kodanda rāma

rāja rāma=Lord Rama the king
sīta rāma=Sita's husband, Rama
kodanda=Rama's bow
tāraka nāma=The Divine Name which takes one across the ocean of transmigration

RĀMAKRISHNA GOVINDA

hari rāmakrishna govinda janārdhana
achyuta paramānanda
achyuta paramānanda nityānanda mukunda

satchidānanda govinda
govinda govinda govinda
gopāla govinda govinda

satchidānanda govinda
achyuta paramānanda

rāma krishna hari rāma krishna hari
rāma krishna hari rāma krishna hari

O Savior of the afflicted, Thou who art Rama, Krishna, Govinda and the Oppressor of the wicked; Thou art the unshakable Supreme Bliss, Eternal Bliss and Bestower of Liberation. Govinda is Existence-Awareness-Bliss Absolute.

RĀMA KRISHNA PRABHUTŪ

rāma krishna prabhu tū
jaya rām jaya rām
yesu pitā prabhu tū
jaya rām jaya rām
allāh īśvara tū allā hū akbar
jaya rām jaya rām
jaya rām jaya rām

Thou art Lord Ramakrishna,
Hail to Ram! Hail to Ram!
Thou art Father Jesus,
Hail to Ram! Hail to Ram!
Thou art the Lord Allah, Allah is Great!
Hail to Ram! Hail to Ram!
Hail to Ram! Hail to Ram!

RĀMA NĀMA TĀRAKAM

rāma rāma rāma rāma rāma nāma tārakam
rāma krishna vāsudeva bhukti mukti dāyakam

The Name of Rama takes one across the Ocean of Transmigration and gives one both material prosperity and Liberation.

jānakī manoharam sarva loka nāyakam
śankarādi sevyamāna divya nāma kīrtanam

That Name has enchanted Sita and is the Support of the whole world. It is being worshipped and sung by gods like Śiva and others.

rāma hare krishna hare
rāma hare krishna hare
rāma hare krishna hare
tava nāma bhajāmi sadānu hare
nāma smarana danyo pāyam
nahi pasyāmo bhava tarane

Rama Hare Krishna Hare! I am always worshipping Thy Name. In crossing the ocean of mundane existence, we see no other means than the Names of the Lord.

KĀYĀ PĪYA

kāyā pīya sukha se soyā
na hakka janna magavāyya
kamala mukha rāma bhajana kodiā

We eat, drink, and sleep comfortably, but we never sing about the lotus-faced Rama.

jā mukha nīsādīna rāma nāma nahi
o mukha katchu na kiyā
kamala mukha rāma bhajana kodiā

The name of Rama never seems to come from our mouths. O mouth, why aren't you singing the songs of the lotus-faced Rama?

laka chorāsi tere pīra dara
sundara tanu magavāyya
kamala mukha rāma bhajana kodiā

Our eyes are not seeing the Lord's beautiful form, and we never sing about the lotus-faced Rama.

kaha ta kabīra suno bāyi sādho
āya vaisā gayā
kamala mukha rāma bhajana kodiā

We come and we go but we never sing the devotional songs of the lotus-faced Rama. Kabir is saying, "O listen, brother sadhus; sing the devotional songs of the lotus-faced Rama."

RĀMA RĀMA RĀJA RĀMA

rāma rāma rāja rāma
sītā rāma śrī raghu rāma
śrī rāma jaya rāma jaya jaya rāma
śrī rāma jaya rāma jaya jaya rāma

RĀMA SMARANAM

rāma smaranam bhāya haranam
raghu rāma gītam ānandam
rāma sevanam agha haranam
raghu rāma nāmam bhava tāranam

Remembrance of Rama destroys fear. The songs about Rama of Raghu's dynasty, are bliss. Service unto Rama destroys sins. The Name of Raghuram takes one across the Ocean of Transmigration.

kausalya nandana daśaratha rāma
suramuni vandita rāghava rāma
rāmachandra hari govinda
ajñāna nāśaka he śaranam

O Son of Kausalya and Dasaratha! O Raghava Rama who gods and ascetics worship, O Ramachandra who is Hari Govinda, O Destroyer of ignorance, grant me refuge!

yāga rakshaka daśaratha rāma
viśvamitra priya raghurāma
rāmachandra hari govinda
ajñāna nāśaka he śaranam

O Dasaratha Rama who protected the sacrifice, O Raghurama, Beloved of Seer Vishvamitra, O Ramachandra...

rāvana mardana daśaratha rāma
vānara rakshaka rāghava rāma
rāmachandra hari govinda
ajñāna nāśaka he śaranam

Slayer of demon Ravana, O Dasaratha Rama, Protector of the monkey army, O Raghava Rama, O Ramachandra...

SADGURU BRAHMA

sad guru brahma sanātana he
parama dayākara pāvana he
janmaja dukha vināśana he
jagado dhārana kārana he
śrī rāmakrishna janārdhana he
bhava bhaya jaladhī tarana he

O Perfect Master, the Eternal Absolute Itself. Supremely gracious, all-purifying One, Destroyer of the sorrows of birth, cause of the uplift of the world. O Sri Ramakrishna who is worshipped by the people, Thou takest one across the fear of the waters of Transmigration.

SARVAM BRAHMA MAYAM

sarvam brahmamayam re re
sarvam brahmamayam
kim vachanīyam kima vachanīyam
kim rachanīyam kima rachanīyam

All is Brahma, all is Brahma! What is worth saying and what is not worth saying? What is worth writing and what is not worth writing?

kim pathanīyam kima pathanīyam
kim bhajanīyam kima bhajanīyam

What is worth learning and what is not worth learning?
What is worth praying for and what is not?

kim bhoktavyam kima bhoktavyam
kim boddhavyam kima boddhavyam

What should be eaten and what not?
What is worth teaching and what not?

sarvatra sadā hamsa dhyānam
karttavyam bho mukti nidānam

Always thy duty is to do deep meditation which will give salvation.

SĪTA RĀM BOL

sīta rām sīta rām sīta rām bol
rādhe śyām rādhe śyām rādhe śyām bol
hari bol hari bol hari hari bol
mukunda mādhava govinda bol

nāma prabhūka he sukha dāyi
pāpa kateng ek shana me bhāri
rāma ki mahima aise bol
mukunda mādhava govinda bol

The Name of the Lord is the Bestower of bliss. It will destroy all sins in a moment. Therefore, sing the glory of Rama and sing "Mukunda, Madhava, Govinda!"

sabari ajāmila saba sukha pāyi
nāma bhajan se mukti pāyi
nāma ki mahima aise bol
mukunda mādhava govinda bol

Devotees like Sabari and Ajamila attained this bliss and finally gained Liberation through the chanting of the Name. Therefore, sing the glory of Ram and sing "Mukunda, Madhava, Govinda!"

bhajare mana tū krishna murāri
nata nākara giridhara banavāri
krishna rasāmrita jīvita bol
mukunda mādhava govinda bol

O mind, worship Lord Krishna, foe of the demon Murari, Dancer and Uplifter of the Mountain. Sing about the deeds of Krishna filled with the nectar of sentiment and sing "Mukunda, Madhava, Govinda!"

SATCHITĀNANDA GURU

satchitānanda guru jaya guru jaya guru
jaya guru jaya guru satchitānanda guru

Victory to the Guru who is Existence-Awareness-Bliss Absolute.

āchāryendra jaya guru jaya guru
dakshināmūrti jaya guru jaya guru
aguna saguna guru jaya guru jaya guru
satchitānanda guru jaya guru jaya guru

Hail to Him who is the King among teachers and who is Dakshinamurti (the first Guru). Hail to that Guru who is both without and with attributes.

guru maharāj guru maharāj
guru maharāj guru maharāj
gurudeva sad guru maharāj
satchitānanda guru jaya guru jaya guru

patita pāvana guru jaya guru jaya guru
param jyoti param brahma jaya guru jaya guru
āgama dhārana guru jaya guru jaya guru
ajñāna timira nāśi jaya guru jaya guru

Hail to the Guru who is the most pure and who is the Supreme Light and the Absolute Itself. Victory to Him who is the Support of the scriptures and who destroys the darkness of Ignorance.

ŚIVA ŚIVA HARA HARA

śiva śiva hara hara
śiva śiva hara hara
meghām bara dhara damaru sundara hara
śiva śiva hara hara
śiva śiva hara hara

O Auspicious One, Destroyer who is clothed in the clouds, the Beautiful One playing the damaru (small drum)...

kara triśūla dhara abhaya suvara hara
bhasma anga dhara jadā jūda dhara
bāla chandra dhara dīna nayana dhara
nāga hara dhara munda māla dhara

Who holds the trident in His hands bestowing fearlessness and boons, who wears ash on His limbs and has matted locks, who bears the crescent moon on His forehead, who has eyes full of compassion, wearing cobras as a garland and a necklace of skulls...

śiva śiva hara hara
śiva śiva hara hara
śankara śiva śankara śiva
śambho mahādeva śankara

O Auspicious One, the Great God...

ŚRI RĀMA RĀMA NĀMAM

śrī rāma rāmā nāmam janma rakshaka mantram
japippavark ānandam paramānandam
bhajikyuka maname nī ninakku salgathi netam
orikyalum mara kāthe bhajikyu kanī

O mind, always chant Rama Mantram which will take one to the Goal of life and which will give Supreme Bliss to one who ever chants It.

enna matta janma metrā mannithil vritha kalanyu
khinnatha kyoranthya minnum vanna tillaho
janma minnu dhanyamākum punya nāma mantra moti
nirmala tvamayi manase chinta cheyukil

Innumerable lives have been spent on this earth but sorrow has not come to an end. By chanting this holy mantra, one becomes pure and the purpose of life will be fulfilled.

śrī raghupati rāmam rāghava śrī rāmam
sritha janāśraya rāmam bhaja maname
danuja ripu rāmam vimala hridaya rāmam
duritha harana nāmam bhaja maname

O mind, worship that Rama who is Raghava and who is the Refuge of those who take refuge in Him. Worship that Rama who is the enemy of demons, who is pure in heart and whose Name removes all miseries.

ŚRI VINĀYAKA

śrī vināyaka guha jananī amba
śrīm harārchita pañcha daśākshari

O Mother of Ganesha and Subrahmanium,
Who art worshipped by the 15 syllable mantra...

hrīm kārini himagiri nandinī
hīrānchita vibusha nāngī
maheśvarī mahisha vināśinī
mām pālaya pālaya varade

O Thou art worshipped with the sound 'Hrim', who art the daughter of the Himalaya Mountain, whose limbs are decorated with diamonds, O Great Goddess, Destroyer of the demon Mahisha, O Giver of boons, please protect me, protect me!

modānvite dama sama dāyinī
nādānkure nalina nivāśini
nītān mamaśoka vināśini
pādāmbuje layamaruluka tāye

O Blissful One who bestows control of mind and senses, who art born of Sound, who dwells in the lotus, only Thou art the destroyer of my sorrows. O Mother. Please bless me to merge in Thy Lotus Feet.

SVĀGATAM KRISHNA

svāgatam krishna śaranāgatam krishna
mathurāpuri sadana mridu vadana madhusūdana

bhoga dāpta sulabha supushpa gandha kalaha
kastūri tilaka mahiba mama kanda
nanda gopa kanda

musthi kāsura chānūra malla
malla viśarada kuvalayā pīda
nartana kāliya mardana gokula rakshana
sakala sulakshana deva
sishta gana pāla samkalpa kalpa
kalpa śata kodi asama barābhava
dhīrā munījana vihāra krishna
dhīrā munījana vihāra madana sukumāra
daitya samhāra deva

madhura madhura rati sāhasa sāhasa
rachayu vatūjana manasa pūjita

sa dapa gari pa gari sada sa
dit tit taga janu tadhi taga janu tata gaja nuta
tari kitā kuku tana kita taka dīm (3 times)

svāgatam krishna śaranāgatam krishna...

VASUDEVA PUTRANE VĀ

vasudeva putrane vā nīla varnna ne vā
ī hridayattin kūrirul nikkuvān

nī kaniyename devā
nī kaniyename

O Son of Vasudeva, blue-colored One, please come. Please bless me by dispelling the darkness of this heart.

amma devikiye
kāttu kollaname
unni krishnane manninu nalkiya
punya mārnnavale devī
punya marnnavale

O Mother Devaki, please protect me, O holy Devi who has given birth to Baby Krishna for the sake of the world.

erakal kulakil
ennum āśrayame
etu kuttavum nī poruttu
nyangalil prīti kollaname
devā priti kollaname

O Holy One, Who art always the Support for Thy supplicants in this world, forgiving any errors, be pleased with us, Lord, be pleased with us...

GAJĀNANA

gajānana he gajānana
gajānana he gaja vadana

O Elephant-faced One...

varana mada hara gajānanā
pārvati nandana gajānanā

kārunyālaya gajānanā
kārana pūrusha gajānanā

O Son of Parvati, Abode of Compassion, Supreme Cause...

vigna vināyaka gajānanā
sajjana sevita gajānanā
chit ghana śyāmala nitya nirāmaya
satphala dāyaka gajānanā

Destroyer of obstacles, who is served by the virtuous, Pure Consciousness, of dark blue hue, Eternal One, bereft of sorrow, Giver of good results...

artta samrakshaka gajānanā
ātmā prakāśā gajānanā
ānandāmrita pūrita moda
surādhipa sevita gajānanā

O Protector of the afflicted, Illuminator of the Self, full of Bliss and worshipped even by Indra...

DARŚAN DENA RĀMA

darśan dena rāma rāma rāma
tadap rahe he hum daśarathe
taras rahe he hum daśarathe
jānakī nātha dayā karo

O Rama, show me Thy Divine form! We are yearning to see Thy form, O Dasaratha's Son! We are thirsty to see Thy form, O Dasaratha's Son! O Lord of Janaki, show us compassion!

sare jag he palan kare
mātā pitā anna dātā thum ho
hum he thumhare hum ko bachāvo
nayya hamāre pār karo
dūr karo sankat ko hamāre

Thou art the Maintainer of the Universe, Thou art our Mother, Father and Nourisher. Protect us, we are Thine! O boat of ours, take us across and remove our sorrows!

VANDE NANDAKUMĀRAM

vande nanda kumāram vande
nanda kumāram navanīta choram
vande vande rādhika lolam
gopī chitta vihāram vande

I salute the Son of Nanda, Stealer of butter, Delighter of Radha, who resides in the minds of the Gopis!

śrīdhara nīśam jagadā dhāram
bhava bhaya dūram bhakta mandāram
vande vande rādhika lolam
gopī chitta vihāram

I salute again and again the Lord who bears the Goddess Lakshmi on His chest, who is the Substratum of the world, Dispeller of the fear of transmigration, Flower of the devotees heart, Delighter of Radha who resides in the minds of the Gopis!

venu vinodam veda susāram
karunālolam kāñchana chelam
kamanīya gātram kamsa samhāram
yamunā tīra vihāram vande

I salute the One Who plays the flute, Essence of the Vedas, who delights in showing compassion, who wears golden color robes, of beautiful Form, Slayer of Kamsa who resides on the banks of the Yamuna River!

vrindāvana sañchāram vande
vande nanda kumāram
vande vande rādhikalolam

I salute that One who moves about Vrindavan, the Son of Nanda, Delighter of Radha!

muni jana pālam mohana rūpam
muralīlolam madana gopālam
yamunā tīra vihāram vande
vrindāvana sañchāram vande

Salutations to the Protector of the sages, of enchanting form, Lover of the flute, beautiful cowherd Boy who stays on the banks of the Yamuna and moves about Vrindavan!

JAGADIŚVARI DAYĀ KARO

jagadīśvarī dayā karo mā
śivaśankarī kripā karo mā
sarveśvarī rakshā karo mā
bhuvaneśvarī dayā karo mā
śivaśankarī kripā karo mā

O Goddess of the Universe, show Thy kindness...
O Auspicious One, bestow Thy Grace...
O Goddess of All, protect us...
O Goddess of the Earth, show Thy kindness...

DEVI JAGANMĀTA

devi jaganmātā jaya jaya devi jaganmātā
devi jaganmātā parāśakti devi jaganmātā

Hail, hail to the Goddess, Mother of the World,
The Goddess of Supreme Energy!

nīla katal karayil tapam cheyyum
nitiya kanya kaye
māri kumāri yamma enakkum
vantu varam taruvai vā

O Eternal Virgin who does penance on the shore of the blue sea at Kanyakumari, come and give me a boon.

jyoti svarūpiniye jñānamaya sundara rūpiniye
satya svarūpiniye svayam śakti ānanda rūpinye

O Thou whose True Nature is Light, whose beautiful Form is made of Wisdom, Truth, Energy and Bliss!

om śri mātā jaya lalitāmbā
om śri mātā jaya lalitāmbā

OM, Hail to the Mother of the Universe!

KAITORUNNEN KRISHNA

kaitorunnen krishna kārunya vāridhe
kaitava mellām akattitane
kandituvān kripa ekuke krishna
kancha dalāyata lochanane

O Krishna, Ocean of Compassion, I salute Thee with joined palms. Please remove all of my sorrows and bless me to be able to see Thee, O Thou with eyes like lotus petals.

kāyāmbūmanivarna komala śri krishna
kālunnen mānasam devā
vārija netra nī poruvān entitra
tāmasam erunnu devā

O Krishna of lovely dark hue like a blue lotus, O Lord, my mind is burning. O Thou with lotus-like eyes, why are Thou so late in coming?

moham valarunnu mohana rūpā nin
śobhana gānam nukarnnituvān
nen chakam tingunna sañchita bhāram ā
sundara rāgattil chertitatte

O Thou of enchanting form, my infatuation is growing to enjoy Thy bright songs. Let all my accumulated burdens, that are swelling within, merge in Thy beautiful tune.

ORUNĀLIL VARUMO

orunālil varumo hridaya śri kovilil
orikkalum anayātta dīpavumāyi

atināyittatiyan alayunnitamme
alaukikānandame amme
alaukikānandame

Won't Thou come one day to the shrine of my heart with an ever-burning lamp? This suppliant is wandering about only for that, O Mother of unearthly bliss.

uyarangalil nyān umayeteti
urukunna chittavumāyi
tarukītum nin karavalliyāl devi
tarumo nin kripa yiniyum

I have searched for the Goddess (Uma) in the heights. O Devi, bless me with the caress of Thy soft hands. O Mother, won't Thou give Thy Grace?

takarunnu nyān talārate
tanaleku mama janani
amarunnu nī yennil enkilum
ariyunna nāl varumo

O Mother, give shelter to me who am collapsing with exhaustion. Though it is true that Thou dwellest within me, when will the day of Realisation come?

PARIHĀSA PĀTRAMĀYI

parihāsa pātramāyi mattunnu enne nī
paribhava mille nikkamme
padatāren hridayattil patiyum boruntākum
paramānandam ketuttalle

Though Thou hast made me into a laughing stock, O Mother, I have no grievances. Only remove not the Supreme Bliss that is experienced when Thy soft Feet are placed in my heart.

mānābhimānagal sarvam tyajichente
mātāve nin darśanārtham
mangāte nin rūpa lāvanya menchittil
tingi variyunna tenno

For the sake of Thy Vision, O Mother, I have sacrificed my honour and self-esteem. When will Thy Beauty overflow without diminishing within my heart?

nyān enna bodham naśichorā sārūpya
bhāvam pakarunna tenno
yāminiyum pakalum marannānanda
sāgare mungura tenno

When will Thou bless me with the identification with Thee wherein the ego is destroyed? O when shall I merge in the Ocean of Bliss, forgetting day and night?

jñāna millāttorī gānam sravichunī
kārunya moterunnellū
chārave van nonnu puñchirichītukil
chetam ninakkilla tellum

Out of compassion come to me hearing this song devoid of pedantry. Thou hast nothing to lose if Thou comest to me with a smiling face.

SADĀ NIRANTARA

sadā nirantara hariguna gāvo
prema bhakti se bhajana sunāvo

rāma krishna ke charaname āvo
mana mandirame dīpa jalāvo
jīvana mayā bhāra lagāvo

Always praise the qualities of God.
Hear bhajans with loving devotion.
Come to the Lotus Feet of Rama and Krishna.
Light the lamp in the temple of the mind.
And thus unload your life's burden.

GOVARDHANAGIRI KUDAYĀKKI

govardhana giri kuda yākki
gopika rādhaye sakhi yākki
gopakumāra en hridayam
gokula mākki

O Cowherd Boy, Thou hast made the Govardhana Hill into an umbrella and hast made Radha Thy dear friend. O Krishna, Thou hast transformed my heart into Gokulam (Krishna's sporting place).

niraline nīla nilāvāyi māttum
karalil mohana nin gānamam
karalil punyam vitarunnu
priyadhara śrīdhara nāmam

O Enchanting Player of the flute, Thy divine music makes even shadows into silverblue moonlight. Thy endearing Name, O Giridhara, will fill the mind with auspiciousness.

araline yellām madhuvāyi māttum
karalil mādhava nin bhāvam
uyiril premam potiyum divyam
sukhakara sundara rūpam

O Madhava, Thy different moods will transform the sorrows of the heart into nectar. Thy beautiful and pleasing Form will fill one's life with love overflowing.

NĪ YENTE VELICHAM

nī yente velicham jīvante telicham
nī yen abhayam alle amme nī yen abhayam alle

Thou art my Light and the clarity of my life. Art Thou not my refuge, O Mother, art Thou not my refuge?

kāyi veti yarute jagadambike
kanivin kedārame amme kanivin kedārame

O Mother of the Universe, forsake me not, O Fountainhead of Compassion.

ninte sthutikal pādu neram
ivarkku tunayāyi nilkename
anugraham ekane sarasvati devi
nin kripa choriyename amme kanivin kedārame

O Mother, Fountainhead of Compassion, be with us when we sing Thy glories. O Goddess Sarasvati, bless us showering Thy grace upon us who worship Thee.

vidyāyil ellām anugraham ekunna
ammaye nyangal stuti chittunen
vīna dhārinī vimalambika nī
nin kripa choriyename amme kanivin kedārame

O Mother who blesses those in their studies, the One with the veena, the Pure One, O Mother, shower Thy grace upon us, O Fountainhead of Compassion.

YEN MAHĀDEVI LOKEŚI

yen mahādevi lokeśi bhairavi
yente yullam telikyātta tentu nī
chinta nī yamame yamen chandike
ninte līlakal oronnum atbhutam

O my Great Goddess, Ruler of the world, O Consort of Lord Śiva, why aren't Thou enlightening my mind? O Chandika, on reflection, each of Thy plays appears wonderful and infinite.

ambe ninte katāksham tarename
amba yellā torāśraya millallo
ambike jaganāyike bhūmi nī
kamba mellā morikenam chinmayi

O Mother, bless us with Thy glance of grace. Other than Thee, refuge we have none. O Mother, Empress of the Universe, Thou art the earth itself. Please rid me of all longings, O Pure Consciousness.

īśvarī nin savidhe vasikkuvān
śāśvatamāya mārgatilutenne
viśva mohini ennum nayikane
sachidānanda mūrte torunnu nan

O Goddess, Enchantress of the Universe, adorations to Thee. Always lead me along the path to Eternity that I may dwell near Thee forever. O Embodiment of Existence, Awareness, and Bliss, I adore Thee with joined palms.

ninte kārunya menkalundākane
tampurātti maheśī maheśvarī
ninte rūpa men chittatil ekiyen
antarātmā vilānanda mekane

O Great Goddess, let Thy grace be upon me. Impressing Thy Form in my mind, bring joy to my inner soul.

KARIMUKAL VARNNAN

karimukal varnnan vannallo
arakerum nīlakkār varnna nallo
mandasmitam tūkum sundara rūpānin
tiruvutal nyangal onnu kantotte

Kanna (Krishna), of the color of a dark rain cloud, has come! O Kanna of dark hue, so lovely art Thou. O smiling Beauty, let me see Thy holy Form.

śāntināyakā mukil varnnā
śāntata yennil nī yekitane
gopakumāraka gokula nātha
kālamāyille māla kattān

O cloud-colored Lord of Peace, give peace to my soul. O Shepherd Boy, Lord of Gokulam, is it not yet time to rid me of sorrow?

devakī sūtanāyi pirannone
gokula bāla śrī krishnā
dushta samhāra sishta samrakshakā
nin pādapadmam namo namaste

O Krishna, Son of Devaki and Child of Gokulam, O Destroyer of the wicked and Saviour of the good, I bow to Thy Lotus Feet.

BHRAMARAME

bhramarame mānasa bhramarame
śuddha madhu tedi alayunnu talarunnu nī

bhramarame mānasa bhramarame

O hummingbird of my mind, searching for pure nectar, you are wandering and becoming exhausted.

tarujālam pūtta tarujālam
bhakti pura tīrattara lillā tānandippū
talaralle chitte karayalle śuddha
hridayattil orunālil anayum nin ambika

The grove of blossomed trees, bereft of all sorrow, resides blissfully on the banks of the river of devotion. O mind, don't be desperate, for your Mother will come to the pure heart one day.

vibudhanmār buddhi kyuraveki śakti
akalattil aralillā tarivāl nīkki
amarunnū ninnil amarunnu
sarva vyatayellām avitekkāyi arppikyunnu

O Sakti, Thou art the spring of intelligence for the wise, removing all sorrows through knowledge. I offer all of my sorrows to Thee in whom everything exists.

eniyenno ninte varavenno ente
karivellām takarumbol varumenno
arūtamme kripa choriyulle
ellā avalambam avidalla tiva narunde

When is that day, O Mother, when Thou wilt come? Art Thou going to come when all of my energy is dissipated? O Mother, do not do that! Won't Thou shower Thy grace on me? Who else is there except Thee as my sole support?

DEVI MAHEŚVARIYE

devi maheśvariye māyā svarūpini ye
ī viśva kārani ye tāye namo namaste

O Divine Mother, Great Goddess, whose nature is Illusion, O Creatress and Cause of the Universe, I bow to Thee again and again.

lokeśi nīlakeśi mahāmāye manoharāngi
bandha mokshangal nalkum bhakta
bandhuvum nī maheśi

O dark-haired Empress of the Universe, O Great Maya of beautiful limbs, O Supreme Goddess, Thou art the Friend of the devotees, granting them both bondage and Liberation.

svarg āpavargangale kodukunna
durge bhagavatiye gaurī ganeshapriye
mat garvam akattīdanam

O Goddess Durga, Bhagavati, who gives heaven and Liberation, O Gauri, dear to Ganesha, kindly rid me of the ego.

moksha sandāyiniye vidya svarūpiniye
sākshāl jaganmāyiye devi sanātaniye

Giver of Liberation, whose very nature is Knowledge, Thou art the Universe itself, O Eternal Goddess.

ambike durge śive mahākālī namo namaste
sumbhādi daitya vadham cheyta yambe namo namaste

O Ambika, Durga, Parvati, O Great Kali, I bow to Thee again and again. O Mother who killed the demon Sumbha, I bow to Thee again and again!

āril udichū sarvam āral nayi chidunnū
āril layikyum ellām ā devī dayāmayiye

In whom everything has arisen, by whom everything is led, in whom everything will merge...Thou art that merciful Goddess.

OM BHADRAKĀLĪ

om bhadrakālī śrī bhadrakālī
sarana mennum ekum deviye mohinī
ambike pāhimām
śrī devī chāmundi
modameki nin janatte kāttukollane

O Bhadrakali, O Goddess who ever gives refuge, Enchantress and Mother, bless me. O Goddess who killed the demon Chamunda, please lovingly protect Thy people giving them delight.

tanka chilampaninnya nin padāmbhujam
anpotati yangal kumpitunnitā
nin katākshameki nī yanugrahikyane
chandike manohari visāla narttaki

We bow to Thy Lotus Feet which are adorned with gold jingles. O Chandika, O Beautiful One, O Great Dancer, bless us with Thy glance of grace.

pātunnū nin gītam
tetunnū nin pādam

dārikante talayarutta vīrabhairavī
tānu vīnu kumpitunnu kārunyāmbudhe

O valiant Bhairavi who has severed the head of the demon Darika, we sing Thy praises seeking Thy Feet. O Ocean of Grace, we bow down to Thee.

PARINĀMAM IYALĀTTA

parināmam iyalātta parameśvarī en
paritāpa makalān nī kanniyename
purameyita parameśan patiyallayo en
purame ninnirul nīkkān arulename

O unchanging, Supreme Goddess, bless me ridding me of misery. Is not Śiva, who burned down the three cities (Tripura) Thy Husband (Lord)? Deign to remove the darkness.

irulinnu pakalenna vidhi yillayo
irulitta hridayam nī ariyillayo
italellām atarunna malarpole nāl
irunnengo marayunnu varikille nī

Won't the night be visited by the full moon? Know Thou not about the darkness of my heart? The days are going by like the dropping of the petals of a flower, yet Thou come not.

cheruvalli kabhayam van mara mallayo amme
cherukunnyin tabhilāsam nīyallayo
cheyyenta tariyilla yivan ambike
chernnitan agatīkku tunayekane

O Mother, is not a huge tree the support of a small creeper? Aren't Thou what a small child really longs for? O Mother, this one knows not what is to be done, so help this forlorn one to merge in Thee.

talarninni marubhūvil maruvunnu nyān amme
taramillang arikattil iranītuvān
tirinnyende gatikan angarikattu nī
tiru pāda gatiyeku sarveśvarī

O Mother, I am pulling on exhausted in this desert unable even to crawl to Thee. O Goddess of All, see my fate and turning towards me, grant me refuge at Thy Feet.

AMMAYALLE ENTAMMAYALLE

ammayalle entamma yalle
kannīr tutakkyum ponnammayalle

Aren't Thou my Mother, O aren't Thou my dear Mother who wipes away the tears?

īreru lakinum ammayalle nī
ī viśva kāranī yammayalle
etranālāyi vilikkyunnu ninne nyān
śakti svarūpinī nī varille

Aren't Thou the Mother of the 14 worlds, the Creatress of the world? Since how many days I am calling Thee, O Thou whose nature is śakti (energy). Won't Thou come?

srishti sthitilaya samhāra mokkeyyum
ishtadāna priye ninnillale
etranālāyi vilikkyunnu ninne nyān
śakti svarūpinī nī varille

O Thou who loves to give the desired things, are not Creation, Preservation and Destruction in Thee? Since how many days...

pañcha bhūtangalum bhūta samastavum
tātanum tāyum nītanne yalle
etranālāyi vilikkyunnu ninne nyān
śakti svarūpinī nī varille

Aren't Thou not the Father, Mother, the Five Elements and the entire world? Since how many days...

vedavum shāstravum vedānta vedyavum
ādi madhyāntavum ninnilalle
etranālāyi vilikkyunnu ninne nyān
śakti svarūpinī nī varille

Aren't the Vedas, Scriptures, Knowledge of Vedanta, the beginning, middle and end all in Thee? Since how many days...

PAURNAMI RĀVIL

paurnami rāvil vāniludikkum
vārtinkal prabha nīyalle
surabhila malar mani manjali lanayum
vasanta rāvum nīyalle

Aren't Thou the splendour of the moonlight that shines forth in the sky on a full moon night? Aren't Thou the spring night that arrives in a lovely, fragrant, flowery palanquin?

tampuruvin mridu tantriyil unarum
sundara nādam nīyalle
kaviyute kalpana ūnnyālātum

taralita gānam nīyalle amme
taralita gānam nīyalle

O Mother, aren't Thou the beautiful sound that awakens in the gentle strings of the tambura? Aren't Thou the lyrical poems in which the imagination of the poet is sporting (swinging)?

erunirangalil eru svarangalil
onnāyi chernnatu nīyalle
pūvin manavum mara villarakum
kāttin kulirum nīyalle amme
kāttin kulirum nīyalle

Aren't Thou that One in which the seven colors and the seven notes have merged? Aren't Thou the fragrance of the flower, the beauty of the rainbow and the coolness of the breeze?

ENTAMME NIN MAKKALE

entamme nin makkale nokkuvān madikyunnu
entānī sādhu cheta tettennu cholka tāye

O Mother, why dost Thou hesitate to look at Thy children? O Mother, please tell the mistake that this poor one has committed.

bodha kuravināle bādhicha tettukale
bodham ulla amma yente māttuvān madikyunnu

O all-knowing Mother, why dost Thou hesitate to remove the errors committed by me due to lack of knowledge?

ādhiyāl angu mingum oti alannyitunna
sādhu vargatti nārā nādhāram cholka tāye

O Mother, please tell me, who is the support for these poor ones who wander here and there due to endless miseries?

muppārum pottuvānāyi kelppullor amme ninte
tripāda seva cheyān kāttirikyunnu nyangal

O Mother who sustains the three worlds, we are waiting to serve Thy Holy Feet.

svarloka tulya māmī hridayattinkal vannu
kalyāna mūrttiyāyi tullasi chītukamme

O Mother, come and shine in this heart which is equal to heaven, O Thou who art the Embodiment of all auspiciousness.

kārunya kātalākum amme ponnambike nī
chāratu vannu ninnu makkale onnu nokkū

O Mother, my beloved Mother, the very Essence of Compassion, kindly come close and cast a merciful glance at Thy children.

pāhimām loka māte pāhimām viśvanāthe
pāhimām pāhimām dehime tval prasādam

O Mother of the world, protect me! O Goddess of the Universe, protect me! Protect me! Protect me! Shower Thy blessings on me!

ANUPAMA GŪNA NILAYE

anupama gūnanilaye devi
aśarana navalambam nīye

O Mother, O Goddess, the Abode of unique qualities, Thou art the Support of those who seek refuge.

āgama vīnute rāgavilole
ekuka tava karunaleśam

O Thou who art modest due to Thy wisdom and gentle due to love, give me a bit of Thy compassion.

ariyān ārivūkal illivanennatu
parayāta vitunnariyumallo

Even without my saying it, know Thou not that I have no knowledge to know anything?

aralāmariyil virumiyeraye
atiyina kātti yanugrahikkyū

Show Thy Feet and bless me who is falling into the ocean of misery.

ELLĀM ARIYUNNA

ellām ariyunna kannanode
onnum parayenda kāryam illa

There is no need to tell anything to the all-knowing Krishna.

kūde nadan ellām kānunnundu
kāryangal ellām grahikkyunnundu

Walking beside us, He is seeing and understanding everything.

antarangattile chinta yellām
ādi nārāyanan kānunnundu

The Primordial Being sees all the thoughts of the innermost self.

tanne maranonnum chetīduvān
ārkkum orikkalum sādhyamalla

It is never possible for anyone to do anything, forgetting Him.

ādi nārāyanan kannan ennum
ārilum kūde vasikkunnundu

The Primal Lord abides in all.

satya svarūpatte nammal ellām
ānanda mode bhaji chidenam

All of us should worship that Embodiment of Truth and Awareness with joy.

KATUTTA ŚOKAMĀM

katutta śokamām tatattil ārttitāte enne nī
patutva milla bhāgya tārakanga lilla yenkilum
kanatta chinta ninnilekkura chitunna tokkeyum
atuttu ninnarinnyu puñchirichu poytolla nī

O Mother, let me not fall into this deep, dark pit of sorrow. I am neither a scholar nor was I born under a lucky star. Even knowing all this, O Mother, when my intense thoughts get fixed on Thee, walk not away simply casting a smile at me.

japichu nin varenya māya vākkukal viśuddhanāyi
tyajichu sarva soukhyavum sadā smarichitunnu nyān
janicha tettu tīruvān yetutta janma māni tennu
rachatokke yorttu māsvasichitunnu śārade

Renouncing all other forms of happiness and constantly remembering Thee endowed with purity, I chanted Thy transcendent Names. O Eternal Auspiciousness, remembering Thy words that this birth is to exhaust all the errors committed in my past births, I console myself.

soubhāgattil modamattu ninne yuttu nokkumen
tamasakatti buddhi suddhi yekane dayāmayī
samatva chinta antarange sīmayil telikane
samasta loka nāyike mahatva sīla dāyike

O Embodiment of Compassion, remove my ignorance and bestow pure intelligence on me who, though in the midst of all these worldly pleasures, is always gazing at Thee without being happy. O Ruler of all the worlds, Giver of greatness, light the lamp of equanimous vision in my innermost self.

svanam marannyorā sushupti vittitum prabhāvame
janam tirannyitunnu ninne viśvamāke ambike manam
telinnyu nokkiyālakattu kanditunna nī
yanugrahikka yenneyum sadāpi nishta nākuvān

O Ambike, who transcends even the state of dreamless deep sleep, people are searching the universe for Thee. O Mother who can be seen within if looked for with a clear mind, bless me to get established in that Supreme Reality.

bhavāni nī ninachu vente bhāvi kārya mokkeyum
bhaya samātti tānetutta vaibhavangal atbhutam
udāramāyi nayichu mārga durghattangal māttane
dayāpare chorinnya moda muttukalkku vandanam

My future is predetermined by Thee, O Bhavani, and amazing are the ways adopted by Thee to get rid of my fears and hopes. O Mother, please guide me in all ways and remove all obstacles which may arise in my path. O Embodiment of Mercy, I bow down to Thee for all the blissful moments that Thou has showered on me.

padāmbuje paranna nannya bhringa mākum en manam
parannitā tirikuvān dalangal kūtiyāl mati
parāpare sudhārasam nukarnnu markitatte nyān
purā morinnya vedasāra pūrame torunnitā

O Mother, the hummingbird of my mind has come flying to Thy lotus-like Feet. Now please fold the petals so as to prevent it from flying away. O Thou who art greater than the greatest, enjoying that nectar of bliss, let me dive deep into it. O Quintessence of all the four Vedas, I bow down to Thee.

kopamākki yennile korukkitunnu snehavum
kathoramā yoratta hāsam ennil susmi tangalāyi
kinākkal mithyenna torttu nyān karannyu pokave
kripāmritam chorinnya ninne verpetilla niśchayam

Thy stream of Love flows towards me in the form of anger and Thy terrific laughter is like a pleasing smile to me. Understanding the unreal nature of the dream-like world, I took leave of it. But I will never get separated from Thee who has showered ambrosial grace upon me.

HARIYUDE KĀLIL

hariyude kālil vīrātārkkum
pari tāpāgni samikkilla
nityam guruve vanangā tārkkum
nirvāna sukham kittilla

Without falling at the Feet of God (Hari), none can extinguish the fire of the sorrow of transmigration. Without bowing forever to the Guru, none will gain the bliss of Liberation.

nāma japattil murukā tārkkum
īśanilettān āvilla
bhakti rasattil layikā tārkkum
muktāvastha labhikilla

None can reach the Lord without getting absorbed in the chanting of the Name. Without merging in the sweetness of devotion, none can attain the state of Liberation.

dhyāna japādikal cheytī tātton
ānandāmrita munnillā
dharmmam dayayum kūtāte sat
karmmam cheyyān kariyilla

He who does not meditate, do japa and other spiritual practices will not partake of the nectar of Bliss. Without righteousness and compassion, good action cannot be performed.

sangam muruvan upekshikkāte
samsārāgni ketukillā
ullil asūya orinnyī tāte
bhagavān neril varukilla

Without renouncing all attachments, the fire of transmigration cannot be put out. Unless the jealousy within is removed, God will not come before us.

nerittīśane darśikkāte
nerentāne nariyillā
ellām īśvara nen nariyāte
alla lotukkān variyillā

Without the direct Vision of God, one will never know what is Truth. Without knowing that all is God, there is no way to end one's misery.

bhaktanu tunayam toranu tāngum
bhagavān allā tingilla
īśvaran nammo tottullapol
āśraya matta varāno nām

In this world, only God is the Friend of the devotee and the Support of the helpless. When He is with us, how can we be without support?

HRIDAYA NIVĀSINI

hridaya nivāsini amme snehamayi amme

O Mother, Dweller in the heart, Embodiment of affection...

onnu muriyā tānāryillame
nin tirunāmangal lallāte

I could utter nothing but Thy sacred Names.

nin charitam pakarnnu nalkuvān
anugraha mekane lokamāte
laukika bhogavum sukhavum vendā
vendatu nirmala bhaktimātram

O Mother of the World, be gracious enough to enable me to tell Thy story. I want neither worldly enjoyment nor pleasure. I want only pure devotion.

janmangal etra karinnyu poyi
trippādam cherāte pārāyi
amme nin apāra kārunyattāl
ī janmam nin tirumumpil etti

nirmala sneha sāgarame
avitutte kenne nyānarppippu
venda onnume vendenikku
ninne yariyātta jīvitam

How many births have been wasted without reaching Thy Holy Feet? Now Mother, due to Thy fathomless compassion, I have reached Thy Holy Presence. O Ocean of Pure Love, to Thee I offer myself. I want nothing nor a life that knows not Thee.

bhārangal enti nyān janma janmangalāyi
ammaye ariyāte natannu
ī janmam ninne kandu nyān ā
bhārangalellām ninakku tannu
sthiramāya tonnume kānunnillamme
ninte chaitanya mallāte
ā chaitanya dhārayil alinnyu
ennile nyān marannitatte

Not knowing Mother, I carried the burden birth after birth. Now in this birth, having seen Thee, I have surrendered all burdens to Thee. O Mother, nothing that is seen is permanent except Thyself. Dissolving in the current of that vibrant Energy, let me forget myself.

randalla nyānum ammayum ennamma
enno totiyirun nennālum
onnāyi kānuvān kelpillenik kennum
paitalā vānānu moham
paitaline ennennum amma
ichayode valarttītum allo
attrikkara sparśattāl ente
pāpangal okke pokum allo

Even though Mother told me that She and I are not two but One, yet I have not the capacity to see so. I want only to be Thy child, O Mother. Mother would always look after a child with care and by the touch of Her hand all my sins would vanish.

entini tāmasam cholka tāye
ī paital avitutte svanta mallo
svantamā nennu ninachu ninachu ñān
nimishangal enni karichitunnu
entini cheyanam ninnil layikkuvān
mārgam iniyum kāttukille
nyān onnume yalla amme ellām
nī tanne nītanne sarvasvavum

Tell me, Mother, is not this child Thy own? Then why this delay? Thinking that I am Thy own, I am counting each moment and wondering what is to be done to come closer to Thee. Won't Thou show me the way? I am nothing and Thou art all that is, Thou alone art all.

KANNUNĪR ILLĀTTA

kannunīr illātta kannu kalenkilum
vingu kayān nente mānasam
onnum uruvitātulla nāvenkilum
tingu kayānu nin mantram amme

Though my eyes are without tears, my mind is throbbing with pain. Though my tongue is not uttering anything, it is full of Thy mantra.

kalpalata vriksha pushpa dalangalil
chutti patarnnu poyi mānasam
attu vittituvān uttu nokkītunnu
nistora māya vilāsam amme

O mystical tree which fulfills desires, our mind is always dwelling on thy flowers. I am looking towards Thee to get detachment from this tree, O Mother.

ennātma manjalil chandanam chartuvān
vanna sumangala yallo amme
nin sneha chandrikā sītala chāyāyil
enne nī dhanya nākku amme enne

The body is a covering of our Real Self. Thou who gives the cooling effect of moonlight, fulfill me with Thy Love!

SUNDARĪ NĪ VĀYO

sundarī nī vāyo
purandarī nī vāyo
śankarī nī vāyo
nirantarī nī vāyo

Please come, O Beautiful One.
Consort of Śiva, please come.
O Auspicious One, please come.
Please come, O Endless One.

kantan tantakkyu vāmākshi nī engum
kānchi pūratte chintum kāmākshi nī
bandhuvāyi kānmorkku svantam nīye
en chintakkyu muravāyi ninnītammā

O Vamakshi, Consort of Lord Śiva, O Kamakshi who radiates brilliance everywhere, to those who look upon Thee as their dear Relation, Thou art their very own. O Mother, please remain as the spring of my inspiration.

onnāyi palatāyi arūpavu māyi
ninnālum jyotirmayi brahmam nīye
nannāyen ullam nī yariyillayo
chonnālum munnil nī varukillayo

Being both of one and of many forms, Thou art the Light of the Absolute. Knowest Thou not my heart well? Won't Thou come before me even though I ask?

SAKALA KALĀ DEVATE

sakala kalādevate sarasvati devī
varamarulukayi innivide ninte dāsaril
panditaralla nyangal pāmararānallo
pandarī ninte kayyile pāvakal mātram

O Sarasvati, the deity presiding over the Arts, grant a boon to Thy servant today. We are not learned but only ignorant ones. O Goddess of Wisdom, we are only puppets in Thy Hands.

lakshākshharangalil onnichirippaval
lakshanamotta visāla manaska nī
lakshyattil ettān sramikkuvor kokkeyum
pakshāntara millātellām kotuppaval

O Thou who sits amongst hundreds of thousands of letters, Ideal of Expansiveness for those trying to reach their goal, Thou art the One who gives everything impartially.

ādyāksharangale nyangal karinnyitū
ādyamāyi nin kripayekane nyangalil
ādiyumantavum ninnil darśippū nyān
ārilum nin kripayekū bhagavatī

We know only the first letter of the alphabet. Therefore, show us Thy Compassion first and immerse us in Thee from beginning to end. O Goddess, show Thy Compassion to all.

PRAPAÑCHAM ENGUM

prapañcham engum nirannyu nilkkum
māyā pratibhāsame māyā pratibhāsame
prabhāmayī en manassil nī yoru
prabhātamāyi varumo ennum
prabhatūki ninnītumo

O Illusory Appearance filling the entire Universe, O Radiance, won't Thou dawn in my mind and stay there shedding Thy Light forever?

nin sneha vātsalya māvolam nukarum nyān
nin chārattanayumbol
nin divya tejassil mungumbol en mana
kleśam ellām akalum en mana
kleśam ellām akalum

I will surfeit myself drinking Thy love and motherly affection. Coming near Thee and sinking in Thy Divine Effulgence, all my mental distress will flee.

ādhāra bindhuvām ninne tirannyu nyān
etra nālāyi alayunnū
ātmāvin ānanda mekuvān entamme
en munnil ettukille amme
en munnil ettukille

Since how many days I am wandering in search of Thee who art the underlying Core of everything. O my Mother, won't Thou come before me and grant me the bliss of the Self, O won't Thou come?

PĀLKKATAL NATUVIL

pālkkatal natuvil vāsam dinavum
pāl moshana parihāsam
kannanu kārmukil niramāyi poyatu
kākolla stana mundatinālo
kāliya damśana mettatumalla
kāliye mechu karutta tutanne

O Thou who dwells in the middle of the Ocean of Milk, yet ridiculed daily for stealing milk! How has Kanna's complexion become so dark? He didn't get bit by the snake Kaliya. Then He must have become dark by grazing the cattle.

mannu bhujichatu koti kūtītā
anda katāham kāttānallā
manninu tendi natannoru vāmana
nundo baliyute dharmmam kannā

He ate mud only due to voraciousness and not in order to show the Universe in the microcosm of His mouth (to His mother Yashoda). How could Mahabali's charity be accepted by Vamana who had gone begging for some earth (land)?

pandoru poril tototiyatil
kuntitam ivanundatu pokatte
pāndava patnikkyekiya vasanam
kandāl gopikal pariparayūlle

O Krishna, I will forget about Thy running back in defeat on the battlefield. Won't the Gopis find fault with Thee (who stole their clothes) when they see the cloth Thou gave to Draupadi?

sandīpaniyute yavil nalkānnyatil
entī priya sakhanotu pinakkam
tīyunmān pasiyettam kannanu
chīrayilatari mrishtānnam

Thou quarreled with Kuchela when he forgot to offer Thee beaten rice given by his guru. O Krishna, Thou art hungry enough to eat fire yet were satisfied to eat a leaf of spinach with relish (from Draupadi).

NĪLAMEGHANGALE

nīla meghangale niṇgal kitengane
netān karinnyinnī nīlavarnnam
vrindāvana tile nanda kumārante
chantamerum nīlaśyāma varnnam

O dark colored clouds, how could you get for yourselves this bluish hue, the same dark complexion as Vrindavan's Son of Nanda (Sri Krishna)?

ningal poyi kanduvo kannanā munniye
tangalil mindiyo punchiricho
nīlāravindatten netrattāl ningale
āpāda chūdham katākshichuvo

Did you go and meet the Baby Krishna? Did He talk to you and smile at you? Did He, with His honeyed, blue lotus-like eyes, cast a glance at you?

kanna ninnen munnilettu mennotiyo
enneyum svāgatam cheyyu mennotiyo
en manaśāntikyāyi ningal tan kaikalil
nalmoritten tellu tannayacho

Did Krishna tell you that He would come to me today? Did He say that He would welcome me? Did He put in your hands a bit of honey-sweet words to pass on to me for my peace of mind?

NIRMALA SNEHAME

nirmala snehame ninne yariyātta
jīvitam entinamma
nitya nirāmayī ninne yariyātta
jīvitam entinamma

O Love Immaculate, O Mother, what is the use of this life without knowing Thee? O Eternal Immutable One, what for such a life?

nistula snehame ninne yariyātta
jīvitam entinamma
mohana rūpame ninne ninakkātta
jīvitam entinamma

O Unequalled Love, what for is this life which knows Thee not? What for is this life which doesn't contemplate on Thee, O Thou of enchanting Form?

moksha sandāyinī ninne labhikkātta
jīvitam dhanyamāno
bhakta jana manohārinī ninnute
darśanam ekukille

O Bestower of Liberation, is life fulfilled without gaining Thee? O Stealer of the mind of the devotees, won't Thou grant me Thy Vision?

OMKĀRA BRAHMATIN

omkāra brahmattin nādam tulumbunno
reto prabhā manjari nī
eto prabhā manjari
chārattu vannitān mohicho renne nī
dūrattil ākitolle amme
dūrattil ākitolle

O unknown bouquet of Effulgence that brings forth the sound OM, the Absolute, keep me not at a distance, O Mother, me who yearns to come close to Thee.

ātmānu rāgattin ādhāra māyulla
premo jvalākārame
premo jvalākārame
nīkkukil īyivan erayāyi tīrnnupom
orkkumo jīvanāthe

O Support of the longing soul, whose Form is the flame of Love, if Thou push me away, I will remain as a helpless soul. Will Thou remember that, Lord of my life?

ātmārpana tināyi āgraha merinin
sūnu nyān kenitunnū
sūnu nyān kenitunnū
nirdoshi yāmenne mrityuvin kaikalil
arpicho rinnyitolle amme
arpicho rinnyitolle

This son of Thine is crying to be able to surrender himself to Thee. Don't offer this innocent one into the hands of Death, O Mother.

PAKALANTIYIL

pakalantiyil etti neram
entamma yingettiyilla
taniye yirinnītuvān
bhayamundi vanen jananī

Time has reached the end of the day but my Mother has not yet arrived. To sit alone, this one is afraid, O my Mother.

karal nontivanetra neram
vila pichalannyu poyi
irul vīsiyippāri tattil
tunayāri vanen janani

How long must this aching heart weep helplessly? Who is there to give company to this one, O my Mother, in this world enveloped in darkness?

kaliyennu ninappato nin
ninavonnu marinnya tillī
gati vanna tinentubandham
tiru nāmam urachitānnyo

Dost Thou take it as a play? If so, I do not understand Thy viewpoint. Why such a fate? Is it because I have not uttered Thy Holy Name?

aralārnni vanepporum nin
padatāru tirannyitunnū
tarikennute hritta tattil
mridu bhakti sudhā rasatte

This one always searches for Thy Lotus Feet with an aching heart. Give me the taste of that sweet nectar of devotion in my heart.

PREMA PRABHO LĀSINĪ

prema prabho lāsinī devī
mātāmritānandinī
prollasal puñchiri tūmalar tenmara
korichoriyum prabhānandinī

O Goddess, the enjoyer of Immortal Bliss, who revels in the brilliance of Love, from whose flower-like smile pours forth the Light of Bliss...

pāpabhayam puralāttoru jīvita
pāta tirannyu varunnavare
prematto tamritānanda pura
olattāl tarukunnaval nī

Thou art the One who carresses with the waves of the River of Immortal Bliss those who search for the Path of a life untouched by the fear of sin.

subhalābha pradamākum
paramātma prabhatingi
potiyum nin bhavanāsa pada tāratil
pranamikkyum hridayattil avināsa prabhatūkū
sakalātma śudhayil nyān vilayichitān

Thy Lotus Feet, thickly enveloped in the Light of the Supreme Self, grant auspiciousness through the destruction of the bondage of Becoming. May Thou cast that Indestructible Light at me whose heart bows down to Thee, so that I may merge in the Universal Soul.

POVUKAYĀYO KANNĀ

povu kayāyo kannā nīyum
povu kayāyo kannā
jagattitil sarvarum kaivetinnyu
povu kayāyo kannā

Kanna, are Thou also going? Everyone in this world has abandoned me. Are Thou also forsaking me?

nīlamani pole mānasa cheppil
ninne sūkshikkyān kotichu...ennum
archana cheyyān kotichu...kannā

I wanted to keep Thee in the chambers of my heart as a blue jewel and wanted to do worship everyday, O Kanna.

nin rūpa nīla katalinte ārattil
muttu perukkā nāsichu...prema
muttu perukkā nāsichu...kannā

Kanna, I wanted to collect the pearls of love from the depth of the blue ocean of Thy Form.

ānanda pakshiyāyi nī virājikkave
ninnil aliyān kotichu...kannā
en jīva dukha vihagam..kannā

When Thou possessed the form of a blissful bird, the mournful bird of my life wanted to merge in Thee, O Kanna.

VARALUNNA HRIDAYATTIL

varalunna hridayattil kulir mara peyyuvān
varanda jīvitam valamāki māttuvān
vannītu kamme ponnambike
vandikkyunnu nyān varumo varumo
ennarikil nī varumo

O Mother, pour forth cool rain on my parched heart that my dry life may blossom. Come, my dear Mother, come. I bow down to Thee. Will Thou come, will Thou come near me?

innu varum amma innu varum enna
āsayode mantrichen hridayam
illa omale illa nyān ninnil ninnum
oru nālum akannu pokayilla

"Mother will come today, yes, Mother will come today!" Thus my heart hopefully chants like a mantra. "No, my darling, no. I will never go away from you."

EN MANASSIN ORU MAUNAM

en manassin oru maunam mani
varnnan varāttatin maunam
kannane kānā turannura nennute
kannina kannīr kutirnnū

Sullen is my mind because Sri Krishna comes not. Not seeing Him, the longing in my heart brings forth a torrent of tears.

kālimekān poyi varānnyato kannan
kāla tunarā tirunnato

kārolivarna nekkānān kotichu nyān
kerunna kāryam marannuvo

Is it because He has not returned from grazing the cattle or is it that He has not yet woken up? Has that dark-colored One forgotten that my heart is weeping in longing for Him?

pāl vennayūnu mutangiyo pinchu
kāl tenniyengānum vīnuvo
nin karalppūkalil ten nukarān bhakta
bhringangal mūtippo tinnyuvo

Perhaps He has not yet had His butter and milk to eat or have His tender feet slipped and He has fallen somewhere? Or have the bee-like devotees crowded around Him to drink the honey of His Feet?

ente varāninna māntam kannan
enne marannu poyenno
kannā varika nī kāroli varnnāyen
kannīr mirikalkku munnil

O, why has Kannan not come today? Hast Thou forgotten me, O Thou of the hue of dark clouds? O please come before these tearful eyes.

DEVI DEVI DEVI JAGANMOHINĪ

devi devi devi jagan mohinī
chandikā devi chanda munda harinī
chāmundeśvari ambike devi
samsāra sāgaram taranam cheyyuvān
nerāya mārgam kāttane devi

O Goddess, Enchantress of the World, Chandika, Destroyer of the demons Chanda and Munda, O Chamundeśvari, Divine Mother, show us the right path to cross the ocean of transmigration.

YĀDAVANE

yādavane mana mohanane
ātma nāyakane venugāyakane
gopi vallabhane śyāma sundarane
gopa bālakane gīta nāyakane

krishna hare jaya krishna hare
murali manohara krishna hare
krishna hare jaya krishna hare
rādhā mādhava krishna hare

yādava=One who is born in Yadu's clan.
manamohana=One who attracts the mind.
ātma nāyakan=Protector
venugāyakan=Player of the flute.
gopivallabhan=Beloved of the Gopis
śyāmasundara=Dark complexioned beautiful One.
gopabālan=Cowherd boy.
gītanayakan=Propounder of the Bhagavad Gita.
murali=Who plays the flute.
hare=Lord Vishnu
rādhā=Sri Krishna's Beloved.
mādhava=Goddess Lakshmi's Consort.

YAŚODA KE BĀLĀ

yaśodā ke bālā yadukula nātha
dvārakavāsi śrī krishna

nanda nandana navanīta priyā
rādhāvilola śrī krishna
dīnā nāthā bālagopālā
nirupama sundarā śrī krishna

hare rāme hare rāma rāma rāma hare hare
hare krishna hare krishna
krishna krishna hare hare

yaśoda ke bālā=The Child of Yasoda.
yadukula nātha=The Lord of the Yadava clan.
dvārakavāsi=Who dwells in Dvaraka.
nandanandana=The Son of Nanda.
navanītapriya=One who is fond of butter.
rādhāvilola=The playmate of Radha.
dīnanātha=Lord of the downtrodden.
nirupama sundara=One whose beauty is incomparable.

VINĀYAKA VINĀYAKA

vināyaka vināyaka
viśvādhāra vināyaka
siddhi vināyaka bhava bhaya nāśa
suramuni vandita śrī ganesha

vināyaka=Destroyer of obstacles.
viśvādhāra=The Substratum of the Universe.
siddhi vināyaka=Who accomplishes.
bhavabhayanāśa=Destroyer of the fear of Becoming.
suramuni vandita=Who is bowed down to by gods and sages.

ŚIVĀYA PARAMEŚVARĀYA

śivāya parameśvarāya
sasisekharāya namo om
bhavāya gunasambhavāya
śiva tāndavāya nama om

śivāya parameśvarāya
chandraśekharāya nama om
bhavāya gunasambhavāya
śiva tāndavāya nama om

Prostrations to Śiva, the Supreme Lord, the one having the moon on His head. Prostrations to that Lord who dances the Cosmic Dance and has all good qualities.

JAI RĀDHA MĀDHAVA

jai rādhā mādhava jai kuñja vihārī
jai gopī jana vallabha jai girivara dhārī
yaśoda nandana vraja jana ranjana
yamunā tīra vanachārī

hare rāma hare rāma
rāma rāma hare hare
hare krishna hare krishna
krishna krishna hare hare

kuñjavihāri=One who sports in the grove of trees.
gopījana vallabha=Beloved of the Gopis.
girivaradhāri=Who held the mountain Govardhana on His hand.

yaśoda nandana=The Son of Yasoda.
vrajajana ranjana=The cause of happiness for the inhabitants of Vraja.
yamunā tīra vanachārī=One who walks in the forest along the banks of the river Yamuna.

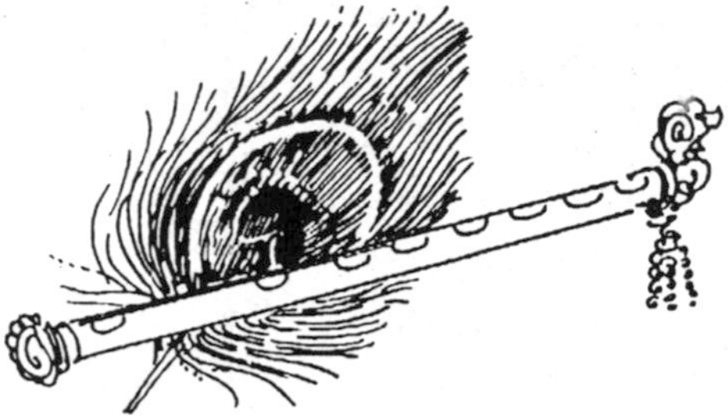

ŚLOKAS & MANTRAS

kāyena vāchā manas endriyair vā
buddhyātma nā vā prakritehe svabhāvāt
karomi yadyad sakalam parasmai
nārayanāyeti samarpayāmi

I dedicate to that Supreme Lord Narayana whatever
I perform with my body, speech, mind, limbs, intellect
Or my inner self either intentionally or unintentionally.

gurur brahmā gurur vishnuhu
gurur devo maheśvaraha
guruhu sākshāt parambrahma
tasmai śrī gurave namaha

The Guru is the Lord Brahma, Vishnu and Śiva.
Guru is the Supreme Absolute Itself.
My obeisance to the blessed Guru!

om saha nāvavatu saha nau bhunaktu
saha vīryam kara vāvahai
tejasvi nāva dhītamastu
mā vidvishā vahai
om śānti śānti śāntihi

OM Lord, protect us as one,
Nourish us Lord, as one.
Let us flourish in Thy strength as one.
Let our knowledge, O Lord, be changed to Light and
Change our hate to love.
OM Peace, peace,peace...

om asato mā sad gamaya
tamaso mā jyotir gamaya
mrityor mā amritam gamaya
om śānti śānti śāntihi

Lead us from untruth to Truth;
From darkness to Light;
From death to Immortality.

om sarveshām svastir bhavatu
sarveshām śāntir bhavatu
sarveshām pūrnam bhavatu
sarveshām mangalam bhavatu
om śānti śānti śāntihi

May perfection prevail on all;
May peace prevail on all;
May contentment prevail on all;
May auspiciousness prevail on all...

om pūrna mada pūrna midam
pūrnāt pūrnam udachyate
pūrnasya pūrnam ādāya
pūrnam evā vasishyate
om śānti śānti śāntihi

That is the Whole, this is the Whole;
From the Whole, the Whole arises;
Taking away the Whole from the Whole,
The Whole remains...

om śrī gurubhyo namaha
harihi om

ŚRĪ LALITĀMBIKA SAHASRANĀMA STOTRAM

DHYANAM

sindūrāruṇa vigrahāṁ tri nayanāṁ
māṇikya mauli sphurat
tārānāyaka śekharāṁ smitamukhīm
āpīna vakṣoruhām
pāṇibhyām alipūrṇa ratna chaṣakaṁ
raktotpalaṁ bibhratīṁ
saumyāṁ ratna ghaṭastha rakta charaṇāṁ
dhyāyet parāmambikām

dhyāyet padmāsanasthāṁ vikasita vadanāṁ
padma patrāyatākṣīṁ
hemābhāṁ pītavastrāṁ kara kali talasad hema
padmāṁ varāṅgim

sarvālaṅkāra yuktāṁ satatam abhayaḍāṁ
bhaktanamrāṁ bhavānīṁ
śrīvidyāṁ śāntamūrtīm sakala sura nutāṁ
sarva sampat pradātrīm

sakuṇkuma vilepanām alika cumbi kastūrikāṁ
samanda hasitekṣaṇām saśara chāpa pāśāṅkuśām
aśeṣa jana mohinīm aruṇa mālya bhūṣojvalām
japā kusuma bhāsurāṁ japavidhau samretambikām
aruṇām karuṇām taraṅgi tākṣīṁ
dhṛta pāśāṅkuśa puṣpa bāṇa cāpām
aṇimādibhir āvṛtām mayūkhai
raham ityeva vibhāvayet maheśīm

She has three eyes; Her hue is like that of red sindura; the diadem of precious stones She wears has a crescent on it shining wonderfully.

That She is easily accessible is indicated by Her benign smile; Her children have an inexhaustible store of the milk of life in Her full breast; the vessel of honey in one hand and the red lotus in the other symbolize joy and wisdom of which She alone is the source; and Her feet placed on the precious pot full of valuable gems indicate that these are not difficult for those who surrender to Her feet and take refuge in Her.

I meditate upon Sri Bhavani Who is seated in the lotus of expansive countenance, Whose eyes are like lotus petals, Who is golden-hued, Who wears a yellow raiment, Who has in Her hand lotus flowers of gold, Who always dispels fear, Whose devotees bow before Her, Who is the embodiment of peace, Who is Sri Vidya Herself Who is praised by the Gods, and Who gives every wealth that is sought . .

I meditate on the Mother Whose eyes are smiling a little, Who has in Her hands the arrow, the bow, the noose and goad, Who bewitches everybody, Who is glittering with red garlands and ornaments, Who is painted with vermillion, Whose forehead is kissed with the mark of musk and Who is red and tender like the japa flower . . .

I meditate on the great Empress who is light red in color, Whose eyes are full of compassion, Who has in Her hands the noose, the goad, the bow and the flowery arrow and Who is surrounded on all sides by powers, such as 'anima,' like rays, as if She is the Self within me . . .

om bhavasya devasya patniyai namaḥ
om sarvasya devasya patniyai namaḥ
om īśanasya devasya patniyai namaḥ

om paśupater devasya patniyai namaḥ
om rudrasya devasya patniyai namaḥ
om ugrasya devasya patniyai namaḥ
om bhīmasya devasya patniyai namaḥ
om mahato devasya patniyai namaḥ

THE THOUSAND NAMES

(OM precedes and NAMAḤ follows all the Names)

Om Śrī mātre namaḥ
Śrī mahā rājñyai
Śrīmat siṁhāsaneśvaryai
Cid agni kuṇḍa saṁbhūtāyai
Deva kārya samudyatāyai
Udyad bhānu sahasrābhāyai
Catur bāhu samanvitāyai
Rāga svarūpa pāśāḍhyāyai
Krodhā kārāṅkuśojjvalāyai
Mano rūpekṣu kodaṇḍāyai 10

Pañcha tanmātra sāyakāyai
Nijāruṇa prabhā pūra majjad brahmāṇḍa maṇḍalāyai
Champakāśoka punnāga saugandhika lasat kacāyai
Kuruvinda maṇiśrenī kanat koṭīra maṇḍitāyai
Aṣṭamī candra vibhrājad alika sthala śobhitāyai
Mukha candra kalaṅkābha mṛganābhi viśeṣakāyai
Vadana smara māṅgalya gṛha toraṇa cillikāyai
Vaktra lakṣmī parīvāha calan mīnābha locanāyai
Nava campaka puṣpābha nāsā daṇḍa virājitāyai
Tārākānti tiraskāri nāsābharaṇa bhāsurāyai 20

Kadamba mañjarī kḷpta karṇapūra manoharāyai
Tāṭaṅka yugalībhūta tapanoḍupa maṇḍalāyai
Padmarāga śilādarśa paribhāvi kapola bhuve
Nava vidruma bimba śrī nyakkāri radanacchadāyai
Śuddha vidyāṅkurākāra dvija paṅkti dvayojjvalāyai
Karpūra vītikāmoda samākarṣi digantarāyai
Nija sallāpa mādhurya vinirbhartsita kacchapyai
Mandasmita prabhāpūra majjat kāmeśa mānasāyai
Anākalita sādṛśya cibuka śrī virājitāyai
Kāmeśa baddha māṅgalya sūtra śobhita kandharāyai 30

Kanakāṅgada keyūra kamanīya bhujānvitāyai
Ratna graiveya cintāka lola muktā phalānvitāyai
Kāmeśvara prema ratna maṇi pratipaṇa stanyai
Nābhyālavāla romāli latā phala kuca dvayyai
Lakṣya roma latā dhāratā samunneya madhyamāyai
Stana bhāra dalan madhya paṭṭa bandha vali trayāyai
Aruṇāruṇa kausumbha vastra bhāsvat kaṭītaṭyai
Ratna kiṅkiṇikā ramya raśānā dāma bhūṣitāyai
Kāmeśa jñāta saubhāgya mārdavoru dvayānvitāyai
Māṇikya mukuṭākāra jānu dvaya virājitāyai 40

Indra gopa parikṣipta smara tūnābha jaṅghikāyai
Gūḍha gulphāyai
Kūrma pṛṣṭha jayiṣṇu prapadānvitāyai
Nakha dīdhiti sañchanna namajjana tamo guṇāyai
Pada dvaya prabhā jāla parākṛta saroruhāyai
Siñjāna maṇi mañjīra maṇḍita śrī padāmbujāyai
Marālī manda gamanāyai
Mahā lāvaṇya śevadhaye
Sarvāruṇāyai
Anavadyāṅgyai 50

Sarvābharaṇa bhūṣitāyai
Śiva kāmeśvar āṅkasthāyai
Śivāyai
Svādhīna vallabhāyai
Sumeru madhya sṛṅgasthāyai
Śrīman nagara nāyikāyai
Cintāmaṇi gṛhāntasthāyai
Pañcha brahmāsana sthitāyai
Mahā padmāṭavī samsthāyai
Kadamba vana vāsinyai 60

Sudhā sāgara madhyasthāyai
Kāmākṣyai
Kāma dāyinyai
Devarṣi gaṇa saṅghāta stūya mānātma vaibhavāyai
Bhaṇḍāsura vadhodyukta śakti senā samanvitāyai
Sampatkarī samārūḍha sindhura vraja sevitāyai
Aśvārūḍhādhiṣṭhitāśva koṭi koṭibhir āvṛtāyai
Cakra rāja rathā rūḍha sarvāyudha pariṣkṛtāyai
Geyacakra rathā rūḍha mantriṇī parisevitāyai
Kiricakra rathā rūḍha daṇḍa nāthā puraskṛtāyai 70

Jvālā mālini kākṣipta vahni prākāra madhyagāyai
Bhaṇḍa sainya vadhodyukta śakti vikrama harṣitāyai
Nityā parākramāṭopa nirīkṣaṇa samutsukāyai
Bhaṇḍa putra vadhodyukta bālā vikrama nanditāyai
Mantriṇyambā viracita viṣaṅga vadha toṣitāyai
Viśukra prāṇa haraṇa vārāhī vīrya nanditāyai
Kāmeśvara mukhāloka kalpita śrī gaṇeśvarāyai
Mahā gaṇeśa nirbhinna vighna yantra praharṣitāyai
Bhaṇḍāsurendra nirmukta śastra pratyastra varṣiṇyai
Karāṅguli nakhotpanna nārāyaṇa daśākṛtyai 80

Mahā pāśupatāstrāgni nirdagdhāsura sainikāyai
Kāmeśvarāstra nirdagdha sabhaṇḍāsura śūnyakāyai
Brahmopendra mahendrādi deva saṁstuta vaibhavāyai
Hara netrāgni sandagdha kāma sañjīvan auṣadhyai
Śrīmad vāgbhava kūṭaika svarūpa mukha paṅkajāyai
Kaṇṭādhaḥ kaṭi paryanta madhya kūṭa svarūpiṇyai
Śakti kūṭaika tāpanna kaṭyadho bhāga dhāriṇyai
Mūla mantrātmikāyai
Mūla kūṭa traya kalebarāyai
Kulāmṛtaika rasikāyai 90

Kula saṅketa pālinyai
Kulāṅganāyai
Kulāntasthāyai
Kaulinyai
Kula yoginyai
Akulāyai
Samayāntasthāyai
Samayācāra tatparāyai
Mūlādhāraika nilayāyai
Brahma granthi vibhedinyai 100

Maṇipūrāntar uditāyai
Viṣṇu granthi vibhedinyai
Ājñā cakrāntarālasthāyai
Rudra granthi vibhedinyai
Sahasrār āmbujārūḍhāyai
Sudhā sārābhi varṣiṇyai
Taḍillatā samarucyai
Ṣaṭ cakropari saṁsthitāyai
Mahāśaktyai
Kuṇḍalinyai 110

Bisa tantu tanīyasyai
Bhavānyai
Bhāvanā gamyāyai
Bhavāraṇya kuṭhārikāyai
Bhadra priyāyai
Bhadra mūrtyai
Bhakta saubhāgya dāyinyai
Bhakti priyāyai
Bhakti gamyāyai
Bhakti vaśyāyai 120

Bhayā pahāyai
Śāmbhavyai
Śāradārādhyāyai
Śarvāṇyai
Śarma dāyinyai
Śāṅkaryai
Śrīkaryai
Sādhvyai
Śaraccandra nibhānanāyai
Śātodaryai 130

Śāntimatyai
Nirādhārāyai
Nirañjanāyai
Nirlepāyai
Nirmalāyai
Nityāyai
Nirākārāyai
Nirākulāyai
Nirguṇāyai
Niṣkalāyai 140

Śāntāyai
Niṣkāmāyai
Nirupaplavāyai
Nityamuktāyai
Nirvikārāyai
Niṣprapañcāyai
Nirāśrayāyai
Nitya śuddhāyai
Nitya buddhāyai
Niravadyāyai 150

Nirantarāyai
Niṣkāraṇāyai
Niṣkalaṅkāyai
Nirupādhaye
Nirīśvarāyai
Nīrāgāyai
Rāga mathanyai
Nirmadāyai
Mada nāśinyai
Niścintāyai 160

Nirahaṅkārāyai
Nirmohāyai
Moha nāśinyai
Nirmamāyai
Mamatā hantryai
Niṣpāpāyai
Pāpa nāśinyai
Niṣkrodhāyai
Krodha śamanyai
Nirlobhāyai 170

Lobha nāśinyai
Niḥsaṁśayāyai
Saṁśayaghnyai
Nirbhavāyai
Bhava nāśinyai
Nirvikalpāyai
Nirābādhāyai
Nirbhedāyai
Bheda nāśinyai
Nirnāśāyai 180

Mṛtyu mathanyai
Niṣkriyāyai
Niṣparigrahāyai
Nistulāyai
Nīlacikurāyai
Nirapāyāyai
Niratyayāyai
Durlabhāyai
Durgamāyai
Durgāyai 190

Duḥkha hantryai
Sukha pradāyai
Duṣṭa dūrāyai
Durācāra śamanyai
Doṣa varjitāyai
Sarvajñāyai
Sāndra karuṇāyai
Samānādhika varjitāyai
Sarva śaktimayyai
Sarva maṅgalāyai 200

Sadgati pradāyai
Sarveśvaryai
Sarvamayyai
Sarva mantra svarūpiṇyai
Sarva yantrātmikāyai
Sarva tantra rūpāyai
Manonmanyai
Maheśvaryai
Mahādevyai
Mahālakṣmyai 210

Mṛḍapriyāyai
Mahārūpāyai
Mahāpūjyāyai
Mahāpātaka nāśinyai
Mahāmāyāyai
Mahāsattvāyai
Mahāśaktyai
Mahāratyai
Mahābhogāyai
Mahaiśvaryāyai 220

Mahāvīryāyai
Mahābalāyai
Mahābuddhyai
Mahāsiddhyai
Mahāyogeśvar eśvaryai
Mahātantrāyai
Mahāmantrāyai
Mahāyantrāyai
Mahāsanāyai
Mahāyāga kramārādhyāyai 230

Mahābhairava pūjitāyai
Maheśvara mahākalpa mahātāṇḍava sākṣiṇyai
Mahākāmeśa mahiṣyai
Mahātripura sundaryai
Catuḥ ṣaṣṭyupa cārādhyāyai
Catuḥ ṣaṣṭi kalāmayyai
Mahā catuḥ ṣaṣṭi koṭi yoginī gaṇa sevitāyai
Manu vidyāyai
Candra vidyāyai
Candra maṇḍala madhyagāyai 240

Cāru rūpāyai
Cāru hāsāyai
Cāru candra kalādharāyai
Carāchara jagannāthāyai
Cakra rāja niketanāyai
Pārvatyai
Padma nayanāyai
Padma rāga sama prabhāyai
Pañcha pretāsan āsīnāyai
Pañcha brahma svarūpiṇyai 250

Cinmayyai
Paramānandāyai
Vijñāna ghana rūpiṇyai
Dhyāna dhyātṛ dhyeya rūpāyai
Dharmādharma vivarjitāyai
Viśvarūpāyai
Jāgariṇyai
Svapantyai
Taijas ātmikāyai
Suptāyai 260

Prājñātmikāyai
Turyāyai
Sarvāvasthā vivarjitāyai
Sṛṣṭi kartryai
Brahma rūpāyai
Goptryai
Govinda rūpiṇyai
Saṁhāriṇyai
Rudra rūpāyai
Tirodhāna karyai 270

Īśvaryai
Sadāśivāyai
Anugrahadāyai
Pañca kṛtya parāyaṇāyai
Bhānu maṇḍala madhyasthāyai
Bhairavyai
Bhaga mālinyai
Padmāsanāyai
Bhagavatyai
Padmanābha sahodaryai 280

Unmeṣa nimiṣotpanna vipanna bhuvanāvalyai
Sahasra śīrṣa vadanāyai
Sahasrākṣyai
Sahasrapāde
Ābrahma kīṭa jananyai
Varṇāśrama vidhāyinyai
Nijājñā rūpa nigamāyai
Puṇyāpuṇya phala pradāyai
Śruti sīmanta sindūrī kṛta pādābja dhūlikāyai
Sakalāgama sandoha śukti saṁpuṭa mauktikāyai 290

Puruṣārtha pradāyai
Pūrṇāyai
Bhoginyai
Bhuvaneśvaryai
Ambikāyai
Anādi nidhanāyai
Hari brahmendra sevitāyai
Nārāyaṇyai
Nāda rūpāyai
Nāma rūpa vivarjitāyai 300

Hrīṅkāryai
Hrīmatyai
Hṛdyāyai
Heyopādeya varjitāyai
Rāja rājārcitāyai
Rājñyai
Ramyāyai
Rājīva locanāyai
Rañjanyai
Ramaṇyai 310

Rasyāyai
Raṇat kiṅkiṇi mekhalāyai
Ramāyai
Rākendu vadanāyai
Rati rūpāyai
Rati priyāyai
Rakṣākaryai
Rākṣas aghnyai
Rāmāyai
Ramaṇa laṁpaṭāyai 320

Kāmyāyai
Kāma kalā rūpāyai
Kadaṁba kusuma priyāyai
Kalyāṇyai
Jagatī kandāyai
Karuṇā rasa sāgarāyai
Kalāvatyai
Kalā lāpāyai
Kāntāyai
Kādaṁbarī priyāyai 330

Varadāyai
Vāma nayanāyai
Vāruṇī mada vihvalāyai
Viśvādhikāyai
Veda vedyāyai
Vindhyācala nivāsinyai
Vidhātryai
Veda jananyai
Viṣṇu māyāyai
Vilāsinyai 340

Kṣetra svarūpāyai
Kṣetreśyai
Kṣetra kṣetrajña pālinyai
Kṣaya vṛddhi vinir muktāyai
Kṣetra pāla samarcitāyai
Vijayāyai
Vimalāyai
Vandyāyai
Vandāru jana vatsalāyai
Vāg vādinyai 350

Vāmakeśyai
Vahni maṇḍala vāsinyai
Bhaktimat kalpa latikāyai
Paśupāśa vimocinyai
Saṁhṛtāśeṣa pāṣaṇḍāyai
Sadācāra pravartikāyai
Tāpa trayāgni saṁtapta samāhlādana candrikāyai
Taruṇyai
Tāpas ārādhyāyai
Tanu madhyāyai 360

Tamo pahāyai
Cityai
Tatpada lakṣyārthāyai
Cideka rasa rūpiṇyai
Svātmānanda lavībhūta brahmādyānanda santatyai
Parāyai
Pratyak citī rūpāyai
Paśyantyai
Paradevatāyai
Madhyamāyai 370

Vaikharī rūpāyai
Bhakta mānasa haṁsikāyai
Kāmeśvara prāṇa nādyai
Kṛtajñāyai
Kāma pūjitāyai
Śriṅgāra rasa saṁpūrṇāyai
Jayāyai
Jālandhara sthitāyai
Oḍyāṇa pīṭha nilayāyai
Bindu maṇḍala vāsinyai 380

Rahoyāga kramārādhyāyai
Rahas tarpaṇa tarpitāyai
Sadyaḥ prasādinyai
Viśva sākṣiṇyai
Sākṣi varjitāyai
Ṣaḍaṅga devatā yuktāyai
Ṣāḍguṇya pari pūritāyai
Nitya klinnāyai
Nirupamāyai
Nirvāṇa sukha dāyinyai 390

Nityā ṣoḍaśikā rūpāyai
Śrī kaṇṭhārdha śarīriṇyai
Prabhāvatyai
Prabhā rūpāyai
Prasiddhāyai
Parameśvaryai
Mūla prakṛtyai
Avyaktāyai
Vyaktāvyakta svarūpiṇyai
Vyāpinyai 400

Vividhākārāyai
Vidyāvidyā svarūpiṇyai
Mahākāmeśa nayana kumudāhlāda kaumudyai
Bhakta hārda tamobheda bhānumad bhānu santatyai
Śiva dūtyai
Śivārādhyāyai
Śiva mūrtyai
Śivaṅkaryai
Śiva priyāyai
Śiva parāyai 410

Śiṣṭeṣṭāyai
Śiṣṭa pūjitāyai
Aprameyāyai
Svaprakāśāyai
Mano vācām agocarāyai
Cicchaktyai
Cetanā rūpāyai
Jaḍa śaktyai
Jaḍātmikāyai
Gāyatryai 420

Vyāhṛtyai
Sandhyāyai
Dvija vṛnda niṣevitāyai
Tattvāsanāyai
Tasmai
Tubhyam
Ayyai
Pañca kośāntara sthitāyai
Niḥsīma mahimne
Nitya yauvanāyai 430

Mada śālinyai
Mada ghūrṇita raktākṣyai
Mada pāṭala gaṇḍa bhūve
Candana drava digdhāṅgyai
Cāṁpeya kusuma priyāyai
Kuśalāyai
Komalākārāyai
Kuru kullāyai
Kuleśvaryai
Kula kuṇḍālayāyai 440

Kaula mārga tatpara sevitāyai
Kumāra gaṇa nāthāmbāyai
Tuṣṭyai
Puṣṭyai
Matyai
Dhṛtyai
Śāntyai
Svasti matyai
Kāntyai
Nandinyai 450

Vighna nāśinyai
Tejovatyai
Trinayanāyai
Lolākṣī kāmarūpiṇyai
Mālinyai
Haṁsinyai
Mātre
Malayācala vāsinyai
Sumukhyai
Nalinyai 460

Subhrūve
Śobhanāyai
Suranāyikāyai
Kālakaṇṭhyai
Kāntimatyai
Kṣobiṇyai
Sūkṣma rūpiṇyai
Vajreśvaryai
Vāmadevyai
Vayovasthā vivarjitāyai 470

Siddheśvaryai
Siddha vidyāyai
Siddha mātre
Yaśasvinyai
Viśuddhi cakra nilayāyai
Ārakta varṇāyai
Trilocanāyai
Khaṭvāṅgādi praharaṇāyai
Vadanaika samanvitāyai
Pāyasānna priyāyai 480

Tvaksthāyai
Paśuloka bhayaṅkaryai
Amṛtādi mahāśakti saṁvṛtāyai
Ḍākinīśvaryai
Anāhatābja nilayāyai
Śyāmābhāyai
Vadana dvayāyai
Daṁṣṭrojjvalāyai
Akṣamālādi dharāyai
Rudhira saṁsthitāyai 490

Kāla rātryādi śaktyaugha vṛtāyai
Snigdhaudana priyāyai
Mahāvīrendra varadāyai
Rākiṇyambā svarūpiṇyai
Maṇipūrābja nilayāyai
Vadana traya saṁyutāyai
Vajrādikā yudhopetāyai
Ḍāmaryādibhir āvṛtāyai
Rakta varṇāyai
Māṁsa niṣṭhāyai 500

Guḍānna prīta mānasāyai
Samasta bhakta sukhadāyai
Lākinyaṁbā svarūpiṇyai
Svādhiṣṭhān āmbuja gatāyai
Catur vaktra manoharāyai
Śūlādyāyudha sampannāyai
Pīta varṇāyai
Ati garvitāyai
Medo niṣṭhāyai
Madhu prītāyai 510

Bandhinyādi samanvitāyai
Dadhyannāsakta hṛdayāyai
Kākinī rūpa dhāriṇyai
Mūlādhār āmbujā rūḍhāyai
Pañca vaktrāyai
Asthi saṁsthitāyai
Aṅkuśādi praharaṇāyai
Varadādi niṣevitāyai
Mudgaudanāsakta cittāyai
Sākinyambā svarūpiṇyai 520

Ājñā cakrābja nilayāyai
Śukla varṇāyai
Ṣad ānanāyai
Majjā saṁsthāyai
Hamsavatī mukhya śakti samanvitāyai
Haridrānnaika rasikāyai
Hākinī rūpa dhāriṇyai
Sahasra dala padmasthāyai
Sarva varṇopa śobhitāyai
Sarvāyudha dharāyai 530

Śukla samsthitāyai
Sarvatomukhyai
Sarvaudana prīta cittāyai
Yākinyambā svarūpiṇyai
Svāhāyai
Svadhāyai
Amatyai
Medhāyai
Śrutyai
Smṛtyai 540

Anuttamāyai
Puṇya kīrtyai
Puṇya labhyāyai
Puṇya śravaṇa kirtanāyai
Puloma jārcitāyai
Bandha mocanyai
Barbarālakāyai
Vimarśa rūpiṇyai
Vidyāyai
Viyadādi jagat prasuve 550

Sarva vyādhi praśamanyai
Sarva mṛtyu nivāriṇyai
Agra gaṇyāyai
Acintya rūpāyai
Kali kalmaṣa nāśinyai
Kātyāyanyai
Kāla hantryai
Kamalākṣa niṣevitāyai
Tāmbūla pūrita mukhyai
Dādimī kusuma prabhāyai 560

Mṛgākṣyai
Mohinyai
Mukhyāyai
Mṛdānyai
Mitra rūpiṇyai
Nitya tṛptāyai
Bhakta nidhaye
Niyantryai
Nikhileśvaryai
Maitryādi vāsanā labhyāyai 570

Mahā pralaya sākṣiṇyai
Parāyai śaktyai
Parāya niṣṭhāyai
Prajñāna ghana rūpiṇyai
Mādhvi pānālasāyai
Mattāyai
Mātṛkā varṇa rūpiṇyai
Mahā kailāsa nilayāyai
Mṛnāla mṛdu dor latāyai
Mahanīyāyai 580

Dayā mūrtyai
Mahā sāmrājya sālinyai
Ātma vidyāyai
Mahā vidyāyai
Śrī vidyāyai
Kāma sevitāyai
Śrī ṣoḍaśākṣarī vidyāyai
Trikūṭāyai
Kāma koṭikāyai
Kaṭākṣa kiṅkarī bhūta kamalā koṭi sevitāyai 590

Śiraḥ sthitāyai
Candra nibhāyai
Bhālasthāyai
Indra dhanūṣ prabhāyai
Hṛdayasthāyai
Ravi prakhyāyai
Trikoṇāntara dīpikāyai
Dākṣāyaṇyai
Daitya hantryai
Dakṣa yajña vināśinyai 600

Darāndolita dīrghākṣyai
Dara hāsojjvalan mukhyai
Guru mūrtyai
Guṇa nidhaye
Go mātre
Guha janma bhuve
Deveśyai
Daṇḍa nītisthāyai
Daharākāśa rūpiṇyai
Pratipan mukhya rākānta tithi maṇḍala pūjitāyai 610

Kalātmikāyai
Kalā nāthāyai
Kāvyālāpa vinodinyai
Sacāmara ramā vāṇī savya dakṣiṇa sevitāyai
Ādi śaktyai
Ameyāyai
Ātmane
Paramāyai
Pāvanā kṛtaye
Aneka koṭi brahmāṇḍa jananyai 620

Divya vigrahāyai
Klīṁkāryai
Kevalāyai
Guhyāyai
Kaivalya pada dāyinyai
Tripurāyai
Trijagad vandyāyai
Trimūrtyai
Tridaśeśvaryai
Tryakṣaryai 630

Divya gandhāḍhyāyai
Sindūra tilakāñcitāyai
Umāyai
Śailendra tanayāyai
Gauryai
Gandharva sevitāyai
Viśva garbhāyai
Svarṇa garbhāyai
Avaradāyai
Vāg adhīśvaryai 640

Dhyāna gamyāyai
Apari cchedyāyai
Jñānadāyai
Jñāna vigrahāyai
Sarva vedānta saṁvedyāyai
Satyānanda svarūpiṇyai
Lopā mudrārcitāyai
Līlā kḷpta brahmāṇḍa maṇḍalāyai
Adṛśyāyai
Dṛśya rahitāyai 650

Vijñātryai
Vedya varjitāyai
Yoginyai
Yogadāyai
Yogyāyai
Yogānandāyai
Yugandharāyai
Icchā śakti jñāna śakti kriyā śakti svarūpiṇyai
Sarvādhārāyai
Supratiṣṭhāyai 660

Sad asad rūpa dhāriṇyai
Aṣṭamūrtyai
Ajā jetryai
Loka yātrā vidhāyinyai
Ekākinyai
Bhūma rūpāyai
Nirdvaitāyai
Dvaita varjitāyai
Annadāyai
Vasudāyai 670
Vṛddhāyai

Brahmātmaikya svarūpiṇyai
Bṛhatyai
Brāhmaṇyai
Brāhmyai
Brahmānandāyai
Bali priyāyai
Bhāṣā rūpāyai
Bṛhat senāyai
Bhāvābhāva vivarjitāyai 680

Sukhārādhyāyai
Śubha karyai
Śobhanāyai sulabhāyai gatyai
Rāja rājeśvaryai
Rājya dāyinyai
Rājya vallabhāyai
Rājat kṛpāyai
Rāja pīṭha niveśita nijāśritāyai
Rājya lakṣmyai
Kośa nāthāyai 690

Catur aṅga baleśvaryai
Sāmrājya dāyinyai
Satya sandhāyai
Sāgara mekhalāyai
Dīkṣitāyai
Daitya śamanyai
Sarva loka vaśaṅkaryai
Sarvārtha dātryai
Sāvitryai
Saccidānanda rūpiṇyai 700

Deśa kālā paricchinnāyai
Sarvagāyai
Sarva mohinyai
Sarasvatyai
Śāstramayyai
Guhāṁbāyai
Guhya rūpiṇyai
Sarvopādhi vinirmuktāyai
Sadāśiva pativratāyai
Saṁpradāyeśvaryai 710

Sādhune
Yai
Guru maṇḍala rūpiṇyai
Kulottīrṇāyai
Bhagārādhyāyai
Māyāyai
Madhumatyai
Mahyai
Gaṇāṁbāyai
Guhyak ārādhyāyai 720

Komalāṅgyai
Guru priyāyai
Svatantrāyai
Sarva tantreśyai
Dakṣinā mūrti rūpiṇyai
Sanakādi samārādhyāyai
Śiva jñāna pradāyinyai
Cit kalāyai
Ānanda kalikāyai
Prema rūpāyai 730

Priyaṅkaryai
Nāma pārāyaṇa prītāyai
Nandi vidyāyai
Nateśvaryai
Mithyā jagad adhiṣṭhānāyai
Mukti dāyai
Mukti rūpiṇyai
Lāsya priyāyai
Laya karyai
Lajjāyai 740

Raṁbhādi vanditāyai
Bhava dāva sudhā vṛṣṭyai
Pāpāraṇya davānalāyai
Daurbhāgya tūla vātūlāyai
Jarā dhvānta ravi prabhāyai
Bhāgyābdhi candrikāyai
Bhakta citta keki ghanāghanāyai
Roga parvata daṁbholaye
Mṛtyu dāru kuṭhārikāyai
Maheśvaryai 750

Mahā kālyai
Mahā grāsāyai
Mahāśanāyai
Aparṇāyai
Caṇḍikāyai
Caṇḍa muṇḍāsura niṣūdanyai
Kṣarākṣarātmikāyai
Sarva lokeśyai
Viśva dhārinyai
Tri varga dātryai 760

Subhagāyai
Tryaṁbakāyai
Triguṇātmikāyai
Svargāpavargadāyai
Śuddhāyai
Japā puṣpa nibhākṛtaye
Ojovatyai
Dyuti dharāyai
Yajña rūpāyai
Priya vratāyai 770

Durārādhyāyai
Durādharṣāyai
Pāṭalī kusuma priyāyai
Mahatyai
Meru nilayāyai
Mandāra kusuma priyāyai
Vīrārādhyāyai
Virād rūpāyai
Virajase
Viśvato mukhyai 780

Pratyag rūpāyai
Parākāśāyai
Prāṇadāyai
Prāṇa rūpiṇyai
Mārtāṇḍa bhairavārādhyāyai
Mantriṇī nyasta rājya dhure
Tripureśyai
Jayat senāyai
Nistraiguṇyāyai
Parāparāyai 790

Satya jñānānanda rūpāyai
Sāmarasya parāyaṇāyai
Kapardinyai
Kalā mālāyai
Kāma dughe
Kāma rūpiṇyai
Kalā nidhaye
Kāvya kalāyai
Rasajñāyai
Rasa śevadhaye 800

Puṣṭāyai
Purātanāyai
Pūjyāyai
Puṣkarāyai
Puṣkar ekṣaṇāyai
Parasmai jyotiṣe
Parasmai dhāmne
Paramāṇave
Parāt parāyai
Pāśa hastāyai 810

Pāśa hantryai
Para mantra vibhedinyai
Mūrtāyai
Amūrtāyai
Anitya tṛptāyai
Muni mānasa haṁsikāyai
Satya vratāyai
Satya rūpāyai
Sarvāntaryāmiṇyai
Satyai 820

Brahmāṇyai
Brahmaṇe
Jananyai
Bahu rūpāyai
Budhārcitāyai
Prasavitryai
Pracaṇḍāyai
Ājñāyai
Pratiṣṭhāyai
Prakaṭākritaye 830

Prāṇeśvaryai
Prāṇa dātryai
Pañcāśat pīṭha rūpiṇyai
Viśṛṅkhalāyai
Viviktasthāyai
Vīra mātre
Viyat prasuve
Mukundāyai
Mukti nilayāyai
Mūla vigraha rūpiṇyai 840

Bhāvajñāyai
Bhava rogaghnyai
Bhava cakra pravartinyai
Chandaḥ sārāyai
Śāstra sārāyai
Mantra sārāyai
Talodaryai
Udāra kīrtaye
Uddāma vaibhavāyai
Varṇa rūpiṇyai 850

Janma mṛtyu jarā tapta jana viśrānti dāyinyai
Sarvopaniṣad udghuṣṭāyai
Śāntyatīta kalātmikāyai
Gaṁbhīrāyai
Gaganāntasthāyai
Garvitāyai
Gāna lolupāyai
Kalpanā rahitāyai
Kāṣṭhāyai
Akāntāyai 860

Kāntārdha vigrahāyai
Kārya kāraṇa nirmuktāyai
Kāma keli taraṅgitāyai
Kanat kanaka tāṭaṅkāyai
Līlā vigraha dhāriṇyai
Ajāyai
Kṣaya vinirmuktāyai
Mugdhāyai
Kṣipra prasādinyai
Antar mukha samārādhyāyai 870

Bahir mukha sudurlabhāyai
Trayyai
Trivarga nilayāyai
Tristhāyai
Tripura mālinyai
Nirāmayāyai
Nirālambāyai
Svātmārāmāyai
Sudhāsrutyai
Saṁsāra paṅka nirmagna samuddharaṇa paṇḍitāyai 880

Yajña priyāyai
Yajña kartryai
Yajamāna svarūpiṇyai
Dharmādhārāyai
Dhanādhyakṣāyai
Dhana dhānya vivardhinyai
Vipra priyāyai
Vipra rūpāyai
Viśva bhramaṇa kāriṇyai
Viśva grāsāyai 890

Vidrumābhāyai
Vaiṣṇavyai
Viṣṇu rūpiṇyai
Ayonyai
Yoni nilayāyai
Kūṭasthāyai
Kula rūpiṇyai
Vīra goṣṭhī priyāyai
Vīrāyai
Naiṣkarmyāyai 900

Nāda rūpiṇyai
Vijñāna kalanāyai
Kalyāyai
Vidagdhāyai
Baiṇdavāsanāyai
Tattvādhikāyai
Tattva mayyai
Tat tvam artha svarūpiṇyai
Sāma gāna priyāyai
Somyāyai 910

Sadāśiva kuṭuṁbinyai
Savyāpasavya mārgasthāyai
Sarvāpad vinivāriṇyai
Svasthāyai
Svabhāva madhurāyai
Dhīrāyai
Dhīra samarcitāyai
Caitanyārghya samārādhyāyai
Caitanya kusuma priyāyai
Sadoditāyai 920

Sadā tuṣṭāyai
Taruṇāditya pātalāyai
Dakṣiṇā dakṣiṇārādhyāyai
Darasmera mukhāmbujāyai
Kaulinī kevalāyai
Anarghya kaivalya pada dāyinyai
Stotra priyāyai
Stuti matyai
Śruti saṁstuta vaibhavāyai
Manasvinyai 930

Mānavatyai
Maheśyai
Maṅgalākṛtyai
Viśvamātre
Jagaddhātryai
Viśālākṣyai
Virāgiṇyai
Pragalbhāyai
Paramodārāyai
Parāmodāyai 940

Manomayyai
Vyomakeśyai
Vimānasthāyai
Vajraṇyai
Vāmakeśvaryai
Pañca yajña priyāyai
Pañca preta mañcādhi sāyinyai
Pañcamyai
Pañca bhūteśyai
Pañca saṅkhyopacāriṇyai 950

Śāśvatyai
Śāśvataiśvaryāyai
Śarmadāyai
Śambhu mohinyai
Dharāyai
Dhara sutāyai
Dhanyāyai
Dharmiṇyai
Dharma vardhinyai
Lokātītāyai 960

Guṇātītāyai
Sarvātītāyai
Śamātmikāyai
Bandhūka kusuma prakhyāyai
Bālāyai
Līlā vinodinyai
Sumaṅgalyai
Sukha karyai
Suveṣāḍhyāyai
Suvāsinyai 970

Suvāsinyarcana prītāyai
Āśobhanāyai
Śuddha mānasāyai
Bindu tarpaṇa santuṣṭāyai
Pūrva jāyai
Tripurāmbikāyai
Daśa mudrā samārādhyāyai
Tripurāśrī vaśaṅkaryai
Jñāna mudrāyai
Jñāna gamyāyai 980

Jñāna jñeya svarūpiṇyai
Yoni mudrāyai
Trikhaṇḍeśyai
Triguṇāyai
Ambāyai
Trikoṇagāyai
Anaghāyai
Adbhuta cāritrāyai
Vañcitārtha pradāyinyai
Abhyāsātiśaya jñātāyai 990

Ṣaḍadhvātīta rūpiṇyai
Avyāja karuṇā mūrtaye
Ajñāna dhvānta dīpikāyai
Ābāla gopa viditāyai
Sarvānullaṅghya śāsanāyai
Śrīcakra rāja nilayāyai
Śrīmat tripura sundaryai
Śrī śivāyai
Śiva śaktyaikya rūpiṇyai
Lalitāmbikāyai 1000

INDEX OF SONGS

Ā JĪVANĀNTAM 59
ABHAYAM ABHAYAM AMMA 165
ĀDI PARĀŚAKTĪ 166
ĀDI PURŪSHA 167
ĀDIYIL PARAMEŚVARIYE 131
ĀDIYIL PARAMEŚVARIYE 74
ĀGAMĀNTA PORULE 81
ĀGATANĀYI 59
AKALATĀ KOVILIL1 67
AKALE AKALE 145
AMBĀ BHAVĀNI JAYA 112
AMBA BHAVĀNI ŚĀRADE 168
AMBĀ MĀTĀ 169
AMBĀ SAHITA 170
AMBIKE DEVI 29
AMBIKE JAGADAMBIKE 170
AMMA AMMA TĀYE 171
AMMA NIN RŪPAM 110
AMMA TAN NĀMAM 122
AMMA YENNULLORĀ 123
AMMAYALLE ENTAMMAYALLE 243
AMMAYIL MĀNASAM 133
AMME BHAGAVATI KĀLIMĀTE 132
AMME BHAGAVATI NITYA 67
AMME KANNU TURAKŪLE 90

AMME ULAKAM 127
AMME YENNU LORU 115
AMRITĀNANDA SVARŪPA 20
AMRITĀNANDAMAYI 9
ĀNANDA MAYI 2
ĀNANDĀMRITA RŪPINI 56
ANANTAMĀM Ī LOKATIL 75
ANGALLĀTI 109
ANUPAMA GŪNA NILAYE 246
ARATI 124
ARIKIL UNDENKILUM 48
ĀRIKULLIL 91
ARUNA NIRAKATI 136
ĀRUNDU CHOLLU VĀN 70
ĀRUTE MAKKAL NYANGAL 85
ATBHUTA CHARITRE 129
ĀTMA RĀMA 173
ATULYA TAYUTE 128
ĀYIYE GURU MAHARĀNI 173
BANDHAM ILLA 53
BHAGAVĀNE 174
BHAJAMANA RĀM 175
BHAKTAVALSALE DEVI 24
BHRAMARAME 238
BOLO BOLO 175
BRAHMĀNDA PAKSHIKAL 111
CHĀMUNDAYE KĀLI MĀ 115
CHANDRAŚEKARĀYA NAMA OM 176

CHILANKA KETTI 104
CHITTA CHORA 176
CHITTA VRINDĀVANAM 177
DAŚARATHA NANDANA RĀMA 179
DARŚAN DENA RĀMA 228
DAYĀ KARO MĀTĀ 165
DEVĪ BHAGAVATI 137
DEVI DEVI DEVI JAGANMOHINĪ 266
DEVI JAGANMĀTA 231
DEVI MAHEŚVARIYE 240
DEVI ŚARANAM 141
DHANYA DHANYE 179
DHIMIKI DHIMIKI 180
DURGA BHAVĀNI MĀ 181
DURGE DURGE 181
ELLĀM ARIYUNNA 247
EN MANASSIN ORU MAUNAM 265
ENNUTE JĪVITA 83
ENTAMME NIN MAKKALE 245
ENTE KANNUNĪR 17
ETRAYO NĀLĀYI 46
GAJĀNANA 227
GANGĀDHARA HARA 182
GHANA ŚYĀMA SUNDARA 183
GIRIDHĀRI JAI GIRIDHĀRI 184
GOPĀLA GOVINDA 18
GOPĀLA KRISHNA 7
GOPI VALLABHA 196

GOVARDHANA GIRIDHĀRI 184
GOVARDHANAGIRI KUDAYĀKKI 235
GOVINDA KRISHNA JAI 186
GOVINDA NĀRĀYANA 186
HAMSA VĀHINI DEVI 187
HARE KEŚAVA GOVINDA 187
HARE MURARE 189
HARIYUDE KĀLIL 250
HE AMBA 112
HE GIRIDHARA GOPĀLĀ 189
HE MĀDHAVA 190
HRIDAYA NIVĀSINI 252
HRIDAYA PUSHPAME 113
HRĪM KĀLI 119
ICHĀMAYĪ 152
IDAMILLA 66
INI ORU JANMAM 191
ĪŚVARI JAGADĪŚVARI 192
JAGADIŚVARI DAYĀ KARO 230
JAI JAI JAI GANANĀYAKA 196
JAI JAI RĀMAKRISHNA 193
JAI RĀDHA MĀDHAVA 269
JAYA AMBE 120
JAYA JAYA ĀRATI 194
JAYA JAYA DEVI 54
JAYA OM ŚRĪ MĀTĀ 195
JAYA RĀMA JĀNAKI RĀMA 196
KAITORUNNEN KRISHNA 232

KĀLINA KĀNĀN 57
KANIVIN PORULE 31
KANNA NĪ YENNE 15
KANNANE KĀNĀN 23
KANNATACCHĀLUM 91
KANNENDE KĀLOCHA 8
KANNILENGILUM 80
KANNUNĪR ILLĀTTA 254
KANNUNĪR KONDU 63
KARĀRAVINDENA 107
KARIMUKAL VARNNAN 238
KARUNĀLAYE DEVI 78
KARUNANĪR KATALE 93
KARUNATAN KATAMIRI 121
KĀRUNYA MURTE 33
KĀRUNYA VĀRIDHE 4
KASTURI TILAKAM 197
KĀTTINU KĀTĀYI 118
KATUTTA ŚOKAMĀM 248
KĀYĀ PĪYA 218
KEŚAVA NĀRĀYANA 198
KERUNNEN MĀNASAM AMMĀ 138
KODĀNUKOTI 199
KRISHNA KANNAYA 200
KRISHNA KRISHNA MUKUNDA 201
KRISHNA KRISHNA RĀDHĀ 202
KRISHNA MUKUNDA 202
KUMBHODARA VARADĀ 203

LAMBODARA PĀHIMĀM 204
MĀDHAVA GOPAL 204
MADHURĀDHI PATE 139
MALARUM MANAVUM 149
MANAME NARA JĪVITAM 65
MANASĀ VĀCHĀ 21
MANASE NIN SVANTAMĀYI 5
MANDAHĀSA 206
MANGALA ĀRATI 206
MANNĀYI MARAYUM 94
MANO BUDDHYA 207
MĀRĀ YADUKULA 148
MARTYARE SAMSĀRA 73
MATHURĀDHIPATE 205
MAUNA GHANĀMRITAM 140
MŪKA GĀNAM 84
MŪKA HRIDAYA 95
NANDA KUMĀRA 209
NANDALĀL 209
NANDALĀLĀ YADU 210
NĀRĀYANA HARI 86
NĪ YENTE VELICHAM 236
NILĀMBŪJA 79
NĪLAMEGHANGALE 259
NIN ORMAKAL 106
NIN PREMAM 15
NIRAMILLA 60
NIRMALA SNEHAME 260

OM BHADRAKĀLĪ 241
OMKĀRA BRAHMATIN 261
OMKĀRA DIVYAPORULE–I 37
OMKĀRA DIVYA PORULE, II 96
OMKĀRA DIVYA PORULE-IV 155
OMKĀRA MENGUM 153
ORU NĀLIL NYĀN EN 106
ORU TULLI SNEHAM 72
ORUNĀLIL VARUMO 232
PAKALANTIYIL 262
PĀLKKATAL NATUVIL 258
PARAMAŚIVA MĀM PĀHI 210
PARĀŚAKTI 211
PARASAHASRA 36
PARIHĀSA PĀTRAMĀYI 233
PARINĀMAM IYALĀTTA 242
PAURNAMI RĀVIL 244
PIRAYENTU CHETU 14
POVUKAYĀYO KANNĀ 264
PRABHU MĪŚAM 212
PRAPAÑCHAM ENGUM 257
PRATILOMA ŚAKTITAN 114
PREMA PRABHO LĀSINĪ 263
RĀDHĀ RAMANA 47
RĀDHE GOVINDA GOPI 164
RĀDHE ŚYĀMA 214
RAGHU NANDANA 214
RĀJA RĀMA 215

RĀMAKRISHNA GOVINDA 216
RĀMA KRISHNA PRABHUTŪ 216
RĀMA NĀMA TĀRAKAM 217
RĀMA RĀMA RĀJA RĀMA 219
RĀMA SMARANAM 219
SADĀ NIRANTARA 234
SADGURO PĀHIMĀM 45
SADGURU BRAHMA 220
SAHASRANĀMA STOTRAM 273
SAKALA KALĀ DEVATE 256
SAMSĀRA DUKHA SAMANAM 108
SARVAM BRAHMA MAYAM 220
SATCHITĀNANDA GURU 222
SĪTA RĀM BOL 221
SKANDA JANANI 150
SNEHA SUDHĀMAYI 1
SRISHTIYUM NĪYE 24
SUNDARĪ NĪ VĀYO 255
SVĀGATAM KRISHNA 226
ŚAKTĪ MAHĀDEVĪ 126
ŚAKTI RŪPE 10
ŚIVA ŚIVA HARA HARA 223
ŚIVĀYA PARAMEŚVARĀYA 269
ŚRĪ CHAKRAM 147
ŚRI KRISHNA ŚARANAM 76
ŚRĪ LALITĀMBIKA 273
ŚRI RĀMACHANDRA 135
ŚRI RĀMA NĀMAMU 70

ŚRI RĀMA RĀMA NĀMAM 224
ŚRI VINĀYAKA 225
ŚYĀMA SUNDARA 49
TAVA SANNIDHĀNATTIL 117
TĀYE TAVA TANAYARIL 113
ULAKATTI NĀDHĀRA 32
UTTAMA PREMATIN 130
UYIRĀYI OLIYĀYI 52
VANDE NANDAKUMĀRAM 229
VANDIKYUNNEN 2
VANNĀLUM AMBIKE 64
VARALUNNA HRIDAYATTIL 265
VASUDEVA PUTRANE VĀ 226
VEDĀMBIKE 61
VEDĀNTA VENAL 35
VIŚVA VIMOHINĪ 34
VINAYA MĀNASAM 151
VINĀYAKA VINĀYAKA 268
YĀDAVANE 267
YAŚODA KE BĀLĀ 267
YEN MAHĀDEVI LOKEŚI 237